IMPORTANT!

W9-AAY-665

HERE IS YOUR REGISTRATION CODE TO ACCESS YOUR PREMIUM McGRAW-HILL ONLINE RESOURCES.

For key premium online resources you need THIS CODE to gain access. Once the code is entered, you will be able to use the Web resources for the length of your course.

If your course is using **WebCT** or **Blackboard**, you'll be able to use this code to access the McGraw-Hill content within your instructor's online course.

Access is provided if you have purchased a new book. If the registration code is missing from this book, the registration screen on our Website, and within your WebCT or Blackboard course, will tell you how to obtain your new code.

Registering for McGraw-Hill Online Resources

TO gain access to your McGraw-Hill web resources simply follow the steps below:

NSU USED

1. USE YOUR WEB BROWSER TO GO TO: **www.mhhe.com/berg1**
2. CLICK ON **FIRST TIME USER**.
3. ENTER THE REGISTRATION CODE* PRINTED ON THE TEAR-OFF BOOKMARK ON THE RIGHT.
4. AFTER YOU HAVE ENTERED YOUR REGISTRATION CODE, CLICK **REGISTER**.
5. FOLLOW THE INSTRUCTIONS TO SET-UP YOUR PERSONAL UserID AND PASSWORD.
6. WRITE YOUR UserID AND PASSWORD DOWN FOR FUTURE REFERENCE. KEEP IT IN A SAFE PLACE.

TO GAIN ACCESS to the McGraw-Hill content in your instructor's **WebCT** or **Blackboard** course simply log in to the course with the UserID and Password provided by your instructor. Enter the registration code exactly as it appears in the box to the right when prompted by the system. You will only need to use the code the first time you click on McGraw-Hill content.

Thank you, and welcome to your McGraw-Hill online Resources!

REGISTRATION CODE

RIRD-2LUG-O64U-18FV-FYRA

Mc Graw Hill **Higher Education**

0-07-310502-3 T/A BERG-WEGER: SOCIAL WORK AND SOCIAL WELFARE, 1E

This is a much-needed series for social work education and the social work profession...one of the best I have seen in decades!

–Mildred C. Joyner, *West Chester University*

Each title is the first of its kind to offer instructors and their students a multidimensional understanding and experience of the world of social work:

- Each book in the series is accompanied by a custom Web site, updated weekly, that allows students to examine events in the news and to think about and discuss those events in the context of what they are reading. The Web site also links students to a wealth of carefully selected internet resources that are constantly updated and refreshed.

- A specially designed online reader, *The Social Work Library,* is also available to students, with over 100 articles and book chapters linked to the key ideas and principles covered in each volume in the series.

- *Practicing Social Work*™, a CD-ROM packaged with each volume in the series, offers complex, richly populated case exercises, with multiple options in text and video for analysis and intervention. The CD gives students a real-world sense of how social workers approach cases from micro, mezzo, and macro perspectives and trains them in the use of social work tools they will likely encounter in their professional lives.

- A free booklet on social work ethics accompanies each text in recognition of CSWE recommendations, and is authored by Kim Strom-Gottfried, University of North Carolina, who is nationally recognized for her educational workshops on the subject.

New Directions in Social Work is a comprehensive effort by a team of accomplished social work educators to move social work education forward. We want to help you enrich and deepen your students' learning experiences. And we want to know what you think! Please email us with your feedback. In the meantime, we welcome your students to a most gratifying, heartbreaking, edifying profession: social work.

Alice A. Lieberman, Series Editor
University of Kansas
e-mail: alicel@ku.edu

Marla Berg-Weger
Saint Louis University
e-mail: bergwm@slu.edu

*Social Work
and Social Welfare*

NEW DIRECTIONS IN SOCIAL WORK: A McGRAW-HILL SERIES

Edited by Alice A. Lieberman, University of Kansas

Technical consultant: Jerry Finn, Temple University

New Directions in Social Work is an innovative series of texts, software, and custom electronic content for the *foundations* courses in the Social Work curriculum. Each title is the first of its kind to offer instructors and their students a multidimensional experience and understanding of the world of social work. Each volume in the series includes a custom Web site, online reader, and *Practicing Social Work,* a unique collection of virtual case studies.

Books in the Series

Social Work and Social Welfare: An Invitation by Marla Berg-Weger

Social Work Practice by Martha P. Dewees

Human Behavior and the Social Environment by Anissa Taun Rogers

Social Welfare Policy by Rosemary K. Chapin

Social Work Research by Judy L. Krysik

Also from McGraw-Hill

Social Work Practice with a Difference: Stories, Essays, Cases, and Commentaries by Alice A. Lieberman and Cheryl B. Lester

The Social Work Experience: An Introduction to Social Work and Social Welfare, Fourth Edition by Mary Ann Suppes and Carolyn Cressy Wells

Social Work and Social Welfare

AN INVITATION

Marla Berg-Weger

Saint Louis University

Boston Burr Ridge, IL Dubuque, IA Madison, WI New York San Francisco St. Louis
Bangkok Bogotá Caracas Kuala Lumpur Lisbon London Madrid Mexico City
Milan Montreal New Delhi Santiago Seoul Singapore Sydney Taipei Toronto

The McGraw·Hill Companies

SOCIAL WORK AND SOCIAL WELFARE

Published by McGraw-Hill, a business unit of The McGraw-Hill Companies, Inc., 1221 Avenue of the Americas, New York, NY 10020. Copyright © 2005 by The McGraw-Hill Companies, Inc. All rights reserved. No part of this publication may be reproduced or distributed in any form or by any means, or stored in a database or retrieval system, without the prior written consent of The McGraw-Hill Companies, Inc., including, but not limited to, any network or other electronic storage or transmission, or broadcast for distance learning.

Some ancillaries, including electronic and print components, may not be available to customers outside the United States.

This book is printed on acid-free paper.

1 2 3 4 5 6 7 8 9 0 FGR/FGR 0 9 8 7 6 5 4

ISBN 0-07-284594-5

Editor-in-chief: *Emily Barrosse*
Publisher and sponsoring editor: *Stephen Rutter*
Special projects editor: *Rebecca Smith*
Developmental editor: *Robert Weiss*
Editorial assistant: *Ann Helgerson*
Marketing manager: *Courtney Cooney*
Lead media producer: *Sean Crowley*
Media supplement producer: *Kate Boylan*
Production editor: *Leslie LaDow*
Senior production supervisor: *Tandra Jorgensen*
Senior designer: *Kim Menning*
Interior designer: *Glenda King*
Cover designer: *Marianna Kinigakis*
Art editor: *Katherine McNab*
Photo research coordinator: *Natalia Peschiera*

Cover image: © *Photodisc*

Produced in association with NASW Press, a division of the National Association of Social Workers. NASW PRESS

This book was set in 9/13 Stone Serif by Interactive Composition Corporation and printed on 60# Focus Matte Book by Quebecor World, Fairfield.

Library of Congress Cataloging-in-Publication Data

Berg-Weger, Marla, 1956-
    Social work and social welfare : an invitation / Marla Berg-Weger.
        p. cm. – (New directions in social work ; 2)
    Includes bibliographical references and index.
        ISBN 0-07-284594-5 (softcover : alk. paper)
        1. Social service–United States. 2. Poor–Services for–United States. I. Title. II. New directions in social work (Boston, Mass.); 2.

HV91.B384 2005
361.3'0973—dc22   2004054256

To all the social workers who have influenced my social work journey and to all those social workers whose journey is yet to come.

AUTHOR BIOGRAPHY

MARLA BERG-WEGER, PhD, LCSW, serves as the associate provost for academic affairs and is an associate professor for the School of Social Service at Saint Louis University, St. Louis, Missouri. Dr. Berg-Weger holds social work degrees at the bachelor's, master's, and doctoral levels. Her social work practice experience includes public social welfare services, domestic violence services, mental health, and medical social work. Her research and writing focuses on social work practice and gerontological social work. With Julie Birkenmaier, she co-authored the textbook *The Practicum Companion for Social Work: Integrating Class and Field Work.*

BRIEF CONTENTS

DETAILED CONTENTS

PREFACE

Social work—before reading further, stop and consider what these words mean to you. The concept has taken on numerous, changing definitions since the idea emerged centuries ago. In our daily lives, you have likely heard of social work and possibly even met social workers, but you may not thoroughly understand the social work profession and its possibilities and contributions to the world.

If you are reading this book, you are probably enrolled in your first social work class. You may have decided to pursue a degree in social work, you may be investigating the possibility of working on a degree in the field, or you may have selected the course as an interesting elective. Regardless of your reasons for taking a social work course, it is my hope that this book will be an introduction to social work that will excite and inspire you about the profession.

Through this book and the electronic content that accompany it, you will be introduced to many facets of social work. You will learn about the profession's origins, the professional knowledge, skills, and values that social workers possess, the myriad settings in which social workers are employed, the ever-widening array of people that social workers serve, and the broad background that the social worker acquires during her or his pursuit of a social work degree.

There are many ways we could approach an exploration into the world of social work. I have chosen to share with you the diverse aspects of social work that have come to be a part of my life as a social worker and that are important to me as a social work educator. Like many of my social work colleagues, I have worked in a variety of settings and with a range of client populations in my two decades as a social work practitioner. What I have come to learn, however, is that the skills and knowledge I gained in my education transfer with each new social work experience. The basic social work knowledge and skills needed for working with older adults are not unlike those used in working in a shelter for women who are survivors of domestic violence and their children. As unlikely as this concept may seem, I hope that this book, with its experiential supplements, will illustrate for you the many possibilities that a career in social work may offer you.

ORGANIZATION OF THE BOOK

You are considering a lifetime career as a generalist social worker. This book provides you with an introduction to the knowledge, skills, and values that are essential for working with individuals, families, groups, organizations, and communities. As you progress through the social work program at your institution, you will complete coursework that will examine each of these areas in greater depth. Consider this book and course as the introduction to what lies ahead for you as you become a social worker.

Chapter 1

A Glimpse into the World of Social Work   We begin our journey into understanding the profession of social work by exploring the definition of social work, the ways that social workers help people, the people with whom social workers work, and the places where social workers practice. We conclude the first chapter of our exploration by examining the contribution of social work to the helping professions and the way that you can become a social worker. In this first chapter, you will meet Emily. Throughout the book, you will follow Emily as she experiences being a social work student and later a social work practitioner. I hope reading about Emily's experiences will help you to learn about the breadth of the social work profession and enable you to gain a sense of the passion that she has for her chosen career.

Chapter 2

History of Social Work and Social Welfare   To understand the profession of social work, you must understand where the profession began and the paths that social work, as a profession, has taken. Our history is one rich in diversity, controversy, and dedication. We begin our exploration of the history of the social work profession with a look at events that occurred as early as the 14th century and examine the highlights all the way to the dawn of the 21st century. Along with reviewing the history of services provided by social workers, we will examine the evolution of the profession itself.

Chapter 3

U.S. Poverty and the Implications for Social Work   An introduction to social work would not be complete if social welfare and its relationship to the profession of social work were not discussed. We will examine the issues related to poverty—what is poverty, who are the poor, what causes poverty, and what are the barriers to moving out of poverty. Understanding the history of the social welfare system in the context of the role that social workers have played is also a focus of this chapter. We end this phase of our journey with an introduction to a sampling of the social welfare programs that are currently in place to serve our society.

Chapter 4

The Social Work Environment   In order to be an effective social worker, it is important to understand the social forces and changes that influence our society and the people with whom social workers work, in particular. Because the demographic profile of our country has changed dramatically during the last century, we begin our exploration of the social work environment by examining such issues as race, ethnicity, age, gender, income (social class), sexual orientation, and religion. We continue our look into the world in which social workers work by considering the political, economic, and social opportunities and challenges facing social workers in the 21st century.

Chapter 5

Diversity in Social Work Practice   Social work, by its very definition and purpose, is committed to serving the entire spectrum of our population. This commitment means that we are often serving those segments of our society that are oppressed, marginalized, or disenfranchised by mainstream life. Therefore, it is incumbent upon us as competent social work professionals to embrace diversity. This requires, however, that we gain self-awareness regarding our own stereotypes and biases. Further, we are obligated to gain knowledge and skills that enable us to work effectively with persons who are different from ourselves. These differences may come in the form of race, ethnicity, culture, religion, sexual orientation, age, or lifestyle—just to name a few. A theoretical framework for understanding diversity is presented along with skills for being a culturally competent social work practitioner.

Chapter 6

Values and Ethics in Social Work Practice   Social work values are the cornerstone of the social work profession. This chapter introduces you to the values on which the profession is built and the ethical principles that guide social work practice. We examine the issues surrounding the ethical dilemmas that often arise as social workers strive to uphold their personal and professional values. These dilemmas include the right to privacy and confidentiality, right to self-determination, boundaries between the social worker and client, self-disclosure, and allocation of resources.

Chapter 7

Social Work Perspectives and Methods   This chapter introduces you to generalist social work practice. The generalist is a professionally degreed and trained social worker who has knowledge and skills grounded in theory and who can competently work at one or more of the three levels considered essential: individuals and families, groups, and organizations and communities. The theoretical frameworks that are woven throughout every aspect of your training as a social worker are introduced in this chapter. You will begin to understand the necessity of seeing people within the context of the environment in which they live and from the perspective of the strengths they possess, and of focusing on solutions rather than problems.

Chapter 8

Fields of Social Work Practice   Critical to your exploration of the social work profession as a possible career path is a picture of the varied clientele and settings encountered in generalist practice. In this chapter you will read narratives from eight social work practitioners. Carroll will discuss her work with older adults. Angela is a social worker in a child welfare agency and works in a school-based setting with children and their families. You will read about Suzanne's work with refugees in a community-based agency. From Jon, you will learn about the world of chemical dependency and addiction treatment with adolescents and note that his work brings him into contact with the legal system. Herbert, in his work in criminal justice, also works within the legal system. Jane will highlight the rewards and challenges of working in a medical setting, particularly her experience working with immigrants and refugees. Barbara discusses her work with victims and perpetrators of domestic violence in a mental health setting. Lastly, Ellen brings the perspective of a social worker whose practice is in a rural community. Learning about the possibilities of working in the areas described by these social workers may serve to narrow or broaden your focus.

Chapter 9

Social Work Practice with Individuals and Families   The opportunity to work directly with individuals and families in social service agencies, nonprofit organizations, hospitals, and schools is often the impetus for students to be drawn to social work. The majority of social workers do work directly with individuals. The skills and knowledge developed at the individual and family level can be used in all areas of social work, including the group level and the organizational and community level. You will be introduced to a model for social work interventions that carries through all three levels of social work practice. In this chapter, the concepts of engagement, assessment, intervention, and evaluation are explored in the context of working with individuals and families.

Chapter 10

Social Work Practice with Groups   For many, the idea of group work prompts an image of a group of people sitting in a circle talking about their problems with a therapist. Although group treatment is certainly an important area of group practice, group work also encompasses advocacy, social goals and change, education, and many other areas. We explore the range of group work models and skills needed to work at this level. Engagement, assessment, intervention, and evaluation will be applied at the group level of social work practice.

Chapter 11

Social Work Practice with Organizations and Communities   Social work practice with organizations and communities is thought by many to be the most exciting and challenging area in which to practice social work. This arena affords you the opportunity to effect change at the community, policy, political, societal, and even global level. Practice with organization and communities does not involve one-on-one client interaction, but it certainly uses both individual and group-level skills. The intersection of these skills is highlighted in this chapter.

Chapter 12

The Social Work Profession   We conclude our introductory journey by examining the issues of professional identification. In other words, where you fit in the profession, and how you become a social worker. Our journey together has come to an end, but yours can just be starting.

A WORD ABOUT LANGUAGE

As you read this book, you will be exposed to a wide range of terms that are integral to social work practice. You will be familiar with some of these terms, but will learn new and expanded definitions for them. For instance, the term *client,* referring to persons or groups being served by social workers, is probably familiar to you. You will also encounter the term *client system,* which may be used interchangeably with the term client to reflect the perspective that individuals are embedded in an environment that includes other individuals as well as groups, organizations, and communities.

You will also be prompted to adopt language that is sensitive to all persons in our society. Social workers strive to use terms that are preferred by the diverse groups in American society. For example, the terms *Latino* and *Hispanic* are both used in this book to refer to persons of Latin American descent, and *Native American* is used to refer to persons of American Indian or First Nation ancestry.

AN INTEGRATED PACKAGE

In addition to the printed material, this book integrates an interactive, online supplement that will enhance your introduction to the social work profession. At the book's Web site, http://www.mhhe.com/berg1, you will find the Social Work Library and more that will challenge and stimulate your learning. The Social Work Library is a compilation of full-text readings that provide an historical as well as contemporary perspective on substantive social work issues. Each chapter contains notations placed in the margins that will direct you to a related reading to enable you to explore in greater depth that particular topic, issues, or concept.

Another component of the New Directions in Social Work package is a case study CD-ROM called *Practicing Social Work*. Using the CD-ROM, you will meet the Sanchez family, a Latino family comprised of ten members. You will come to know each of the members through descriptions and situations that will bring to life the social work knowledge, skills, and values you are gaining. *Practicing Social Work* offers multiple options in text and video that will give you the opportunity to learn about engagement, assessment, intervention, and evaluation and termination. Through hands-on, interactive exercises, you will gain a sense of the approaches that social workers use in their professional activities.

IN SUM

My hopes for your experience with this book and the companion experiential supplement are that you gain an understanding of the passion that makes social work the rewarding profession that it is, the skills required to be an effective social worker, and the rich diversity and variety that make social work an exciting career choice. Social work is a meaningful, vastly satisfying profession in human services that provides invaluable help to people and communities and enables you to feel you are really making a difference. The skills and knowledge that you acquire during your training can prepare you to work in health care, mental health services, services to older adults, child welfare, political advocacy, the legal system, schools—the possibilities are almost limitless!

ACKNOWLEDGMENTS

I would like to extend my appreciation to the many social workers who helped this book to become a reality. To Alice Lieberman and the other authors of this book series, Rosemary Chapin, Marty DeWees, Judy Krysik, and Anissa Rogers, I thank you for your vision, support, and feedback through this enriching and invigorating process. To my colleagues at Saint Louis University, Julie Birkenmaier, Ellen Burkemper, Sue Tebb, and Sabrina Tyuse, I appreciate your willingness to provide resources, review chapters, and serve as a sounding board for my ideas. To the practitioners who contributed their "voices from the field," I am grateful for your willingness to share the stories of your professional lives. To the three reviewers, Pam Huggins, Becky Garrison, and Helen Glik, thank you for your diligence in completing multiple reviews of the book. Your input was invaluable. Lastly, to the editors and staff at McGraw-Hill, thank you for your guidance and expertise.

CHAPTER 1

A Glimpse into the World of Social Work

ASK SOCIAL WORKERS WHAT DREW THEM TO THE PROFESSION, and you will hear one common message: They liked the idea that they would be helping to better people's lives. Although they might have considered one of the other helping professions, such as psychology, sociology, teaching, or medicine, they chose social work. As you will learn throughout this book, social work is unique among other helping disciplines because of its broad scope of concern, its strong core values, and its commitment to social and economic justice.

Social work has goals and methods in common with other helping disciplines, and social workers have adopted useful knowledge from many of these professions. From psychology, social workers learn to understand the impact of emotional and psychological factors on the individual. From sociology, they gain insight into populations of people. From the medical professions, they learn of the relationships between biological functioning and health/illness and the impact of these factors on psychosocial well-being. The health professions also emphasize the value of the interdisciplinary team approach. Social work and other helping professions certainly overlap; however, social work is also distinctive in a number of ways (see Table 1.1).

The social work profession emphasizes a holistic, or interpersonal, perspective as opposed to the individual (intrapersonal) perspective of other helping professions. The **National Association of Social Workers (NASW)**, the professional organization for the social work profession, issued a policy statement supporting "the delineation of social work as distinctly different from other human service disciplines (such as counseling, clinical psychology, nursing, and marital counseling) as it focuses on the intra- and inter-personal aspects of clients' lives" (National Association of Social Workers [NASW], 2000–2003a).

A hallmark of providing social work services to people is to consider their **social environment:** their family, home, work, state of health, community, and the interactions that they have with all those areas of their life. Perhaps the most important distinction between social work and other helping professions

	DISCIPLINE	SIMILARITIES WITH SOCIAL WORK	DIFFERENCES FROM SOCIAL WORK
TABLE 1.1 *What Makes Social Work Unique*	**Psychology**	(1) Both are practice professions. (2) At the graduate level, both are trained to provide psychotherapy. (3) Both may work in the same settings with the same clients.	(1) Psychology focuses on internal issues as the source of the problem; social work focuses on the person within the environment (PIE). (2) Psychology focuses on the individual as the target of the intervention; social work interventions encompass the individual and those in his/her environment. (3) Psychologists administer and interpret psychological tests; social workers are typically not trained in this area of practice. (4) In some states, psychologists can prescribe medications; social workers cannot. (5) Clinical practice often requires a PhD for psychologists and an MSW for social workers. (Social workers are licensed to practice as BSWs in many states.)
	Sociology	(1) Both are interested in the patterns of behaviors of people.	(1) Sociology is not a practice profession, but a social science that considers the population, often in the context of communities.
	Health Professions (nursing and medicine, in particular)	(1) Both are practice professions. (2) Both recognize the influence of health on well-being. (3) Both work in community/hospital settings with the same patients. (4) Both have generalist and specialist expertise.	(1) Health professions often focus primarily on physical health issues; social work assessments routinely include biological, psychological, and social perspectives/factors. (2) Social workers are expert about community resources. (3) Physicians and some nurses can prescribe medications; social workers cannot.

DISCIPLINE	SIMILARITIES WITH SOCIAL WORK	DIFFERENCES FROM SOCIAL WORK	**TABLE 1.1** *continued*
Marriage and Family Counseling	(1) Both are practice professions. (2) At the graduate level, both are trained to provide psychotherapy. (3) Both have licensing and certification requirements. (4) Both can conduct clinical practice with a master's degree. (5) Neither discipline can prescribe medications.	(1) Like psychologists, counselors focus primarily on the individual as the source of the problem for assessment and intervention. (2) Counselors are not typically trained in community practice (for example, advocacy, organizing); social work training emphasizes competence at the individual/family/community levels.	

Note: Additional sources used here include Ginsberg, 2001; Peck, 1999.

is the emphasis on social action through advocacy for those oppressed or discriminated against by society. Although social workers help people by providing services in an agency setting, the profession also advocates addressing social conditions such as homelessness, hunger, teen pregnancy, poverty, and discrimination. This chapter will illustrate the meaning of social work. In the remaining chapters, a more detailed picture will emerge of what social work is and what you need to learn to be an effective social worker.

The Social Work Library

Read Greenwood's article to gain an historical perspective on the social work profession.

A DEFINITION OF SOCIAL WORK

Developing an accurate and comprehensive definition of social work requires an expansive view of the profession and the positions that social workers hold. As you might already know, social workers are employed in such helping institutions as schools, hospitals, mental health facilities, older-adult service programs, and children's residential settings. You might not know, however, that social workers also work in banks, large corporations, theater groups, community gardens, military installations, and police stations. Social work professionals work with people in all segments of society, from those who are disenfranchised or devalued by society and living in poverty to those in the middle and upper socioeconomic segments of society. They work with the young and the old, with people in good health and poor health, and with people from diverse cultures and backgrounds.

Let us see how the profession itself defines social work. In 1973, the National Association of Social Workers established a definition of **social work** that remains relevant today:

The Social Work Library

Review the article by Tillich to learn his perspective on the social work profession.

> Social Work is the professional activity of helping individuals, groups or communities to enhance or restore their capacity for social functioning and creating societal conditions favorable to this goal. (p. 4)

The NASW definition includes four basic goals for the profession: (1) linking people to resources; (2) providing direct services to individuals, families, and groups; (3) helping communities or groups provide or improve social and health services; and (4) participating in relevant legislative processes (NASW, 1973, pp. 4–5). In other words, the goal of social work is to empower people to optimize their abilities and quality of life, whether through working directly with people or through taking action to change society. The openness and flexibility of this definition enable social workers to respond to those needs that exist within their communities. The populations, health crises, social conditions, and ethical dilemmas with which social workers are engaged may vary, but the work transcends time and individual circumstance because of its all-encompassing nature. This diversity and the activist bias attract many people to the social work profession.

THE WORK OF SOCIAL WORK

Consider the experiences of a midcareer social worker named Emily. Like many of her professional counterparts, Emily has worked in a number of different social work positions and settings. Early in her career, she worked in the public welfare system in several different areas ranging from child protective services, to services for older adults and persons with visual impairments, to outreach work in a domestic violence program. Later, Emily obtained a graduate degree and, over the years, held social work positions in a mental health center, home health agency, hospital, and medical outpatient clinic.

One of the things that Emily has found especially rewarding about her profession is the variety of experiences she has had because she has degrees in social work. When she worked in the domestic violence program, for instance, she responded to calls from emergency rooms where women had gone after being battered by their partners. Emily met the woman at the hospital and assessed her current situation, abuse history, safety needs, and resources. She then arranged housing either at the shelter or at a safe house for the woman and her children. Emily worked with the woman during her stay to explore options and make long-term plans. Sometimes, this effort involved helping the woman leave her partner for a new life, but other times it meant watching her return to the relationship. In these cases, Emily always worked out a safety plan with the woman in the event the violence occurred again. Emily used a number of social work skills in this position: crisis intervention, interviewing, assessment, providing information and referral, brokering, intervention planning, evaluation, and documentation.

At the mental health center, Emily conducted intakes for persons requesting therapy services. She met with those persons for an hour-long assessment of their presenting concern, social situation, and mental health status. After completing this assessment, she dictated a report and recommended a treatment plan. In this job, Emily used such skills as assessment, diagnosis, preparation of documentation, and crisis intervention.

As a medical social worker in a hospital, Emily provided services to patients and their families upon the request of the medical staff. She often assisted the patient and her or his family in making discharge plans. This process could include arranging for financial assistance, home health or hospice services, residential care, medications, medical equipment, and possible relocation. Emily was also there to support families when a patient died. When she was on call for the social work department, she covered the emergency room, which could involve just about any situation. Her crisis intervention skills clearly were a major asset here.

Because social work training provides a core set of knowledge and skills that can be applied in a variety of settings with a diverse population, Emily has been able to work in a number of challenging but rewarding positions: investigating adult and child abuse and neglect, working with battered women and their children, conducting assessments for therapy in a mental health center, arranging discharge plans for hospitalized patients, and providing therapy for persons experiencing such conditions as depression, a new medical diagnosis, or family and marital problems. You can see that Emily has enjoyed a broad and diverse career that was made possible by her social work degrees. She thrives on the opportunity to work with different types of people who are experiencing different life *situations. In addition, she welcomes the opportunity to move into a new position if she chooses. Most of all, Emily enjoys being able to help people through difficult life experiences.*

What Social Workers Do

A federal government study found that approximately 468,000 people were employed as social workers in 2000 (U.S. Department of Labor, 2002b). More than two-thirds of them are engaged in **direct practice**, in which they work with individuals, couples, families, and small groups (Gibelman & Schervish, 1997). Most social workers who responded to a 1995 survey reported that they provided mental health services (38 percent), family services (26 percent), or health-related services (13 percent)—all of which are types of direct practice. In fact, social workers in the United States provide more mental health and therapy services than any other discipline does, including psychology or counseling (NASW, 1996). In this field of practice, social workers provide crisis intervention and counseling services to individuals, families, and groups experiencing difficulty in coping with a life crisis or transition, such as a relationship problem, death or injury, divorce, or illness.

A significant number of social work professionals are engaged, in whole or in part, in policy development and analysis, advocacy, and in supervisory, administrative, and fund-raising activities. In fact, the second-highest ranked category of primary social work function (area in which the person spends the majority of her or his time) is program/agency administration and personnel management (Gibelman & Schervish, 1997). Almost one-third of the social workers surveyed did not have just one primary function; rather, they were engaged in multiple areas and levels of social work activities. Supervision and teaching are the most frequently mentioned secondary areas of work. In the areas of administration and policy, social workers are often the initiators of new social programs because they have been in the field and are able to see where the needs exist. This experience also helps social workers to understand and influence social policies because they have observed the impact of those policies on the client systems with whom they work. Social workers can share real-life stories with legislators to help them understand the effects of their votes on constituents.

Social workers' skills enable them to work in a broad range of areas and specializations (Barker, 2003; NASW, 2004c):

- Conducting needs assessments, providing information and referrals, and accessing resources in **social casework/case management.**

- Serving as a case manager and counseling around specific health-related issues in **medical social work.**

- Working with students and their families on emotional, social, and economic concerns to enable them to focus on the student's education in **school social work.**

- Counseling individuals, families, and groups in such settings as hospitals, schools, mental health facilities, and private practices in **clinical social work.**

- Supervising programs and people in **administration and management.**

- Working to influence the development, implementation, and evaluation of policies aimed at creating social justice for those impacted by the policies in **policy practice.**

- Working with groups and communities to identify conditions and develop strategies to address them in **community organization.**

- Analyzing conditions, programs, and policies and conducting and studying research in an effort to improve the social service system in **social policy research.**

On a daily basis, social workers may find themselves engaged in these common work activities:

- Determining the social, emotional, and economic concerns and needs of persons for whom they provide services.

- Providing services to address the needs of people, or referring clients for appropriate professional or community services.

- Developing resources, programs, and social policies to address unmet community needs.

- Assessing, diagnosing, and/or treating mental health and emotional conditions.

- Working to improve social programs and health services by conducting research and encouraging communities and organizations to be responsive to identified needs.

- Helping people improve personal and/or social functioning by providing or referring for education, training, employment, and personal growth services.

- Coordinating and working with governmental, private, civic, religious, business, and/or trade organizations to combat social problems through community awareness and response programs.

- Researching, planning, and developing social and health policies and programs.

BOX 1.1

Who Needs a Social Worker?

YOU'LL NEED A SOCIAL WORKER . . .

When you come into the world too soon

When you can't find anyone to play with

When you are left home alone

When you hate the new baby

When you don't think your teacher likes you

When you are bullied

When you don't want your mommy and daddy to divorce

When you miss your big brother

When you don't like how the neighbor touches you

When you get into fights at school

When you don't make the team

When your best friend moves away

When you get poor grades

When you always fight with your siblings

When your friends pressure you to get high

When you can't adjust to the move

When you can't talk to your parents

When you want to quit school

When your friends don't like you anymore

When you didn't want this baby

When you feel like running away

When your friend swallows an overdose

When you are the only one that thinks you're fat

When you can't find someone who speaks your language

When you can't forget the assault

When you can't decide on a career

When your family pressures you to marry

When your boss is hitting on you

When you can't stick to a budget

When you want to adopt

When you wonder if you are drinking too much

When you can't find good day care

When you think you are neglecting your kids

When you are hated because of who you are

When you lose your baby

When your community has gang problems

When your kids want to live with your ex

When your partner is unfaithful

When you want to meet your birthparent

When your disabled child needs friends

When your step-kids hate you

When your mother won't speak to you

When you can't face moving again

When your spouse wants a divorce

When you want to be a foster parent

When your city officials don't respond

When your best friend has panic attacks

When you find drugs in your son's room

When your job is eliminated

When your mother-in-law wants to move in

When your neighborhood needs a community center

When you find there is no joy in your life

When your car accident destroys your career

When you sponsor a refugee family

When your legislature passes a bad law

When your brother won't help care for dad

When your partner has a mid life crisis

When you are stressed by menopause

BOX 1.1
continued

When your mom gets Alzheimer's

When you are caring for parents and children

When you want to change careers

When you lose your home in a fire

When you are angry all the time

When your nest really empties

When your partner insists you retire

When you can't afford respite care

When you can't find a job and you're sixty

When your kids demand that you move in with them

When your daughter suddenly dies

When you are scared about living alone

When you can't drive any more

When your children ignore your medical decisions

When your retirement check won't pay the bills

When you learn you have a terminal illness

When you need a nursing home

LIFE'S CHALLENGES - SOCIAL WORKERS ARE THERE FOR YOU!

Source: © 2001, Darlene Lynch and Robert Vernon. For free distribution information visit: http://hsmedia.biz

Social workers' skills afford them the opportunity to work with any population in any situation or setting.

Who Is Served by Social Workers

If you are interested in being a social worker, you need to understand that many of the people with whom you will work are struggling to function within their setting. Fortunately, most people have strengths on which to draw, and activating those strengths is the social worker's specialty. From the beginnings of the profession, social workers have worked one-on-one primarily with persons facing discrimination because of ethnic background, race, gender, ability, or age, or with those experiencing life crises, or physical or mental health issues. When asked to identify where they focus their professional resources, many social workers indicate a desire to work with family issues and with persons who have limited incomes (Gibelman & Schervish, 1997). However, the scope of practice and service boundaries for social workers have expanded throughout history to keep up with societal needs. Today, for example, social workers assist teens with pregnancy and HIV/AIDS prevention and sex education. Box 1.1 provides some insight into the range of people who might find themselves in need of a social worker's services.

As an adult service worker in the public welfare agency, Emily once started off a typical day by visiting Mrs. H., a 70-year-old widow with no family. Mrs. H. lived alone in a small house that Emily could see was not well maintained or clean. Mrs. H. was referred to Emily's agency by her minister because he was concerned about her. Mrs. H. had a visual impairment due to glaucoma, severe arthritis, and diabetes. She had been trying to cover up for her increasing debilitation by isolating herself and not participating in her usual social activities.

These may seem like insurmountable problems, and the only reasonable response might seem to be, at first blush, to put Mrs. H. in a nursing home. However, Mrs. H. desperately wanted to continue living independently. Moreover, she was financially independent, and she had a small circle of caring people, such as her minister and neighbors, who provided social support. Through Emily's social assessment, which included family, financial, and health information, she concluded that Mrs. H. was a candidate for a number of social services: homemaker/chore (help with housekeeping tasks), home health services (nursing assistance to monitor her diabetes), services for persons with visual impairments (a rehabilitation teacher to help her adjust to her visual impairment), and telephone reassurance services (a daily telephone check-in service). With the help of these services, Emily's ongoing case management, and a willingness to build on her strengths, Mrs. H. remained independent and functional until her death 10 years later.

Where Social Workers Work

Emily's social work degrees and experience have enabled her to change positions within the social work field. Her social work training prepared her to work with varied groups of people in direct practice—children, families, older adults, and persons with disabilities or persistent illness. Her knowledge and skills have also enabled her to facilitate groups and to work at the administrative and educational levels. Emily values the learning she has gained in each of these settings.

Nevertheless, she has developed her preferences. Emily's social work experience began with a community service assignment in her introductory social work course. She found an opportunity at a nursing home, helping older adults. With her undergraduate degree in social work, Emily found a job in the public welfare system. However, Emily developed an extensive knowledge of the public welfare system that was an asset in being accepted into graduate school and in being hired to work in a shelter program for women who have been abused and their children. Her experiences in public welfare and domestic violence were viewed favorably when she applied for a position at the mental health center.

Although each setting offered a different experience and enabled her to develop her knowledge and skill as a social worker, Emily also found that her personality was better suited for some settings than others. For example, she learned that she enjoys working in an agency in which she has a large group of co-workers with whom she can interact on a daily basis.

Like Emily, most social workers gain experience in a variety of settings. Such settings include (1) organizations that primarily provide social services; (2) **host settings**, or secondary organizations such as schools, correctional facilities, or health care facilities; (3) voluntary nonprofit agencies; and (4) governmental or public agencies. Although some social workers are in private practice, most work in an organization. As for specialty, Exhibit 1.1 describes the settings in which most practicing social workers were employed in the year 2000. Social workers most frequently work in such settings as mental health agencies, child welfare programs, and elementary and secondary schools (Doelling, Matz, & Kuehne, 1999).

Between one-half and two-thirds of all social workers are employed in the private social service sector (Gibelman & Schervish, 1997). A majority work in nonprofit settings such as social service agencies, hospitals, residential care facilities, home health agencies, health centers, and criminal justice programs. These privately funded agencies are administered by boards of directors, and their profits are retained or reinvested in the programs to enhance service delivery. These agencies raise funds through individual and corporate donations, grants, fundraisers, and public sector contracts. In addition, an increasing number of social workers are working in for-profit settings such as corporations (for example, in employee assistance programs) and private schools (U.S. Department of Labor, 2002c). The private social service delivery system in the United States consists of approximately 102,000 organizations (U.S. Department of Labor, 2002a).

Although a majority of social workers are employed in the private sector, public or governmental settings remain an important source of jobs for social workers. Reports suggest that between one-third and one-half of social workers are employed in publicly funded settings that provide services in the areas of mental health, social services, child welfare, housing, education, and corrections (U.S. Department of Labor, 2002b). The overwhelming majority of social

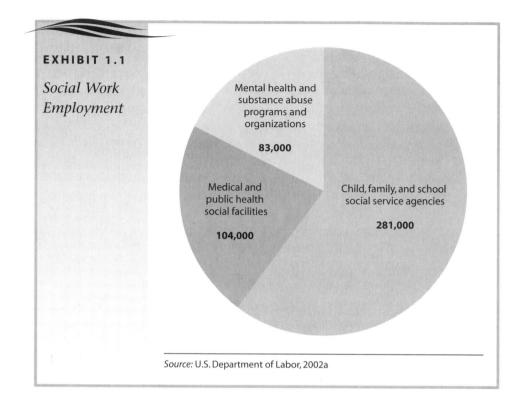

EXHIBIT 1.1

Social Work Employment

Mental health and substance abuse programs and organizations

83,000

Medical and public health social facilities

104,000

Child, family, and school social service agencies

281,000

Source: U.S. Department of Labor, 2002a

workers in the public sector are employed at the state and local levels, with a smaller number working in programs at the federal level. These local, state, and federal settings include state-funded public welfare/human service departments; mental health agencies; child welfare agencies; housing programs; veterans' administration organizations; military installations; local, state, and federal court/justice systems; public schools; hospitals; and policy-making organizations. The number of social workers in the public sector is decreasing due, in large part, to cutbacks in local, state, and federal budgets (Gibelman & Schervish, 1997). However, the public setting remains an important arena for social workers to assist with enhancement of welfare programs.

PATHS TO BECOMING A SOCIAL WORKER

Emily's path to becoming a social worker is her own, but it is typical for many social workers. It began with a significant personal experience. Emily married shortly after graduating from high school, and she clearly did not expect that domestic violence would occur in her marriage. But when it did, Emily ended the marriage in a relatively short time. With her family's support, Emily headed off to college. She had no idea what she wanted to major in, but she was influenced by her past life experiences.

Emily was intrigued by a psychology course she took to fulfill her university's general education requirement. She liked the idea of trying to understand the ways that people think and behave. She had always been the person among her friends in whom others confided—maybe because she was a good listener. Next, Emily took sociology and anthropology courses. She was drawn to the idea of thinking about people within their societies, but she also liked the possibility of being able to help people.

One of Emily's instructors commented that she seemed to enjoy these classes, and she asked if Emily had considered social work. Emily had never met a social worker, but she began to investigate the social work program. The rest, as they say, is history. Emily went on to get her bachelor's and master's degrees in social work, and she has worked in a variety of settings. And yes, she has worked in many situations that involved domestic violence. Because of her training as a professional social worker, Emily recognized the importance of exploring her own life experience in relation to her professional work, and she has continued to do just that throughout her career.

Emily's story is not an uncommon example of a social worker's journey into the profession. Many social workers come to the profession through interest in helping people, a psychology course, or past personal experiences. Emily happened to have all three. The psychology course helped her to find a connection with one of her strengths—an interest in helping people. Her personal experience as a survivor of domestic violence helped her tap into a reservoir of empathy to help others. Knowing your strengths and developing skills for working with people are essential for considering a career in social work.

You might wonder, though, why Emily decided to major in social work instead of psychology or sociology. Had it not been for that insightful faculty member, Emily would likely have graduated with a psychology degree. Having a degree in psychology could have taken Emily down a different career path. She might have gone on to complete a graduate degree in psychology, which would have led her to focus primarily on psychological testing. A doctorate in psychology could have taken her into private practice, research, or academic life. You can see how psychology can overlap with social work, but there are differences, too. Emily can become a therapist with a master's degree in social work and a clinical credential (license). In psychology, she would require a doctorate.

SOCIAL WORK EDUCATION

To practice social work, social workers need the proper credentials. Professional social work can be performed only by a person who has been awarded a bachelor's or master's degree from a college or university social work program that is accredited by the **Council on Social Work Education (CSWE).** NASW has issued a policy statement that conveys the importance of the title of social worker being used only for persons who hold social work degrees (NASW, 2003–2006). In fact, many states have passed title protection legislation stipulating that only persons with social work degrees from CSWE-accredited programs may refer to themselves as social workers. In addition, all states have enacted social work credentialing legislation that enables degreed social work practitioners to obtain a license or certification to practice social work. These laws vary from state to state and by area of practice expertise. Further, NASW actively advocates against laws and rules that do not stipulate that social work positions must be filled by degreed social workers.

Perhaps the social workers of your state have lobbied for legislation to protect the title of social worker or require social work positions to be filled by degreed social workers. You can check with your state's NASW chapter.

U.S. social work programs grant three types of degrees:

- **Bachelor of Social Work (BSW)** prepares the graduate for generalist social work professional practice.

- **Master of Social Work (MSW)** prepares the graduate for advanced professional practice in an area of concentration.

- **Doctorate of Philosophy in Social Work (PhD or DSW)** is typically considered a research-oriented degree with a focus on preparing the graduate for a teaching and/or research career. However, several programs offer a doctorate degree in social work that emphasizes clinical practice.

Social work education is multifaceted, interdisciplinary, and diverse. The BSW exposes students to a wide range of content areas. A liberal arts background provides students with basic knowledge and skills that are an asset in social work practice, including an appreciation for scientific methods and historical development; skills for effective communication and critical thinking; awareness of the human condition and the contribution of the arts to society; openness to diversity, difference, and improvability; and knowledge of human biological function. For their elective coursework, many undergraduate social work students gravitate to courses that will strengthen their knowledge of human behavior or social policy development. An area of growing interest is fluency in a second language, such as Spanish or American Sign Language (ASL). As our society becomes increasingly ethnically diverse, bilingual skills will become more important within the social work profession. Within the BSW program, an array of courses covers the areas that have been identified as essential for the professional social worker (Council on Social Work Education [CSWE], 2001a):

- Values and ethics

- Social work practice

- Diversity

- Populations at risk

- Social and economic justice

- Human behavior and the social environment

- Social welfare policy and services

- Research

- Field work

Among the helping professions, social work is the leader in preparing graduates with a bachelor's degree to work effectively in social services. The BSW permits such quick entry into professional practice for three reasons: (1) students in the BSW program are required to participate in two or three service-learning experiences in a social service agency; (2) the BSW program is accredited by a professional body; and (3) the BSW enables graduates to obtain a state license or certification (no other discipline credentials baccalaureate-level professionals) (Boyd, 1996).

The distinction between the BSW and the MSW is primarily in the areas of content, program objectives, and depth, breadth, and specificity of knowledge and skills (CSWE, 2001a). According to one NASW survey, 86 percent of practicing social workers that responded possess an MSW degree, while 10 percent of respondents had the BSW as their highest degree (Gibelman & Schervish, 1997). Social workers with BSWs and MSWs often work in the same settings and with the same client systems, but each functions at different levels and performs different tasks.

For example, at the BSW level, Emily worked directly with women and children in the domestic violence program. She helped them gain admittance to a safe-house program and to obtain legal, financial, health, and mental health services. In contrast, at the MSW level, Emily actually provided mental health treatment for the women and children in the shelter.

FIELD EXPERIENCES

Whichever level of social work education you might pursue, you can expect the theory learned in the classroom to be integrated with actual practice. The field education experience promotes the application of knowledge, skills, and values through at least 400 hours of supervised practice in a social work setting. This training enables social workers to work effectively and ethically with people facing real challenges. Members of the profession feel strongly that social workers should be mentored and supervised by other social workers.

✗ Actual experience is invaluable. In fact, one strategy for determining whether social work might be the profession for you is to gain exposure to social work through a volunteer experience. Whether or not you have engaged in community service in the past, now is an excellent time to seek a learning experience through volunteer service with the aim of working with and observing social workers as they perform their activities. Take full advantage of this opportunity to challenge yourself. Seek out a population with whom you are familiar, or even not familiar, and imagine yourself as a social work professional in that setting. If you are not required to engage in a community project as part of your introductory coursework, do it anyway. In addition to providing an opportunity for you to gain experience, your community service can be an asset in other ways (Dale, 2001):

- Helping you to identify interests (or areas in which you are not interested) and goals.

- Enhancing your resumé, future marketability, and social work network.

- Building self-confidence and guiding your career directions.

Most social service agencies welcome—and actually rely on—the contributions of volunteers. Here are some suggestions for learning about service opportunities in your community:

- Consult with faculty members, your academic advisor, and/or the field education department.
- Contact your state's NASW chapter office.
- Contact your local United Way.
- Check your university's community service or volunteer clearinghouse office.

Like Emily, you may find yourself unexpectedly drawn to the profession of social work. And, like Emily, you will find that every little bit of experience helps. In each of the jobs in which Emily has worked, she has used the skills that she learned during her training and in previous jobs. Each job led to the next, and each job built on the last.

CONCLUSION

We have arrived at the end of the first chapter of this book. In this chapter, you have been introduced to the definition of social work, areas in which social workers practice, and the education required for becoming a social worker. I hope your perception of the social work profession is beginning to encompass the diversity and breadth that the profession itself encompasses. After reading this chapter, you may have developed more questions about the social work profession than you had when you began.

In this chapter, you have gained more insight into this career you are exploring, but we have a long way to go. We will continue our journey through the social work profession by exploring the history of social work, current challenges that influence social work, areas of practice, cultural competence, values and ethics, theoretical frameworks for guiding practice, fields of practice, and the possibilities for the future of the social work profession.

As you proceed, keep in mind the following, written by an MSW student (Walton, 1996, p. 63). Her words not only capture her enthusiasm for her new profession, but they also provide a sense of the work that social workers do.

Social work is a career you can't leave at the office. You are committed to facilitating change in people's lives and the environment in which they live. You

BOX 1.2

Top 10 Reasons for Being a Social Worker

10. Help People
9. Do What Counts
8. Practice Your Principles
7. Foster Success Stories
6. Match Skills with Life's Challenges
5. Change the Future
4. Make the World a Better Place
3. Satisfaction Guaranteed
2. World-Class Peers
1. Career of Champions

often work with, or on behalf of, individuals who have difficult problems and lack the resources with which to cope. It can be inspiring to see your client help themselves out of a crisis using skills you helped them find within themselves.

I hope that you, too, can be inspired and that you are now beginning to consider whether you want to be a social worker. Check out the top 10 reasons for being a social worker in Box 1.2 for some insight into a profession whose mission is to help others, make the world a better place, and perform meaningful work.

MAIN POINTS

- Social work is a professional activity that provides the opportunity to work with individuals, families, groups, organizations, and communities. Almost a half-million people in the United States are practicing social workers.

- Other professions, such as psychology and sociology, have contributed to the development of social work, but the profession of social work also has unique values, knowledge, and practice skills.

- Social workers provide an ever-changing array of services such as counseling, advocacy, case management, education, prevention, support, and crisis intervention.

- Social workers work with persons throughout all areas of our society, including children, adolescents, and adults experiencing life changes or crises; persons who are struggling with an illness, disability, addiction, or homelessness; and persons who are the victims of oppression, discrimination, or social injustice.

- Social workers work in a variety of settings, including schools, hospitals, mental health facilities, chemical dependency treatment programs, advocacy programs, and residential facilities for children, youth, persons who are homeless, and older adults.

- Social workers can obtain degrees at the bachelor's, master's, and doctoral levels. The National Association of Social Workers (NASW) and the Council on Social Work Education (CSWE) have defined the criteria for competence in a degreed social worker.

EXERCISES: PRACTICING SOCIAL WORK

Meet the Sanchez Family

In this exercise, you will meet the Sanchez family. Click on Program Introduction to meet the Sanchez family. Review how this program can be used. Activate each button to familiarize yourself with the interactive case study. Spend some time exploring the biographies of Sanchez family members.

Unanswered Questions

Continuing on with the Sanchez family interactive case study, click on Engage. Click on View Your Tasks in this section. Complete Task #1 to better understand the needs of the Sanchez family.

"Listening" to the Client System

Complete Task #2 in the Engage portion of the interactive case study to learn more about the Sanchez family.

After you have completed Task #2, use the notebook to reflect on the roles that a social worker can play; describe the types of things a social work professional might be able to do to help the Sanchez family.

EXERCISES: THE SOCIAL WORK LIBRARY

Attributes of a Professional

After reading "Attributes of a Profession" (Greenwood, 1957) in the Social Work Library, respond to the following:

1. Describe the five attributes of a profession.

2. Compare Greenwood's conceptualization of social work as a profession with your current perception of social work.

The Philosophy of Social Work

After reading "The Philosophy of Social Work" (Tillich, 1962) in the Social Work Library, respond to the following:

1. How does Tillich define social work?

2. In Tillich's conception of social work, what is the role of the caseworker?

3. Compare the conceptualization offered by Tillich with your current perception of social work.

OTHER EXERCISES

Paths to Learning about Professional Social Work

Visit one of the following Web sites to obtain information about the social work profession:

1. National Association of Social Workers, www.naswdc.org. Click on "State Chapters" to get information about NASW programs in your state, including community service opportunities.

2. Council on Social Work Education, www.cswe.org.

Journal Entry #1—Self-perception

Describe yourself (character, traits, and values) in terms of how you perceive the world and human nature. Discuss how these qualities may impact your professional work.

CHAPTER 2

History of Social Work and Social Welfare

T HE EXACT BEGINNINGS AND ORIGINS OF THE PROFESSION OF social work are difficult to determine, but ample evidence throughout history suggests that what has come to be recognized as social work has been performed for thousands of years. This work, often performed by persons affiliated with religious institutions, usually took the form of providing tangible goods and services to impoverished people confronted with health problems. As you will learn in this chapter, this "charity" work evolved over the centuries to include the provision of mental health services, community organization and development work, and advocacy for groups of people experiencing oppression whose voices are not heard by decision makers.

Imagine what it was like, though, to be one of the pioneers who began to practice social work before it had a name. What would it have been like to pursue social work before much of society acknowledged the idea that we should care for all our citizens? Try to grasp the struggles that these heroes and heroines faced. Imagine that you are in 17th-century England trying to help poor families obtain enough food to eat; in 18th-century America trying to gain support to open that first orphanage; in 19th-century America working in one of the new settlement houses helping immigrants adjust to their new home; in 20th-century America working for school desegregation, elimination of domestic violence, or one of the other new areas for social work. In the 21st century we are still working in the same areas—new challenges, but the same areas.

As we begin this discussion of the history of social work, clarifying the difference between social work and social welfare is important. Although the terms are often used synonymously, they are not the same. As you learned in Chapter 1, social work is the practice of a professional activity of helping individuals, groups, and communities. In contrast, **social welfare** is a system aimed at creating social and economic justice. Social welfare services and programs have been part of society for centuries, and they provided the cornerstone for the emergence and development of the social work profession. Our discussion here will include a chronicle of the history of social welfare programs and services in which many social workers are active as well as the history of the social work profession. It will end with an overview of the development of social work education. The NASW publication *Milestones in the Development of Social Work and Social Welfare* (1998) is a primary resource used in compiling the following historical perspective.

DEVELOPMENT OF SOCIAL SERVICES

The roots of the social work profession lie within the religious community and the religious teachings of a range of different religious groups. For many centuries, the provision of charity (or alms) was entirely within the purview of churches. As early as 1200 BC, religious leaders urged Jews to help the poor of their communities. Reflecting those tenets, historical Jewish documents describe charitable services that actually resemble modern-day mediation and casework (Senkowsky, 1996b). A man named Stephen, working as a representative of his religion, has been called the "first" social worker. Seven Jewish deacons were selected by Christian leaders to see to the needs of Jews who had been enslaved. One of these seven men, Stephen, was particularly effective in this mission. Along with his six peers, his efforts have been described as the first social work because he collected food and money for distribution to the "needy." These activities themselves were not innovative; however, designating specific persons to do the work was innovative. Stephen was commended by many for his work, but the leaders of Jerusalem were not in support of his work. He was tried by the High Court of the Great Temple and executed for his values and beliefs by the religious leadership (Marson & MacLeod, 1996). For examples of the influence of religious doctrine on modern-day social services, see Exhibit 2.1.

Beginning in the 14th century, social changes in Europe began to transform attitudes toward the poor and the provision of charity. The feudal system of payment for services in land was beginning to shift to a more wage-based economic and social system, which led to increased trade within the towns and cities, thus creating a new "middle class" (Reid, 1995). In 1349, the Statute of Labourers was established in England to create a distinction between the "worthy" and the "unworthy" poor. Under this law, only the elderly and people with disabilities were deemed worthy to receive charity.

Two centuries later, this concept was expanded into the Henrician Poor Law of 1536. Through this law, Henry VIII created even more restrictive categories of persons eligible to receive aid. He also developed governmental regulations for the collection and disbursement of mandatory donations (taxes) from the general citizenry. One effect of this law was to transfer the responsibility of charity from the church to the state. Together, the Statute of Labourers and the Henrician Poor Law established the precedent for public social services and provided the framework for the enactment of the Poor Laws of 1601.

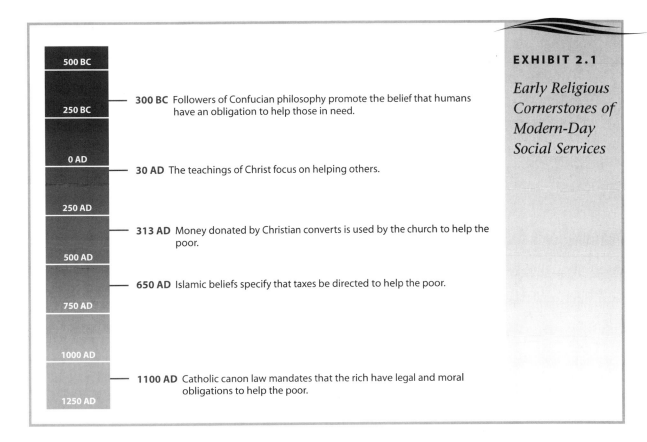

EXHIBIT 2.1

Early Religious Cornerstones of Modern-Day Social Services

300 BC Followers of Confucian philosophy promote the belief that humans have an obligation to help those in need.

30 AD The teachings of Christ focus on helping others.

313 AD Money donated by Christian converts is used by the church to help the poor.

650 AD Islamic beliefs specify that taxes be directed to help the poor.

1100 AD Catholic canon law mandates that the rich have legal and moral obligations to help the poor.

500 BC
250 BC
0 AD
250 AD
500 AD
750 AD
1000 AD
1250 AD

Elizabethan Poor Laws of 1601

A defining point in the history of social services was the passage of the Elizabethan Poor Laws of 1601. These laws are thought to be the single most significant event that defined the social service and welfare delivery system for the next 300 years. Many historical accounts of the development of the social work profession actually begin with the institution of these history-making laws.

Advancing the philosophy of Henry VIII toward caring for those persons in need, the Poor Laws of 1601 were established in England during the reign of Queen Elizabeth I. Building on the efforts of the previous century that were aimed at placing responsibility for charity with the government and categorizing levels of charity based on worthiness, the **Poor Laws** employed the concept of mandatory taxation to fund social and financial assistance. Public assistance was provided to persons deemed eligible in three distinct categories: (1) monetary help for poor people who were deemed unemployable (older persons and persons with disabilities); (2) work for persons of limited income who were not elderly or disabled; and (3) apprenticeships for orphaned and dependent children. In order to receive assistance, recipients were often required to live in a residential institution such as a workhouse or poorhouse for adults and orphanages for children. Known as "indoor relief," this practice continued well into the 19th century and in some areas of Europe and the United States, could be found into the mid-20th century.

The European social and political climate was changing due to an increasing number of persons being displaced from rural areas as a result of restrictions on their rights to farming land. Known as the Enclosure Laws, these restrictions resulted in increased unemployment and homelessness. Such changes served as the impetus for the creation of the Poor Laws. These laws were an attempt to (1) extricate the church from the delivery of social services, (2) eliminate begging and criminal behavior, (3) centralize assistance within the government, and (4) standardize the types and amounts of assistance provided for the growing class of workers. The Poor Laws made a significant, long-term impact on the development of policies for providing aid to those persons in need by creating a clear-cut distinction between persons deemed worthy of receiving assistance and those deemed unworthy of receiving help. Persons deemed unworthy of aid were considered to be responsible for their situations. This belief continues to be at the core of the debate regarding funding for social programs. The Poor Laws represent a clear shift away from the private sector involvement in social service (that is, by the church) to governmental responsibility for the poor. This controversy over private versus public responsibility also continues to the present day. A form of the Poor Laws was eventually adopted in the North American colonies, as you will see in the next section.

Social Services in the 17th and 18th Centuries

Despite the overarching pervasiveness of the English Poor Laws, other events and advances that occurred during the next two centuries also had a profound effect on the future of social services in Europe and, later, in North America. For example, in the early 1600s, Father Vincent de Paul founded charity and religious organizations in France that established formalized structures for providing food, clothing, and financial support for those persons in need. The St. Vincent de Paul Society operated solely on voluntary contributions from parishioners, a model that prevails in the social service delivery system today. You might recognize the name, as the Society itself is still active in many communities.

Also during the 1600s, the Protestant ethic was gaining popularity in England and other parts of Europe. The **Protestant work ethic**, a belief system and way of life, emphasizes self-discipline and frugality and has had a significant influence on societal attitudes toward the poor. This perspective has taken on a negative connotation, as many people believe that all persons, through hard work and discipline, should be able to care for themselves at all times without help from others. Such thinking often translates into opposition to funding for social service and domestic programs.

Further efforts in 17th-century England to restrict access to aid by the poor took the form of the 1662 Law of Settlement, which stipulated that aid was based on one's place of residence. This law discouraged aid recipients from moving to other areas where they might find work (Reid, 1995).

Meanwhile, in England's North American colonies, the colonists began formulating social welfare policy in the form of poor laws fashioned after those in England. By 1657, Boston was home to the first private social welfare agency, the Scots' Charitable Society. In 1729, the first residential facility for orphans was opened in the French colony of New Orleans, and the first psychiatric institution was established in 1773 in Williamsburg, Virginia. As you can see, even while the colonists were focused on expanding into new territory, establishing themselves in a new world, and grappling with the issue of colonization versus independence, they also devised plans to care for poor, sick, and disadvantaged persons. Most of these newly created organizations were private and often religiously affiliated.

Soon after independence, the government of the United States made its first major efforts to create public social and health services. A governmentally funded orphanage opened in Charleston, South Carolina, in 1790, and the U.S. Public Health Service was established in 1798 by a legislative act aimed at creating a health care system for merchant seamen. The Public Health Service still exists today to provide health care and mental health care to underserved populations around the world, to prevent and control disease, and to conduct research.

In sum, the 17th and 18th centuries were a time of expansion for social services. Although the primary focus of most charitable programs was the alleviation of poverty by providing financial aid, they helped to educate future generations regarding the importance of addressing other aspects of the individual's life in order to facilitate a move out of poverty. The seeds for modern-day social casework and clinical treatment were being planted even at this point in our history in an effort to help those living in poverty to gain economic stability. A social system was literally built from scratch in the American colonies, becoming institutionalized as the country gained independence from England. However, as you will see, the belief in public responsibility for social and health services among American citizens would wax and wane from this point on—and it continues to be a source of controversy in the 21st century.

The 19th Century—a Defining Era in the United States

The 1800s were a boom time for the development of social welfare programs and the social work profession, particularly in the United States. This century witnessed progress in such areas as the creation of public and private agencies and organizations to address the country's growing social problems. During this century, the United States grew substantially in both size and population. In addition, the population became more diverse due to the increasing rates of immigration. The country endured the Civil War and its aftermath, and it had to survive a fluctuating economy that produced many periods of depression.

19th-Century Advances in Social Services in the United States

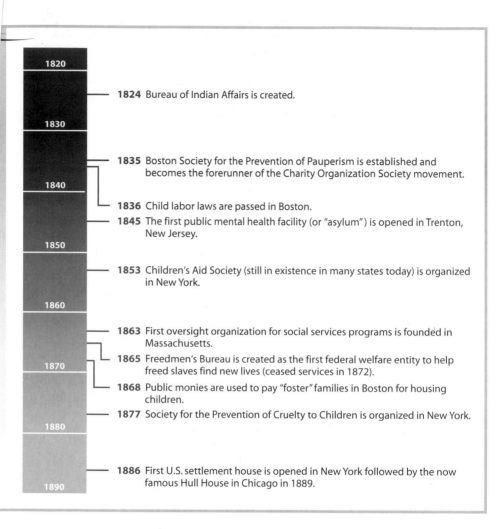

1820

1824 Bureau of Indian Affairs is created.

1830

1835 Boston Society for the Prevention of Pauperism is established and becomes the forerunner of the Charity Organization Society movement.

1840

1836 Child labor laws are passed in Boston.
1845 The first public mental health facility (or "asylum") is opened in Trenton, New Jersey.

1850

1853 Children's Aid Society (still in existence in many states today) is organized in New York.

1860

1863 First oversight organization for social services programs is founded in Massachusetts.
1865 Freedmen's Bureau is created as the first federal welfare entity to help freed slaves find new lives (ceased services in 1872).

1870

1868 Public monies are used to pay "foster" families in Boston for housing children.
1877 Society for the Prevention of Cruelty to Children is organized in New York.

1880

1886 First U.S. settlement house is opened in New York followed by the now famous Hull House in Chicago in 1889.

1890

Thus, the time was ripe for the formation of a more organized system of social service delivery. With the growth of the social service system came a dawning awareness that qualified and trained persons were needed to provide these services and to work with the increasingly diverse populations.

Exhibit 2.2 highlights some of the advancements that were made in our country's burgeoning system for taking care of all our citizens. Most important was the fact that a belief was developing during this time that certain groups within our population needed help in having their voices heard. The new United States was becoming humane with respect to the needs of those citizens living in poverty. Still, children, African Americans, widows and children of war veterans, persons with mental illnesses, and people devastated by disasters were just a few of the groups whose voices were then—and are now—often not heard by the majority of society. Advocates faced considerable adversity as they defended the rights of these marginalized groups. They often risked their reputations, safety, and personal funds to start programs to enhance the quality of life for these groups.

Although still considered by many authorities to be the preferred method for providing aid, indoor relief eventually gave way to "outdoor relief," the provision of services outside the institutional setting. From this paradigm shift came the founding of two movements that are of particular importance in the 19th-century history of social work and social welfare. The settlement house and Charity Organization Society movements, similar in intent but different in function, changed the nature of social service delivery and are proclaimed as being responsible for the birth of the social work profession. Both movements share a philosophy that has become synonymous with American culture—individualism and personal freedom. However, efforts to integrate capitalistic individualism and charitable altruism have not always been successful, often resulting in a "patchwork of programs" (Reid, 1995, p. 2209). Nonetheless, settlement houses and charity organizations became the cornerstone of the American social service delivery system, despite the contradictions.

Settlement House Movement   Originating in England, the **settlement house** is a facility based in a geographically bound neighborhood whose purpose is to provide a center for the neighbors to come together for educational, social, and cultural activities. Settlement houses also provided social services and financial assistance. The first settlement house, Toynbee Hall, opened in London in 1884. It was not long before this model spread across England and the United States. In fact, just two years later, the first American settlement house began operation in New York under the leadership of a former resident of Toynbee Hall, Stanley Coit. The best-known U.S. settlement house is Hull House, opened in Chicago in 1889 by Jane Addams and colleagues. See Exhibit 2.3 to learn more about Jane Addams.

The settlement house idea is based on three concepts: (1) social change can occur, (2) social class distinctions can be narrowed through information and education, and (3) change can come only when social workers immerse themselves in their clients' community (Blank, 1998). Simply stated, settlement houses were created as an attempt by socially minded persons to engage in "friendship with the poor through sharing their lives" (Kendall, 2000, p. 16). A key belief of this movement is that the social structure and society overall are responsible for individual problems. Originally aimed at serving the growing immigrant population, the early settlement houses focused on education and socialization into the American culture of the time (Blank, 1998). Jane Addams described her approach to the settlement house movement this way:

> Teaching in a Settlement requires distinct methods, for it is true of people who
> have been allowed to remain undeveloped and whose facilities are inert and
> sterile, that they cannot take their learning heavily. It has to be diffused in a social

EXHIBIT 2.3

Profile in Innovation: Jane Addams (1860–1935)

Synonymous with the origins of social work in the United States, Jane Addams opened Chicago's Hull House in 1889. Partnering with Ellen Gates, Addams established Hull House after visiting the original settlement house, Toynbee Hall, in London. Ever the activist, Addams fought for improved sanitary conditions in Chicago and, as a result, was appointed neighborhood sanitation inspector. A Quaker and staunch pacifist, her contributions go far beyond the work of Hull House. She was a community organizer, peace advocate, 1931 co-winner of the Nobel Peace Prize, and one of only two social workers inducted into the Hall of Fame of Great Americans. Her dedication to the issue of world peace resulted in her active involvement in a number of peace organizations, including the Women's Peace Party, the National Progressive Party, and the Women's International League for Peace and Freedom. She accomplished all of this despite the fact that as a woman she did not acquire the right to vote until 1920.

Source: Barker, 2003; Quam, 1995

atmosphere, information must be held in solution, in a medium of fellowship and good will . . . It is needed to say that a Settlement is a protest against a restricted view of education. (Urban Experience in Chicago)

The Social Work Library

To read Jane Addams' own account of Hull House, visit the Social Work Library.

Settlement house workers were typically young, well-educated adults (mostly women) interested in social issues and the arts. Because settlement house workers lived in the same neighborhoods as those with whom they worked, they could not ignore the mounting social concerns. These workers found the living and sanitary conditions, housing, child care, education, and worker exploitation in these neighborhoods to be unacceptable. The settlement house workers found themselves at the forefront of controversial and much-needed social change and advocacy for marginalized groups. They also instituted training programs that would later become a component of the social work profession.

The settlement house concept is still in existence today, but it has undergone considerable reconstruction. The centers where idealistic, youthful volunteers lived and made efforts at teaching the arts and literature have been replaced by neighborhood-based community centers that provide a wide array

BOX 2.1

*Grace Hill
Neighborhood
Services: A
Settlement
House*

Grace Hill Neighborhood Services, located in St. Louis, Missouri, can trace its origins to a decision in 1844 by leaders of the town of North St. Louis to donate land for a church. Grace Episcopal Church was built in a neighborhood in which most residents were Episcopalians. As wealthier residents moved out of this neighborhood, it became home to a middle-class and then a low-income population, including many recent immigrants. In response, Grace Episcopal Church founded the Holy Cross Mission in 1903 to meet the changing needs of the neighborhood.

To expand their mission into the delivery of health care services, the Episcopal Diocese began the Holy Cross Dispensary in a nearby location in 1906. In 1914, Holy Cross Mission was incorporated. In 1923, the organization joined with the Community Fund (now United Way) to provide kindergarten, health clinics, recreation, and classes in crafts, dance, athletics, and music. From 1938 to 1944, Grace Hill gained recognition as a settlement house and instituted such changes as accepting African Americans and replacing religious staff with social workers. By 1965, Grace Hill had established its first Head Start program for preschool education. Shortly thereafter, Grace Hill, using neighbors (residents of the neighborhood) as advisors to program operations, began a meal program for older adults and developed a 10-year neighborhood improvement plan that resulted in the construction of low-cost apartments and the rehabilitation of existing housing stock.

By the 1980s, the philosophy of the agency was that the neighbors should be involved in developing training programs, forums, a resource bank, self-help groups, and communication centers. Today, the neighborhood is populated largely by African Americans. Currently, Grace Hill serves 11 neighborhoods in the St. Louis area. Keeping the settlement house model alive, services are now provided in the areas of health care, child and older-adult care, housing for low-income persons and families, self-help, job skills training, and shelters and housing relocation for persons who are homeless.

of goods and services, including food and clothing, health care, after-school and summer recreation, crisis intervention, and counseling. The basic ideal on which the settlement houses were founded still exists today—change is most effective if it comes from within the community itself. One example, Grace Hill Neighborhood Services, is profiled in Box 2.1.

Charity Organization Society   During the same period that the settlement houses were improving life for immigrants and influencing the formation of social welfare services in the United States, another movement that would impact the future of social work was under way. Like those of the settlement houses, the roots of charity organizations can also be found in 19th-century England. The London-based Society for Organising Charitable Relief and Repressing Mendicity provided the framework for the first North American **Charity Organization Society (COS)** in Buffalo, New York, in 1877. The concept of a charitable service that did not involve living with the persons being served quickly spread throughout the country; by 1892 there were 92 such societies in operation (Brieland, 1995).

The philosophical underpinning of the charity society movement was a morally based belief that the person was responsible for his or her own difficulties but could be rehabilitated through individual sessions with a "friendly visitor" as opposed to a financial handout (Brieland, 1995). "Not alms but a friend" was the motto of the early COS workers, who believed that extending friendship and sympathy would enable persons living in poverty to feel better about themselves and rise out of poverty (Kendall, 2000). The first workers in the movement that would eventually become modern-day social services were primarily middle-class women who voluntarily ventured into neighborhoods in which persons of low income lived in order to share their wisdom and advice on good living. Organizers of this movement believed that visiting people in their homes and encouraging them to live a moral life was a more effective method of intervention than giving them financial aid. As a result, the COS entities engaged in such activities as individual assessments and registration of those "worthy" of receiving charity and, ultimately, employment and legal services (Brieland, 1995). Although the value-laden component of these early social services continued and became a pervasive part of social work for many decades, the work of these well-intentioned volunteers laid the groundwork for such advancements as social casework and the formation of family and children's service agencies.

Contributions of the Settlement House and Charity Society Movements   To grasp the significance of the events of 19th-century social services, let us compare and contrast these two major movements. The settlement house movement taught the importance of assessing and understanding the conditions in which client systems live as well as their cultures, the impact of environmental conditions on the quality of people's lives, and the effectiveness of empowerment through education, information, and group work. The friendly visitors of the Charity Organization Society movement taught the value of assessing each individual situation and developing an intervention specific to the individual, coupled with the knowledge that money alone does not always facilitate change. Although both movements—in particular, the COS movement—have been criticized for being short-sighted and judgmental, together they provided the first steps that enabled the social work profession and society to move forward in our treatment of poor, abused, and oppressed groups.

Social Services in the 20th Century

The dawning of the 20th century brought with it even more changes in our society, in general, and the social services community, in particular. Economically, the country was emerging from the depression of the late 1800s. The first two decades of the 1900s were a time of economic prosperity. Socially and politically, the 1890s and early 1900s, known as the Progressive Era, were a time of significant reform in such far-ranging areas of women's rights (specifically suffrage), health care and social service programs, education, political practices, occupational and consumer safety, child and social welfare laws, environmental preservation, and socialization for immigrants. The leaders of the progressive movement successfully advocated for changes in social insurance, government regulation, and the professionalization of helping professions (Reid, 1995, p. 2212).

By this time, social work was established as a profession that responds to current economic, political, and social events and trends. Therefore, in times of economic booms, leaders in the social service movement had the opportunity to focus on coordinating services and organizing coalitions to enhance service delivery. The Progressives, a group of social and political activists that included Jane Addams, founder of Hull House, encouraged a number of social changes during this time. The Progressives gained national recognition for the need to establish a federal infrastructure for financial assistance, public health interventions, and social work professionalization that would concretize the delivery of social services for many years to come (Reid, 1995).

During the early decades of the 1900s, social workers and government officials formed organizations and government agencies that solidified the place of social services in U.S. society. Three organizations that grew out of the progressive movement and had an impact on the work of social workers were the National Urban League, the Children's Bureau, and the Child Welfare League of America. Although the influence of such organizations on social work may not be readily apparent, the endorsement of governmental agencies and the merging of smaller groups into larger groups strengthened the position and voice of those committed to serving the poor.

Of particular importance during this period was the implementation of workers' compensation and the Mother's Pensions program that provided assistance for women and children. Recipients of the Mother's Pensions were typically Caucasian widowed mothers. Modeled after traditional charity programs in which the financial benefits were minimal and the goal was moral reform, this program was the first nationwide public program that provided financial assistance to women who were rearing families on their own and attempted to destigmatize recipients (Seccombe, 1999).

Developments during the Depression and the New Deal   The stock market crash of 1929 sent the country spiraling downward into an economic and social depression that would last through the next decade. The Great Depression of the 1930s was a time of suffering and unrest. Nevertheless, as had become the tradition for the profession, social workers once again rose to the occasion. When Franklin D. Roosevelt, a Democrat, was elected to the presidency in

1932, nearly one-third of Americans were living in poverty, manufacturing and agriculture had been devastated, and the breadlines were long and getting longer. In response, the Roosevelt administration instituted a number of New Deal programs that would have a lasting effect on our society.

Probably the most important New Deal legislation was the Social Security Act of 1935. Originally championed by members of the progressive movement since the early years of the century, the Social Security Act was passed as a measure to alleviate the poverty of the elderly, widows and widowers, the unemployed, persons with disabilities, and dependent children. The legislation became the foundation of our public welfare and retirement systems. In addition to providing a retirement income for older adults, the Social Security Act ultimately resulted in the development of public assistance programs that would include such services as health care, employment services, transportation, and child day care for persons living in poverty and with disabilities, as well as impoverished women and children (known as Aid to Dependent Children and later, **Aid to Families with Dependent Children—AFDC**). The Social Security Act and other New Deal reforms affirmed the role of the federal government in the administration of social services. This development would later serve U.S. society well, because structures were in place during times of economic crisis.

Other social and economic programs implemented during the New Deal include

- *Works Progress Administration (WPA):* Founded by social worker Harry Hopkins, the WPA created employment from 1935 to 1943 for over eight million people in such diverse areas as construction of roads and bridges to development of cultural programs.

- *Civilian Conservation Corps (CCC):* In existence from 1933 to 1942, the CCC was designed to conserve and develop the nation's natural resources, while creating employment opportunities for unemployed men.

- *National Youth Administration (NYA):* Out of concern for ensuring that the country's high school and college students be able to complete their education, the NYA provided funding for part-time employment.

Developments during World War II and the 1950s   As often occurs during wartime, the United States experienced an economic recovery during the 1940s. World War II had a significant impact on the social work profession as well. For example, social workers developed and administered mental health programs for military personnel. This activity ultimately led to the creation of the nationwide, community-based mental health system that remains the basis for the provision of mental health services (Reid, 1995).

Nevertheless, there was little expansion of the social welfare system during the latter half of the 1940s. The focus during these years was on the returning veterans, who used the 1944 GI Bill of Rights to acquire a college education and purchase homes. This period provided a segue into the 1950s, which was clearly a strong economic period as well as a relatively conservative era in politics.

One of the most important 1950s events for social welfare and social work was the creation of the cabinet-level Department of Health, Education, and Welfare (HEW) in 1953, during the administration of Republican president Dwight D. Eisenhower. This was the first acknowledgment by the federal government that the well-being of all people in the United States was a high priority. This department—which in 1979 was divided into the Department of Health and Human Services (HHS) and the Department of Education—has been instrumental in formulating and administering virtually every federally funded social welfare program in existence in this country.

Other than establishing HEW, the 1950s, like the 1940s, are not well known for advances in the social service arena. Historically, the combination of Republican presidential administrations with prosperous times often means little attention (and funding) is devoted to the social service community; the 1950s are a prime example of that historical pattern.

Developments during the 1960s and 1970s   The 1960s have become well known as a tumultuous time on many fronts. In 1960, the nation elected a Democratic president, John F. Kennedy. The civil rights movement was heating up. The war in Vietnam would soon take center stage, bringing with it civil unrest here at home. The youth were headed in a different direction from those of the previous decades. Many young people opposed the Vietnam War and military service in general, participated in the sexual revolution, and experimented with illicit drugs.

From the social work perspective, the 1960s were an interesting time, indeed. Many social workers feel that the 1960s were one of the most significant times for the profession due to the creation of a number of social programs, advances in civil rights, and the willingness of U.S. citizens to confront injustices in a public way. The Kennedy administration established the Peace Corps in 1961 and encouraged Congress to pass the 1963 Community Mental Health Center Act. Kennedy's successor, Lyndon B. Johnson, another Democrat, oversaw passage of the Civil Rights Act of 1964 as well as the Economic Opportunity Act of 1964—an array of social welfare legislation known collectively as the Great Society. Although some critics consider Johnson's War on Poverty and the Great Society to have been a failure, the 1964 legislation was responsible for the creation of numerous social programs, many of which still exist in some form today: the Job Corps, Head Start, Volunteers in Service to America (VISTA—the domestic version of the Peace Corps), and the Neighborhood Youth Corps.

Four major social programs were enacted during the Great Society that enhanced—and perhaps saved—the lives of the people they serve:

- *Medicare:* Health insurance for those who receive Social Security passed in 1965.

- *Medicaid:* Health insurance for those who receive public welfare benefits also passed in 1965.

- *Older Americans Act:* A nationwide system of community-based services for older adults was created in 1965.

- *Food Stamp Act of 1964:* This Department of Agriculture program provides food assistance to people living on limited incomes.

Although not as glamorous and exciting as the 1960s, the 1970s were a decade of progress in social services. Despite the ultimate downfall of the Republican administration of Richard M. Nixon, a significant number of programs were created under his leadership. The focus of his administration was a traditional Republican one in that "charity" was not endorsed, but work incentives were supported (Reid, 1995). The laws passed during the administrations of Nixon and his successor, Gerald Ford, that had far-reaching effects on social service delivery include

- Supplemental Security Income (SSI) was made available in 1972 for older persons and people with disabilities whose income was still well below poverty standards.

- The 1974 Comprehensive Employment and Training Act (CETA) program provided educational and job opportunities for persons of limited income.

- The Education for All Handicapped Children Act (1975) required all public schools to provide educational experiences for children with disabilities that are comparable to those available to children without such disabilities.

- The Title XX amendment to the Social Security Act (1975) provided funds for the purchase of social services, training, and housing for persons who qualified based on their income.

- The 1974 Child Abuse Prevention and Treatment Act created a comprehensive approach to the prevention, investigation, and treatment of child abuse that was expanded in 1978 to address inadequacies of the adoption system.

Developments during the 1980s and 1990s   Those in the social work community do not typically view the 1980s with favor. The Republican administrations of Ronald Reagan and George H. W. Bush followed the traditional pattern of decreased spending on domestic and social programs. Specifically, two legislative acts passed during Reagan's first term severely cut social service funding: the Omnibus Budget Reconciliation Act (OBRA) of 1981 and the Tax Equity and Fiscal Responsibility Act of 1982. OBRA gave more authority and less funding to states for administration of public assistance programs and made it more difficult for those living in poverty to access services, as states could individually determine eligibility and access. The 1982 law resulted in decreased Medicare, Medicaid, AFDC, SSI, and unemployment funds. Continuing in his predecessor's footsteps, Bush advocated for increased privatization of the social service system based on a belief that the public should not be responsible for the welfare of the general population.

Ironically, it may be argued that the attempts of Reagan and Bush to disempower the social welfare system resulted in a strengthening of sorts. Increased funding and management options at the state level and a renewed interest in the nonprofit sector helped bring the attention of the general public to the need for a centralized social service system (Reid, 1995).

President Bill Clinton's campaign platform in the early 1990s was designed to redirect the public's attention to domestic issues. Clinton's presidential years focused on reviewing and revamping a number of domestic programs. His administration took on such intractable social issues as health care, family health and well-being issues, abortion, discrimination against gays and lesbians in the military, welfare reform, and distressed communities (Green & Haines, 2002). In spite of changes pursued by the Clinton administration, many people question whether real change occurred and, if so, who benefited from that change. For example, homosexuality was publicly addressed for the first time by the military with the creation of the "don't ask, don't tell" policy. This policy, which meant that the military could not officially inquire about a service member's sexual orientation, and service members could not offer that information, was viewed as a setback by the gay and lesbian rights movement.

For social workers, the most significant issues addressed during the 1990s were welfare reform and community development. The 1996 Personal Responsibility and Work Opportunity Reconciliation Act (PRWORA) became law, replacing Aid to Families with Dependent Children with **Temporary Assistance to Needy Families (TANF).** TANF continues to provide cash assistance to poor women and children, but with greater restrictions, mandated work requirements, and a five-year lifetime cap on the receipt of benefits. Proponents believe that the welfare-to-work programs created by welfare reform are responsible for positive changes, while others (mostly those on the front lines) believe they are a deterrent to getting out of poverty. Many former welfare recipients gained employment during the prosperous 1990s, but many critics question whether this trend can be maintained during weaker economic times (Green & Haines, 2002). Many persons working full time for minimum wage still live in poverty without health care and other resources.

Social Services in the 21st Century and Beyond

The new millennium saw the inauguration of a Republican president whose campaign platform let us know that he is not a supporter of increased funding for social programs. In fact, one of George W. Bush's early efforts in this area was to make federal monies available to faith-based social services. In many ways, this is a continuation of the agenda promoted by his father, George H. W. Bush, who launched the 1,000 Points of Light project in which private-sector agencies were showcased for their efforts. Both efforts aim at increasing the private sector's responsibility for social programs.

Although historical trends can be a guide, predicting what will happen in the coming years would still be speculation. However, we can predict which issues among the current social, economic, and political challenges that confront our social service system will affect social work practice. For example, welfare reforms, changing family demographics, restricted access to benefits, and an aging society are all expected to provide opportunities for social workers to test their skills. Here are some observations from current research:

* Approximately two-thirds of our population will use public assistance benefits at some point in their adult life (Rank & Hirschl, 2002). More funding will be needed to support welfare-to-work programs, particularly for single, female-headed households.

* The population will continue to become older, creating new challenges for the families of older adults as well as for society (Kosberg & Kaufman, 2002).

PROFESSIONAL EDUCATION IN SOCIAL WORK: AN HISTORICAL PERSPECTIVE

As you have seen, the social work profession has been evolving for centuries. However, the term "social work" was not commonly used and formalized social work education did not exist until the late 1800s and early 1900s. In a sense, social work education began in the early settlement houses, which served as "social laboratories" for university students. As Exhibit 2.4 shows, though, not all the training originated at the university.

The term social work was first used in 1900 by an educator, Simon Patten, to refer to the work of friendly visitors and settlement house workers. This bit of social work trivia indicates that the emergence of the profession coincided with the growth of these two movements during the late 1800s.

Educating Social Workers

As in England, U.S. social work training emerged from the COS and settlement house movements, taking the form of apprenticeships and in-house training.

EXHIBIT 2.4

Profile in Innovation: Octavia Hill (1838–1912)

A little-known charity organization worker from an upper-middle-class English family, Octavia Hill entered the charity world by working with young girls in a toy-making project under the guidance of her mentor, social reformer John Ruskin. Hill soon became aware of the appalling conditions in which the girls lived. By 1869, she had moved from the toy project into recruiting and training other volunteers to help improve housing for low-income persons. These female volunteers, known as Housing Estate Managers, collected rents and engaged in individual work that would later be known as social casework.

Hill's contribution to the development of the social work profession around the world is that she trained the volunteers to work with tenants on an individual basis in a caring, respectful manner, affirming their dignity and autonomy—the cornerstone of what we now know as social work. In fact, Hill's group discussions about cases, facilitated by a mentor, were the origins of organized social work training. Hill is also credited with establishing an organization that became the model for the Charity Organization Society movement.

Source: Barker, 2003; Kendall, 2000

The leadership of the burgeoning profession quickly determined that more formal training was needed. By 1893, a call had been issued for "formal education in applied philanthropy" because the "on-the-job" training offered within the agency setting was deficient in the provision of principles and theory (Leighninger, 2000, pp. 1–2). In 1894, the first social welfare textbook, *American Charities,* was published. Exhibit 2.5 discusses Mary Richmond and the textbook that she developed two decades later.

The idea of formalized social work training quickly gained appeal throughout the United States. These early educational ventures were agency based, but within a brief period, the training programs were increasingly located in university settings, with input provided by agency personnel (Frumkin & Lloyd, 1995). Many people believed that the early British social work educational approach was more advanced than U.S. methods because the training was entirely university based. Many English social workers, however, considered the slower-developing American system—with its independent schools of social work heavily influenced by community agencies—to be superior to their university-based system (Kendall, 2000).

EXHIBIT 2.5

Profile in Innovation: Mary Richmond (1861–1928)

The "foremother" of American professional social work, Mary Richmond was a social activist and prolific writer on social issues. Starting out as a treasurer for a Maryland COS, Richmond also served as a friendly visitor. In 1897, Richmond, then secretary of the Charity Organization Society of Baltimore, delivered a speech at the National Conference of Charities and Corrections in which she said, "We owe it to those who shall come after us that they shall be spared the groping and blundering by which we have acquired our own stock of experience." Richmond argued that workers needed training as "relief and child-saving agents" with "shoulder-to-shoulder contact which makes cooperation natural and inevitable." She went on to state that theory and practice should be concurrent, with students beginning in a general

area of study and moving into a specialization—the model still used as the basis of social work education today.

Richmond's call for the formalized training of charity workers had previously been made by a Massachusetts community activist, Anna Dawes, but it was not acted on until 1898 when the New York School of Philanthropy (now the Columbia University School of Social Work) offered a six-week summer school session that was extended in 1910 to two years. Richmond went on to become a faculty member in this program. She is best known for her 1917 book, *Social Diagnosis,* which became the primary textbook used by early social work educators.

Source: Brieland, 1995; Kendall, 2000; Longres, 1995; Richmond, 1897, p. 181

The founding of the program considered to be the first social work training program in the United States occurred in 1895 at the Chicago School of Social Economics at Chicago Commons. By 1903, the program was known as the Chicago School of Civics and Philanthropy (which later became the University of Chicago School of Social Service Administration) and was offering a year-long training program. By 1918, seventeen social work training programs had been established (Frumkin & Lloyd, 1995)—an average of one new program per year. Most programs emphasized a casework curriculum, thus carving out a niche for clinical social work. Despite the rapid growth of educational endeavors, however, the profession was still in its infancy, and it was generally unorganized and fragmented.

Abraham Flexner (1866–1959), an educator who was not a social worker, made a major contribution to the growth of the social work profession, although his efforts initially were viewed as devastatingly negative. His 1915 critique on the profession resulted in some of the most important advancements in the profession's history. At the time of his analysis, Flexner was the assistant secretary of the General Education Board for New York City. Speculation has been offered that the profession's leadership asked Flexner, an educational reformer, to offer his thoughts on the social work profession because they had already begun to realize that the profession needed to change (Leighninger, 2000). Although the enhancements that Flexner recommended took many years to achieve, and, in fact, are ongoing, his report did serve to solidify social work as a profession. Flexner recommended that social work become better organized, and he identified a set of criteria that he viewed as minimal for any discipline to be considered a profession. Flexner's report states that a profession must

- Involve intellectual operations with large responsibility.
- Derive raw material from science and learning and apply it to a practical and definite end.
- Possess educationally communicable techniques.
- Have self-organization.
- Be altruistic in motivation.

Recognizing that social work possessed character, practicality, a tendency toward self-organization, and altruism, Flexner stated that it was not yet a profession due to deficits in individual responsibility and educationally communicable techniques (Syers, 1995).

Social work professionals of the time rallied in an effort to strengthen the profession. As a result of Flexner's critique, social work training programs became more formalized. In addition, social workers began to conduct their own research, thus generating their own theories. Finally, the profession began to articulate its own methods of practice and focused on organizing social workers into a professional group. One response to Flexner's concerns was Mary Richmond's 1917 book, *Social Diagnosis*, which outlined assessment techniques for use with clients.

By 1917, seventeen of the social work education programs that were in operation in the United States and Canada came together to establish the Association of Training Schools for Professional Social Work. Reorganizing later, the group became known as the American Association of Schools of Social Work

The Social Work Library

Visit the Social Work Library to read the original Flexner presentation.

(AASSW). By 1952, the AASSW joined forces with the National Association of Schools of Social Administration to become the Council on Social Work Education (CSWE)—the organization that now accredits bachelor and master of social work programs. In addition, the National Association of Social Workers was established in 1955 when seven previously separate professional social work organizations joined to form one national organization that could represent the interests of the profession.

Expanding Professional Boundaries

Establishing social work education was not the only activity of the social work profession that was occurring during the late 19th and early 20th centuries. Professional social work was gaining recognition in three fields of practice: medical social work, psychiatric social work, and child welfare. In 1905, the first hospital social work department was organized at Massachusetts General Hospital, and just two years later, the same institution offered psychiatric social work services. Interestingly, the title "psychiatric social worker" was not used until 1914.

In the realm of child welfare services, a variety of practice activities were emerging. Social workers were being trained in the area of mental health diagnosis at the same time that juvenile court systems were being established to address the issue of juvenile crime and delinquency (Brieland, 1995). Social workers were also making their presence felt in the public school systems, where they worked with children whose home lives were dysfunctional. These areas remain a central part of social work today.

An additional area of activity for the social work profession was the creation of professional associations. See Exhibit 2.6 for some of the highlights of the profession's organizational efforts.

In 1977, a special issue of the journal *Social Work* was devoted to defining, describing, and discussing conceptual frameworks that were pertinent to social work practice at that time. This effort to further refine the definition of the profession of social work addressed such issues as the mission, objectives, professional oversight, knowledge and skills, and educational implications associated with the profession (Minahan, 1981).

This special issue generated such attention that a second special issue appeared in 1981. This second effort to frame social work as a strong profession included a working statement on the purpose of social work. I want to share the complete statement with you so that we can use this as a point from which to build our collective understanding of the social work profession (Minahan, 1981, p. 6):

> The purpose of social work is to promote or restore a mutually beneficial interaction between individuals and society in order to improve the quality of life for everyone.

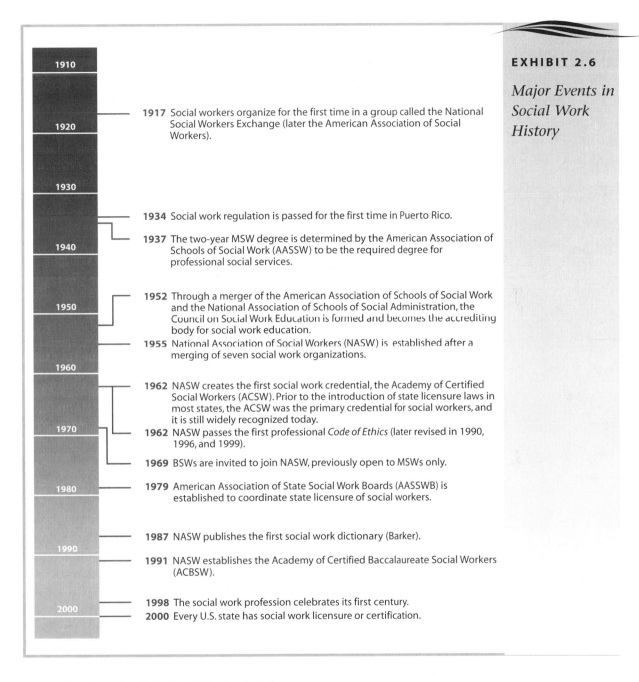

EXHIBIT 2.6

Major Events in Social Work History

1917 Social workers organize for the first time in a group called the National Social Workers Exchange (later the American Association of Social Workers).

1934 Social work regulation is passed for the first time in Puerto Rico.

1937 The two-year MSW degree is determined by the American Association of Schools of Social Work (AASSW) to be the required degree for professional social services.

1952 Through a merger of the American Association of Schools of Social Work and the National Association of Schools of Social Administration, the Council on Social Work Education is formed and becomes the accrediting body for social work education.

1955 National Association of Social Workers (NASW) is established after a merging of seven social work organizations.

1962 NASW creates the first social work credential, the Academy of Certified Social Workers (ACSW). Prior to the introduction of state licensure laws in most states, the ACSW was the primary credential for social workers, and it is still widely recognized today.

1962 NASW passes the first professional *Code of Ethics* (later revised in 1990, 1996, and 1999).

1969 BSWs are invited to join NASW, previously open to MSWs only.

1979 American Association of State Social Work Boards (AASSWB) is established to coordinate state licensure of social workers.

1987 NASW publishes the first social work dictionary (Barker).

1991 NASW establishes the Academy of Certified Baccalaureate Social Workers (ACBSW).

1998 The social work profession celebrates its first century.

2000 Every U.S. state has social work licensure or certification.

Social workers hold the following beliefs:

- The environment (social, physical and organizational) should provide the opportunity and resources for the maximum realization of the potential and aspirations of all individuals, and should provide for their common human needs and for the alleviation of distress and suffering.

- Individuals should contribute as effectively as they can to their own well-being and to the social welfare of others in their immediate environment as well as to the collective society.
- Transactions between individuals and others in their environment should enhance the dignity, individuality and self-determination of everyone. People should be treated humanely and with justice.
- Clients of social workers may be an individual, a family, a group, a community or an organization.

The social workers who developed this working statement also conceptualized a list of objectives that were (and still are) essential for the practice of social work (Minahan, 1981, p. 6). These objectives include

Social workers focus on person-and-environment *in interaction.* To carry out their purpose, they work with people to achieve the following objectives:

- Help people enlarge their competence and increase their problem-solving and coping abilities.
- Help people obtain resources.
- Make organizations responsive to people.
- Facilitate interaction between individuals and others in their environment.
- Influence interactions between organizations and institutions.
- Influence social and environmental policy.

WHERE WE HAVE COME FROM AND WHERE WE ARE GOING

The Social Work Library

To learn from another pioneer, read Bertha Caper Reynolds' perspective on social casework.

We began this odyssey into the history of social work and social welfare more than 3,000 years ago with the concept that we, as citizens, have a moral obligation to help others. You have seen, throughout the centuries, the ways in which an entire profession has been molded from those early hints of altruism. In just the past 100 years alone, the term social work came into use, and the definition of a social worker has evolved from "anyone involved in activities with a social purpose" (Kendall, 2000, p. 93) to a professional who has completed a degree from an accredited social work program and who is engaged in a theory-based practice of helping others to optimize their potential in life. As a profession, social work has moved from a belief system that blamed the individual for creating her or his pauperism to an understanding that environmental conditions are the precursors for poverty. In addition, both social action and individual casework are now recognized parts of the profession (Kendall, 2000).

Having made the journey from the origins of the profession to the present day, you can see that a long and rich history will guide social workers into the future.

CONCLUSION

This chapter has described the history of the social work profession. Many innovative and courageous women and men have helped shape the profession that is so integral to our modern-day society. I hope that this gives a meaningful context to learning about the values and ethics embraced by the profession, the fields of practice in which social workers engage, and some of the skills needed to be a professional social worker.

The history of social work and social welfare has been and continues to be linked to the events of the time. As social workers respond to the changing needs of the client systems that they serve, new knowledge and skills are developed. One thing that we now know about social work is that our history still serves as a guide to our future. A statement from the NASW *Code of Ethics* (1999) says it all:

> A historic and defining feature of social work is the professional focus on individual well-being in a social context and the well-being of society. Fundamental to social work is attention to the environmental forces that create, contribute to, and address problems in living.

MAIN POINTS

- Social welfare is the system of programs and services that respond to social and economic needs and injustices. The first organized attempt at mandating the provision of social services was the 1349 Statute of Labourers that designated categories of need in England.

- The Elizabethan Poor Laws of 1601 established an approach to the delivery of financial and social aid that continues today. Intended to transfer the authority for charity from the church to the government, standardize aid programs, and decrease criminal activity, these laws dictated that public aid could be given to the unemployable, but that the employable must work and children that were orphaned or dependent would serve as apprentices.

- The roots of the U.S. social service system can be found in the British system's settlement houses and charity organizations. In the settlement house movement, young people lived and worked in poor neighborhoods to help improve living conditions; in the charity organization movement, caseworkers focused on helping individuals overcome their problems.

- The 20th century saw the formalization of the social work profession and growth in the social service delivery system. The Depression of the 1930s prompted a shift of services from the private to the public sector. The civil unrest of the 1960s and 1970s prompted new social initiatives created to address issues of poverty and the needs of women, children, and older adults.

- Demographic changes in the 21st century are creating a society with widening economic gaps and an older, more diverse population with greater social, economic, and physical needs.

- In existence for a century, social work education has continued to change in response to societal needs. Flexner's 1915 report on the profession had the effect of solidifying social work as a profession.

EXERCISES: PRACTICING SOCIAL WORK

History of a Social Service Agency

You will note in the Sanchez family case study that Celia Sanchez utilizes the food bank at her church as a resource for her family. The Catholic Church has a long and venerable history of caring for the poor in its communities. Describe a faith-based organization in your community that offers services to persons with limited incomes. How does it differ from sectarian institutions that offer the same or similar services?

An Historical Perspective on Service Delivery

Select one of the concerns or needs identified in the Sanchez family interactive case study. Citing examples from this chapter, speculate on the ways that the concern or need would have been addressed in different eras.

The History of a Policy

Review the profile of Hector Sanchez. You will note that Hector was given amnesty under a 1986 federal amnesty program. Using the internet, conduct a search to learn about federal amnesty programs.

EXERCISES: THE SOCIAL WORK LIBRARY

Is Social Work a Profession?

After reading "Is Social Work a Profession?" (Flexner, 1925), provide your own synopsis of this critique on social work as a profession. Then, referring back to the article by Greenwood (Chapter 1), compare and contrast the two models used by Greenwood and Flexner to define the elements of a profession.

The First Days at Hull House

Using the Social Work Library, visit the Hull House library link and click on The First Days at Hull House. After reading Addams' account of the beginnings of Hull House, reflect on the following:

1. What was Jane Addams' goal in establishing Hull House?

2. Describe the challenges she and her colleagues encountered in reaching their goals.

3. Describe the strengths of Addams' approach in creating a settlement house

Client or Community?

After reading section I of "Between Client and Community: A Study of Responsibility in Social Casework" (Reynolds, 1934), respond to the following:

1. What is the premise of Bertha Capen Reynolds' question: client or community?

2. Do you agree or disagree with Reynolds' premise? Provide a rationale.

3. Based on your understanding of contemporary social work, compare Reynolds' depiction of social work with your perception of social work.

CHAPTER 3

U.S. Poverty and the
Implications for Social Work

How did I get to be eighty
   And
      Never
         Get over
            Being
               Poor?
When I was little
   I was poor.
      But playing
         And
            Dreaming
         Kept some of the pain
          Of
              Being poor
               Away
     And my folks
       Kept
           Lots of the worries from me.
When I was a teenager
   I just knew I'd marry a good man
      With work
        And
           Things would be all right.
And I did.
But he was poor, too.

Work was steady for a while,
   But so were the children.

There were good days
   And warm times
But there were lots of times
   When his work died off
      And
        His worrying
          Brought pain.

He worked any kind of job
   In
       Any kind of weather
        Till
     The fever got him
       And
     The Lord took him
        And I had to go to welfare.
   Then
       They cut that—some.

Reverend,
   Do people born poor?
     Have
   To stay that way—always?
Ain't there any other way—
         Even when we get to be eighty?
Does "poor" always have to be
      A
        Life sentence?

From *If . . . A Big Word with the Poor*
By Don Bakely
Reprinted by permission.

This 1976 poem, composed by a social activist, focuses on the plight of an impoverished 80-year-old woman. At the same time, the poem raises a number of issues that continue to plague our society more than 25 years after its publication. The woman in this poem contacted Don Bakely for help one Thanksgiving Day because she was out of food and fuel. His powerful words move us as we read this poem because they address the issues of lifelong poverty, being elderly and poor, and the inadequacy of the public welfare system. His words, however, also capture the hope that this woman continued to have throughout her life—a phenomenon we do not usually associate with chronic poverty and advanced age.

The social issues raised in this poem provide us with a beginning point for a discussion of the needs of many persons in our society and the approaches that have been devised to address those needs. Specifically, we will continue our journey through the social work profession by discussing the issues of poverty and society's historical response to eliminating poverty. Understanding poverty, welfare programs, and social services is critical for all social workers. As noted in Chapter 1, the mission of social workers is to enhance the capacity of their clients. To be an effective social worker, you need to understand your clients' concerns, challenges, and needs—whether they are related to poverty, health, employment, or safety. This chapter covers the origins of poverty, the ways in which the public and private sectors have attempted to minimize poverty and its effects, and the role of a social worker in optimizing clients' capacities.

DIMENSIONS OF POVERTY

Emily did not have much experience with or knowledge of poverty before deciding to be a social worker. Actually, Emily had no personal experience with poverty. She certainly knew there were people in the world and in her community who lived in poverty, but she did not think about their situations, so they were not real for her. She had no insight into the realities of living in poverty. She had heard people say that poor people could escape poverty simply by "pulling themselves up by their bootstraps." Not being sure about the truth of that adage, Emily found herself wondering about the reasons for so many people to become impoverished.

Emily's first experience with persons living in poverty came during her community service for her introductory social work course. She was working at Oasis House, a shelter for families who are homeless. There, she began to gain insight into poverty and the ways in which living in poverty affected people. As she worked with children on their homework, they shared with her stories about having utilities cut off, being hungry, getting evicted, and living in the car—all because a parent was laid off from her or his job. Emily learned that poverty is not simple or just, and it is not caused by a lack of motivation. Rather, poverty is a complicated phenomenon that has many faces, some that are 9 years old.

If asked What does being poor mean? Who are the poor? How do people get to be poor? What keeps people in poverty? many people in our society would have opinions, but those opinions are often not fact based. The definition of poverty, profiles of those who live in poverty, and the causes of poverty have been and continue to be emotional and value-laden issues with which our society struggles in the political, social, religious, and public and private social service arenas.

Defining Poverty

A simple definition of **poverty** would be having inadequate financial resources. Stated more poignantly:

> Poverty is hunger. Poverty is lack of shelter. Poverty is being sick and not being able to see a doctor. Poverty is not being able to go to school and not knowing how to read. Poverty is not having a job, is fear for the future, living one day at a time. Poverty is losing a child to illness brought about by unclean water. Poverty is powerlessness, lack of representation and freedom. (Worldbank Group, 2003)

In 1964 the federal government devised the poverty line as an official measure of poverty. The **poverty line** is the amount defined by the federal government as the minimal income level at which a family or individual can meet their basic needs. The measure was originally based on research from 1955 that suggested that people spend one-third of their post-tax income on food (Sherraden, 1990). Known as the Thrifty Food Plan, the government thus calculated the poverty line by identifying the amount needed for the minimum subsistence diet and then multiplying that number by three. Based on this formula, in 2002 a family of four fell below the poverty line if their total income was less than $18,400 (U.S. Department of Health and Human Services [DHHS], 2003). Data from the 2000 census indicate that the income of a typical person living in poverty was $2,813 less than the poverty line (Center on Budget and Policy Priorities [CBPP], 2003c).

Current spending patterns differ dramatically from what they were in 1964. Today families spend a smaller percentage of their income on food and a much larger percentage on transportation, housing, and medical care. Moreover, poverty is measured on income before taxes are deducted, and some nonmonetary items (such as food stamps) can be considered a part of income. These strictly economic measures of poverty (though still used) are considered out dated by welfare rights advocates, and many social workers think that poverty can best be understood in social, political, economic, and emotional terms.

Economically, "absolute" poverty occurs when an individual's income is less than the amount needed to obtain the minimal necessities for living. On an emotional level, "relative deprivation" is the perception that an individual does not possess as many assets as others (Hopps & Collins, 1995). Both types of poverty are real and interrelated, and both can be devastating for the individual and the family.

Who Are the Poor?

Many people believe the stereotype that people who are poor are nonwhite unemployed single mothers with lots of children, who subsist on welfare and are homeless or live in dilapidated housing in "bad" areas. Most unfortunate is the widespread myth that people who live in poverty are lazy and unmotivated to change their situations. Many people living in poverty are employed, have two or fewer children, and are very motivated to move out of poverty. In spite of this, the percentage of Americans living in poverty increased from 11.7 percent in 2001 to 12.7 percent in 2002 (U.S. Census [U.S. Census], 2003), and nearly 10 percent of all families in the United States do not have incomes that bring them above the poverty line.

By age 65, some 64 percent of Americans will require assistance from at least one form of a social welfare or "social safety net" program such as Medicaid, food stamps, and cash assistance (Rank & Hirschl, 2002). The fact is that a

The Social Work Library

For more on the safety net concept, read Rank & Hirschl's article in the Social Work Library.

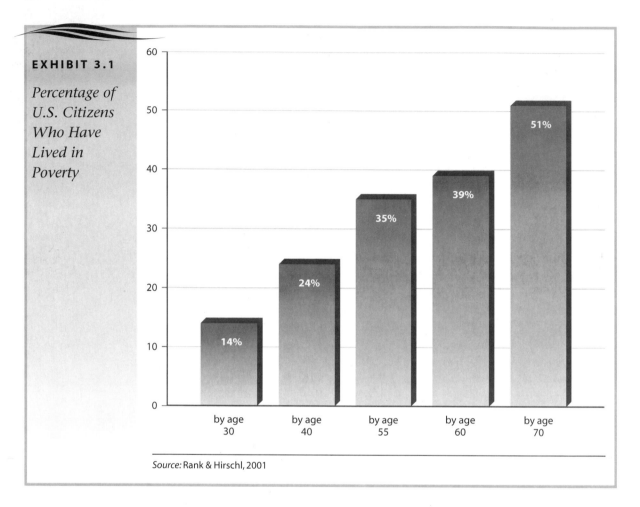

EXHIBIT 3.1

Percentage of U.S. Citizens Who Have Lived in Poverty

Source: Rank & Hirschl, 2001

large percentage of U.S. citizens will live in poverty at some point during their lives (see Exhibit 3.1).

Although many of the stereotypes of poverty are unfounded, the reality is that certain groups are vulnerable for living in poverty. For example, women are more likely to experience poverty than men. Over one-fourth of female-headed households in which there is no husband/father present have incomes that fall below the poverty line (U.S. Census, 2003). Women at each end of the age continuum are particularly at risk for living in poverty, with 17 percent of women aged 18 to 24 and 14 percent of women aged 75 and over living in poverty (DHHS, 2002). Nonwhite women are at the greatest risk for poverty among all groups.

In addition to gender, another significant factor in being poor is race and ethnicity. For example, in 2002, 24 percent of African Americans and 21 percent of Hispanics/Latinos were reported to have incomes below the poverty line as compared to 8 percent of non-Hispanic whites (U.S. Census, 2003). Moreover,

Annual income from full-time employment at $7.00/hour	$14,000	**TABLE 3.1**
Minus tax deduction	($1,071)	
Plus tax credit	$3,612	*Income of the*
Total annual income	$16,541	*Working Poor*

Source: Lazere, Frernstad, & Goldberg, 2002

38 percent of African American female-headed households in which no husband is present have incomes that are less than the poverty line. By age 75, ninety-eight percent of African American women and 96 percent of African American men with less than a high school education will have spent at least one year of their lives living in poverty, compared to 65 percent of white women and 74 percent of white men (Rank & Hirschl, 2001).

Age is also a factor. Approximately 11.5 million children live in poverty in the United States (Lazere, Frernstad, & Goldberg, 2002). Of these poor children, 7.3 million have at least one working parent (Johnson, 2001). Within the older-adult population, approximately 10 percent have incomes below the poverty line (U.S. Census, 2003).

Employment is no guarantee that a person will escape poverty. In fact, approximately two-thirds of poor families had at least one adult employed full time, but over half of those families still fall under the poverty line (CBPP, 2003c; National Public Radio/Kaiser/Harvard [NPR], 2001). Clearly, working full time in a minimum-wage position does not raise an individual above the poverty line. In fact, consider the situation for a family of four represented in Table 3.1. As you can see, based on $18,400 being the poverty line for a family of four, this four-person family falls short of the poverty line by $1,859 each year despite the fact that the "breadwinner" is working full time. By the way, the wage earner is making $7.00 per hour, while the federal minimum wage is currently only $5.15 per hour. Moreover, seven states do not have a minimum wage. However, 11 states and the District of Columbia have enacted laws that require higher minimum wages, ranging from $6.15 in Rhode Island, Delaware, and the District of Columbia to $7.15 in Alaska (Lazere et al., 2002; U.S. Department of Labor, 2003). Finally, did you know that the minimum wage would have to be $6.60 per hour to have the same purchasing power as it did in the 1970s?

Causes of Poverty

One of the most controversial issues in U.S. society today concerns the causes of poverty. Most opinions will be in one of two directions: (1) the individual is responsible, or (2) society is responsible. We will examine both arguments.

Relating back to the philosophy of the Charity Organization Society movement, the first approach, known as the *individualistic perspective,* views the individual as the cause of his or her impoverished situation (Seccombe, 1999). This philosophy, which is sometimes referred to as "blaming the victim," is rooted in the belief that all individuals can and should be self-sufficient and should not require any outside assistance for themselves or their families. Further, in a survey conducted by a team of researchers, half of all persons surveyed believed that those living in poverty are not working hard enough to bring themselves above the poverty line (NPR, 2001). This belief system presents an ongoing challenge for those who advocate for the poor, particularly when funding decisions are at stake. Voters and policy makers who adhere to the "pull yourself up by your bootstraps" philosophy are typically less supportive of spending tax dollars on programs to combat poverty. Interestingly, these views fall neatly along political lines. Examining beliefs by political affiliation suggests that Republicans typically believe that lack of hard work and an unwillingness to be employed are the major causes of poverty, whereas Democrats more often cite external circumstances as the cause of poverty (NPR, 2001).

The alternative view places the blame for poverty on society. Much like the founders of the settlement house movement, proponents of this approach believe that a number of external factors over which the individual has no control make certain individuals vulnerable to a life of poverty. Known as the *social structural perspective,* this view maintains that poverty is caused by economic and social inequities that occur within society's social structures (such as its institutions, organizations, or the economy) (Seccombe, 1999). The prevalence of low-paying employment opportunities that do not offer adequate benefits and the possibility for advancement creates situations in which low-income persons cannot gain economic stability. As one example, even in economic boom times, there is no guarantee that jobs will be accessible to those who lack training and technical sophistication. In addition, as you have seen, when jobs become available to such people, the salaries are frequently insufficient for these workers to climb out of poverty. Other causal factors related to poverty include being female, nonwhite, too old, or too young; being a victim of domestic violence as a child, an adult, or both; being a victim of institutional oppression or discrimination based on disability or social class.

Poverty has many different faces; therefore, distinguishing the types and longevity of poverty adds a useful dimension to our definition. Poverty can be delineated into three types: transitional, marginal, and residual (Segalman & Basu, 1981):

- Poverty experienced on a temporary basis is **transitional poverty.** Examples of transitional poverty occur when people are laid off from their jobs, have a short-term disability, or are enrolled in a training program. These people rely on public assistance until they are able to rejoin the labor force. Thus, they live in poverty only for a short period of time. Recent immigrants who receive public assistance until they find work also fall into this category.

- **Marginal poverty** occurs because the person lacks stable employment, has inadequate skills or limited education, and as a result, is underemployed. Often referred to as the **working poor**, this group is typically employed, but poverty occurs when the job is only part-time or does not compensate the employee enough to move above the poverty line, resulting in the individual being marginally poor.

- **Residual poverty** is chronic and may continue through multiple generations. Possible causes of residual poverty are (1) physical or mental illness or substance abuse that prevents consistent employment; (2) lack of adequate education or training for obtaining or retaining consistent employment; (3) retention problems due to inappropriate work behaviors; and (4) being employed in an industry that has frequent layoffs. Being reared in a family that receives public assistance places individuals at risk for this type of poverty cycle (Rank, 1994). Education also plays a role: People with less than a high school education are at much higher risk than those with high school or higher for living in poverty (Rank & Hirschl, 2002).

CHALLENGES AND BARRIERS TO MOVING OUT OF POVERTY

Living in poverty can become chronic and cyclical for those individuals who begin their lives in poverty and may later move in and out of poverty, particularly with changes in employment, health, and child care status. To understand this concept, recall the elderly woman in the poem at the beginning of the chapter. She was born into poverty, a life that may not provide adequate opportunities for health care, education, or career choices. She probably did not complete high school. She and her husband worked in a series of low-paying jobs that did not offer opportunities for upward mobility or even stability and certainly not for saving for old age or their children's education. Her children grew up in an environment of deprivation and lack of choices, thereby creating another generation of a family who will rear their children in poverty. Thus, the cycle continues.

Consider the teenaged girl who experiences an unplanned pregnancy and applies for public assistance (welfare) as a single parent. As a result of her pregnancy, she may not be able to complete high school or pursue any post–high school education. If she obtains full-time employment, she will lose the financial assistance that she currently receives for child care. Moreover, if her car breaks down, she may not be able to afford the repairs. In such a case, she could lose her job due to absenteeism and may consequently be forced to reapply for public assistance. Thus, the cycle continues.

The Social Work Library

Read Abramovitz's article to see what she has to say on this issue.

Another scenario to consider is the woman who married at a young age and had several children. Her husband insisted that her job was to take care of the children, so she did not work outside the home. Over the years, the husband's occasional outbursts of violence became more frequent until he was physically abusing her on a regular basis, mostly when he was drunk. When he turned his violence toward the children, the woman decided she and the children had to leave. She sought safety for herself and the children in a shelter for battered women. The shelter staff helped her to apply for public assistance, food stamps, and housing and to file for divorce. The court ordered her husband to pay child support, but payment was erratic at best. Because the woman had never held a full-time job, she had no work history or discernible skills to market to potential employers. She found a few minimum-wage jobs, but she was always the first worker to be laid off. Between her frequent layoffs and unreliable child support, she moved in and out of the welfare system. Even when she was able to survive without public assistance, she could never move herself out of poverty. Thus, the cycle continues.

These are just three examples of the challenges of moving out of the cycle of poverty. To gain insight into the role of the social work profession in helping poor people receive services to meet basic needs and in working toward change in society to alleviate poverty, let us now turn to a review of the approaches that have been adopted in the United States to address the issue of poverty.

APPROACHES TO POVERTY IN THE UNITED STATES

Defining the best strategy for eliminating poverty has long been a hotly debated issue in the United States. Strategies for raising people's incomes above the poverty line are controversial because public tax dollars are the primary funding source for welfare programs. As you know, the issue of helping the poor is a value-laden one. This already emotional issue is further complicated by the fact that all U.S. taxpayers have a vested interest in the way their money is spent. For this reason, funding for social programs is a consistently volatile issue for politicians, special interest groups, and those agencies responsible for implementing the programs.

Let us not forget, though, the group that has the most vested interest in the ways in which public funds are spent—the persons themselves who are living in poverty. Unfortunately, this group often has the least influence over the decisions that affect their well-being.

Another group that has a keen interest in social welfare programs is social workers. It is much easier for social workers to fulfill their mission of empowerment if they have adequate funding to do so.

Before reviewing the strategies that have been employed here in the United States, it is important to understand the philosophy that underpins the strategies. Let us start by reviewing definitions that are relevant for our discussion of social welfare.

Terminology of the Social Welfare System

In its literal interpretation, the word *welfare* means "good health, prosperity and social respect" (Albelda, Folbre, & the Center for Popular Economics, 1996). However, in the context of our discussion, the modern-day intent of **welfare** is a societal effort to help people achieve and maintain physical, emotional, and financial well-being. Since the early 1900s, when social services were being formalized in the United States, the term welfare has come to have a negative connotation and has become synonymous with poverty and the public assistance programs that provide cash assistance to single mothers and their children (AFDC, now known as TANF). Although typically associated with programs for low-income persons, welfare, if taken in its literal sense, also comes in the form of corporate and realty investor tax benefits, corporate bailouts, home mortgage deductions, tax abatements for home ownership in economically depressed areas, and farm and low-income housing development subsidies.

The term social welfare has also taken on a dual meaning. Following the literal definition for *welfare,* social welfare describes a group's level of stability. However, it also refers to our country's system of programs, benefits, and services that support those in need of financial, social, and health care support. The term **public welfare**, often used synonymously with *public assistance,* also refers to the policies that a country develops to provide for the well-being of its citizens.

Social welfare programs are guided by **social policy**, defined as governmental rules and regulations that are used to develop and guide the practices and procedures related to social issues. These policies guide social workers' practice. Social policies address programs in such areas as education, health, corrections, and social welfare, but are aimed at creating resources needed to meet the basic needs of society. Social policies can be of two types: residual and institutional. **Residual social policies** address a social need that is specific to a population and will continue to exist regardless of the policies' effectiveness or ineffectiveness. Services for pregnant women and disabled persons are examples of programs that result from residual social policies. In contrast, **institutional social policies** address a social need that is universal to a population. Social Security is an example of an institutional social policy that provides retirement insurance for all older adults who have invested in that system. The work of the social work profession is inextricably linked to the social policies (perhaps even dependent on the policies) that underlie the laws, funding, insurance reimbursements, and authority to enact, implement, and oversee the programs.

A subset of social policies, **social welfare policies** allocate financial, social, and health resources. Social workers' activities are impacted by social policies, in general, and social welfare policies, in particular.

Now that you have acquired a basic understanding of the terms that are so integral to any discussion of social welfare issues, let us examine the historical underpinnings of our modern-day social welfare system. As you know from Chapter 2, the social welfare system in the United States is based on the English model but adapted by the United States. As the country was founded on the principle of independence and autonomy, it is not surprising that the basis of the welfare system is "competitive individualism and the validity of market-based economics" (Hopps & Collins, 1995, p. 2268). The historical review of the social work profession in Chapter 2 focused on the development of the social service structure. For our review of the evolution of the public welfare system, we will again take a tour through history, but this time we will target the important events that led to the creation of our contemporary programmatic approaches to social needs.

Social Welfare in the 17th–19th Centuries

Although considerable progress was made in social service–related areas in the first two centuries of our country's history, much of the accomplishment was in the private sector. Before 1862, all welfare benefits provided by the government were administered at the local, rather than the federal, level. However, the widespread disability and death rates caused by the Civil War created the need for a comprehensive national response. Therefore, in 1862, the federal government enacted legislation to provide pensions for Union soldiers and their dependents or survivors in the event of a soldier's death (Albelda et al., 1996). Other public assistance programs triggered by the Civil War included the Freedmen's Bureau, which provided help for freed slaves from 1865 to 1872, and an 1890 law that awarded pensions to all veterans who served in the Union army.

Social Welfare in the 20th Century

During the late 19th and early 20th centuries, in addition to the emergence of the settlement house and Charity Organization Society movements, public programs were being created to combat the results of the economic depression that had beset the country in the 1890s. Many of these programs were initiated at the state level, but they spread from state to state. Groups such as orphaned or fatherless children and older adults were being marginalized by the lack of a comprehensive approach.

BOX 3.1

*New Deal
Programs*

1933—The Federal Emergency Relief Act (FERA) provided temporary financial support to unemployed persons.

1933—The Civilian Conservation Corps (CCC) was an early, federally funded employment program that became the forerunner to the Job Corps program of the 1960s.

1935—The Social Security Act provided assistance to fatherless families through the Aid to Families with Dependent Children (AFDC) program. AFDC became the cornerstone of the public response to poor families and remained essentially unchanged until the 1990s.

1935—Aimed at creating employment opportunities, the Works Progress Administration (WPA) employed eight million workers in the building of parks, bridges, and roads.

In addition, a new paradigm for assisting the increasing populations of children, single mothers, and older adults was introduced during these years. In 1909, a White House Conference on Children recommended that children should remain with their parents whenever possible (Albelda et al., 1996). As a result, public funds were shifted toward providing services in homes versus automatic institutionalization. One law that reflected this new approach was the 1921 Sheppard-Towner Act, the first federal program to fund maternal and child health care for low-income women and children, thought by many to be the forerunner to modern-day public assistance for single women and their children.

New Deal Welfare Reforms   The drastic times of the Great Depression of the 1930s called for drastic measures. To alleviate the suffering of millions of Americans, the administration of Franklin Roosevelt created a number of public welfare programs. With nearly one-third of the workforce unemployed at the height of the Depression, a stronger, more comprehensive federal response was necessary. Perhaps the most famous federal initiative from this period is the Social Security Act of 1935. However, under the umbrella of Roosevelt's New Deal, a number of welfare programs were established (see Box 3.1).

With the exception of the Social Security legislation, most of these interventions were repealed or discontinued following the Depression. Programs developed to address crisis situations are typically intended to exist only for the duration of the crisis. Social Security is the exception, and it created a comprehensive system for providing an income for older adults and later for the children of deceased workers and workers that suffered disabilities.

Social Welfare from World War II through the 1970s   Welfare programs established during the economically prosperous late 1940s were primarily aimed at war veterans and their dependents and survivors (although it is doubtful whether many people considered these programs to be welfare). The Servicemen's Readjustment Act of 1944—more popularly known as the GI Bill of Rights—provided funds for education, home and business loans, health care, and employment counseling, training, and placement.

The 1950s continued to be a prosperous decade for the United States, with moderate growth in the development of social welfare programs. The Social Security Act was expanded in 1950 to include benefits for low-income children and the disabled. The U.S. Housing Act of 1954 prompted urban renewal projects across the country. In 1953, the Department of Health, Education, and Welfare (HEW) was created as a cabinet-level department to oversee funding and programs in these three areas.

From a public welfare standpoint, the 1960s were a boom time. As part of Lyndon Johnson's War on Poverty, new programs were established through the Economic Opportunity Act of 1964. The Economic Opportunity Act funded training and community action programs such as the Job Corps, which provided employment training for youth; Volunteers in Service to America (VISTA), which sent volunteers into poor neighborhoods; Community Action Programs (CAPs), community-based antipoverty programs; and **Head Start,** the program that provides early childhood development services to low-income children. Additional efforts included the food stamps program, which helped low-income people to purchase food, and the Older Americans Act of 1965, which dispersed funds to communities to develop programs for older adults.

Despite the fact that new programs were being created to decrease the numbers of persons receiving public assistance, the welfare rolls increased in both size and composition. AFDC recipients were increasingly families headed by single mothers and families of color. Opponents of welfare programs called for making the benefits more restrictive and requiring welfare recipients to work. In an effort to respond to the criticisms of public assistance programs, the Work Incentive Program (WIN) was established to provide training, job placement, child care, and transportation. But the program failed due to lack of adequate funding to provide the comprehensive services that were intended.

In contrast to the 1960s, during the 1970s, few new programs were introduced. Rather, adjustments were made to existing programs. For example, the 1975 Title XX amendment to the Social Security Act provided additional funding for personal social services for low-income persons, including services to promote economic independence (for example, employment training and placement), child and elder abuse and neglect prevention, and community-based services to prevent institutionalization of older adults and persons with disabilities. The exception is the **Supplemental Security Income (SSI)** program, established in 1972. This program provides public financial assistance for low-income persons who are elderly, visually impaired, or have disabilities.

Unlike Social Security, assistance is not based on previous employment, but on current income.

Following the demise of the Nixon administration, Presidents Ford and Carter endeavored to continue the "welfare revolution" begun in the 1960s but had only moderate success. The number of recipients of welfare programs was reduced, but at a high financial cost to taxpayers because social welfare program funding was increased using tax dollars. Proponents of the work-ethic school of thought perceived that these programs were only increasing the dependence of the poor on public assistance and were not reforming them (Reid, 1995). The "revolution" as such ended with the election of Ronald Reagan in 1980.

Turnabout: Social Welfare in the 1980s and Beyond   The Reagan and Bush (senior) administrations of the 1980s and early 1990s focused on decreasing resources for public welfare programs. Both administrations subscribed to the philosophy that welfare should be a private business, not a public responsibility. To implement this philosophy, Reagan proposed, and Congress passed, the 1981 Omnibus Budget Reconciliation Act (OBRA), which eliminated public-service jobs, decreased benefits for low-income workers and AFDC recipients, and granted authority for resource distribution to the states (Albelda et al., 1996). The Family Support Act of 1988 emphasized work requirements and brought support for the perceived need to make welfare benefits more punitive and restrictive by making eligibility more limited. Issues such as AFDC, homelessness, and AIDS took a backseat to supporting corporate America and military spending (Segal & Brzuzy, 1998). Many critics contend that the policies adopted by the Reagan and Bush administrations constituted a significant setback for the gains that had been made in social welfare policy throughout the 20th century.

The 1990s brought a renewed focus on public responsibility for social needs. Clinton's election strategies focused on returning the nation's attention to domestic issues, specifically, health and education. During the 1990s Congress passed several laws that had economic implications for impoverished families, people with disabilities, and minority populations. For example, the 1990 Americans with Disabilities Act, the Civil Rights Restoration Act, the 1993 Family and Medical Leave Act, the Brady (gun control) Bill, and the Anti-Crime Bill were all aimed at enhancing the quality of life for large groups of Americans and, in many cases, the quality of their economic well-being (Segal & Brzuzy, 1998).

The tides soon shifted again, however. Promoted by Newt Gingrich, a member of the House of Representatives, the Republican-based Contract with America was introduced in the mid-1990s. The Contract was an effort by political conservatives to reverse the more liberal social welfare policies of earlier decades (for example, the Great Society). This shift resulted in the introduction of welfare reform legislation. After numerous revisions, the Clinton administration agreed to support the Personal Responsibility and Work Opportunity Reconciliation Act (PRWORA) in 1996, which replaced AFDC with Temporary Assistance to Needy Families (TANF). The PRWORA was intended to decrease dependence on welfare. Moreover, because the federal government would fund TANF through block grants to the states and would not provide a uniform set of guidelines, the PRWORA authorized each state to determine (1) the ways that funds would be allocated and the amounts that would be awarded, (2) time limits for cash assistance, and (3) eligibility requirements for Medicaid health coverage. States that did not comply with general federal regulations regarding the restrictions for receiving TANF benefits jeopardized continued funding. One condition of the PRWORA was a five-year lifetime cap on public assistance benefits. In addition, TANF recipients are required to be engaged in a work-related activity for at least 30 hours per week. The first five-year period ended on September 30, 2002.

Concern for the well-being of TANF recipients who would have difficulty gaining and maintaining employment motivated welfare rights advocates to lobby state legislatures to reauthorize TANF benefits. Since the TANF authorization expired in 2002, Congress has yet to permanently reauthorize the block grants that are awarded to each state. However, Congress has authorized several temporary extensions of TANF funding until a compromise can be reached (CBPP, 2003b; NASW, 2003).

A fierce debate continues between those who emphasize decreasing welfare rolls and increasing employment, and those who stress alleviating poverty through the provision of funding for training and employment (Peterson, 2002). There has been considerable concern and controversy over the impact of TANF legislation. Advocates for children and welfare recipients fear that the lives of these individuals will get worse instead of better because states that have not budgeted well for a particular year can refuse or decrease the amount of aid granted for each applicant (Segal & Brzuzy, 1998).

Although many people agreed that the welfare system was in need of reform, opponents of the new TANF program view it as coercive regarding work requirements, inflexible regarding time limits, and shortsighted about middle-aged women who are terminated from TANF when their children are no longer eligible due to their age (Abramovitz, 1997). Critics view welfare reform as based on what they consider to be an incorrect assumption that poverty is a temporary situation that can be rectified by a stable national and global economy (NASW, 2003–2006).

Other criticisms leveled against the reforms suggest that little change has occurred since the passage of the PRWORA. Requiring TANF recipients to work has only minimally decreased national poverty rates, primarily because TANF recipients have been unable to obtain employment with wages high enough to lift them out of poverty (Danziger, 2002). Therefore, the next steps to supporting TANF recipients in their struggle for self-sufficiency are to focus on the factors that would help them find well-paying jobs (for example, education, training, physical and mental health conditions, and transportation needs) and to advocate for higher overall wages (Danziger, 2002).

IMPACT OF THE CHANGING APPROACHES TO POVERTY ON SOCIAL WORK

This brings our discussion to the present day. As you have learned, sentiments regarding public welfare resources and programs are complex and closely linked to the political, economic, religious, and social spheres of U.S. society. Our discussion raises the question What are the implications of this changing tide for the social work profession? Social and economic needs inevitably prompt a societal and political response. This response, in turn, determines the amount of money that politicians, bureaucrats, private foundations, and individual donors will spend. This availability of funding determines the extent to which social workers will be engaged (funded) to provide social work services.

The public child welfare system provides an example of this model. When the political climate is unfavorable for public social services, funding is decreased, and the number of social work positions is lowered. Although the demand for social work services in this case may remain high, the funding is not adequate to support all the positions required to meet this demand. Such situations result in fewer workers with larger caseloads. During these times, politicians often suggest that the private sector should fill the gap created by decreased public funding.

There will always be a role for social workers regardless of the political and economic climate. However, social workers' jobs may become more or less challenging depending on the political affiliation of the people or group in the political majority, the state of the economy, and the prevailing sentiments regarding social welfare programs. In the most recent policy statement, the National Association of Social Workers calls for social workers to advocate for plans that will

- provide assistance to people who are poor when the five-year lifetime cap has been reached on their eligibility for benefits;

- create a safety net for persons that are experiencing poverty;

- help persons living in poverty to build personal and financial assets through such programs as individual development accounts;

- enable those persons living in poverty to integrate work, education, and family life; and

- promote research to better understand the underlying economic causes of poverty, including the impact that such factors as substance abuse, domestic violence, health problems, and illiteracy play in preventing an escape from poverty. (2003–2006, pp. 343–344)

One of the roles of an effective social worker is to facilitate the client system's access to services. When functioning in this role, the social worker assists client systems of all sizes in identifying and connecting to all the resources for which the client is eligible. For example, helping a family locate in-home services to avoid placing their elderly mother suffering from dementia in a long-term care facility is an example of linking a client to needed resources. To fulfill that objective, social workers must possess a working knowledge of existing social welfare programs and keep themselves updated on the ever-changing policies, eligibility requirements, application protocols, and benefits associated with these programs.

Although programs come and go with political and funding changes, a core group of programs have seemingly weathered the political and economic storms. These programs fall into one of two general categories: universal or selective. Let us look at a sampling of both types of programs with which social workers need to be familiar.

Current Universal Programs

All persons in a particular group are deemed eligible for a universal program. These programs can be either cash or service based. Two major universal programs are Social Security and Medicare.

- Authorized by the Social Security Act of 1935, **Social Security** provides a retirement income for all workers who have paid into the system during their years of employment. The benefit that a person receives is based on the amount that she or he "invested." The act also provides income to survivors (spouses and children) of deceased workers and to workers who become disabled, if they have worked long enough to qualify.

- Part of the Great Society movement of the 1960s, **Medicare** is health care coverage for persons who receive Social Security benefits. Any person who receives any type of Social Security payments is automatically eligible for Medicare.

Current Selective Programs

In contrast to universal programs, selective programs provide benefits only to individuals or families who meet specific criteria that are determined by the federal or state government agency responsible for administering the program.

Eligibility is often based on income, assets, and/or family composition. Here is a sampling of eligibility-based social welfare programs in existence today:

- Temporary Assistance to Needy Families (TANF) provides monthly cash assistance to eligible low-income families with children under age 18. Within the first two years of benefits, TANF recipients who are able-bodied must be engaged in work or work-related activities (for example, job training or seeking) or lose benefits. Over a lifetime, an individual can receive benefits for a total of five years only. Because each state determines the eligibility criteria and amount of assistance received, TANF benefits vary from state to state. However, the average monthly cash benefit is $349 overall ($356 for a single parent with two children), with the range extending from $141.49 per month in Alabama to $627.31 per month in Alaska (based on 2000 data from DHHS, 2003).

- Funded through the Social Security program, **Social Security Disability (SSD)** provides cash assistance for persons deemed to be unable to work for a period of at least one year for reasons of physical or mental disability. Restrictions enacted as part of the Contract with America deemed workers who become disabled due to drug or alcohol addiction to be ineligible for SSD (Dickinson, 1997).

- Begun in 1972 as a merging of several different federal and state programs, **Supplemental Security Income (SSI)** provides cash assistance to low-income adults, older adults, and persons with disabilities or visual challenges who meet income and health standards. SSI funds are administered by the Social Security Administration, but the funding is separate from the funds allocated for other Social Security programs. SSI recipients can receive other benefits (such as Medicaid and food stamps) while receiving SSI. The federal government bears the cost of this program, but a number of states add to that amount.

- Introduced in 1965 along with Medicare as an amendment to the Social Security Act, **Medicaid** is the health coverage that is available to some recipients of the eligibility-based programs (TANF, SSI, and SSD). Social Security recipients may also receive Medicaid, but eligibility is based on need; that is, recipients must qualify based on their income. Each state sets the criteria for Medicaid.

- Instituted in 1964, the **food stamps** program administered by the Department of Agriculture provides coupons that can be used to purchase food items. This program is intended to supplement a family's income and is based on the assumption that families spend 30 percent of their total income on food. The program allows recipients to spend an average of 78 cents per person per meal (Albelda et al., 1996). Approximately

80 percent of TANF recipients receive food stamps. The average monthly allotment is $224, but amounts range from $163.68 per month in Massachusetts to $377.18 per month in Hawaii (DHHS, 2003).

- Aimed at enhancing the physical health of poor women, infants, and children, **Women, Infants, and Children (WIC)** has been in operation since 1974. Primarily a federally funded program, it provides vouchers to poor women who are eligible based on their income and current health status. They can purchase certain foods for themselves and their children. Mothers and their children can receive WIC benefits along with other assistance programs such as TANF and Medicaid.

- For those low-income adults who do not qualify for any other cash assistance programs, states have historically made small, short-term cash benefits available through **General Assistance (GA)**, sometimes called general relief. As welfare cuts and reforms have proliferated, many states have opted to eliminate this program.

- In effect since 1975 and expanded in 1986, 1990, 1993, and 2001, low-income working persons are eligible to receive the **Earned Income Tax Credit (EITC)**, a refundable tax credit based on the number of children and the total household income. The federal EITC program, which is administered through the Internal Revenue Service, is designed to help the working poor retain a larger percentage of their income. Because applicants simply request these funds when they submit their federal tax returns, this program involves less paperwork than many others. One in every seven individuals and families that submit federal income tax returns applies for federal EITC, making this program the most successful government effort for alleviating poverty for children (CBPP, 2003a). The maximum federal EITC benefit for a family with one child is $2,547 and $4,204 for a family with two children. In addition to the federal program, 17 states have enacted state-level EITC programs (CBPP, 2003a). In these states, families can receive additional credits of $382 and $631, respectively.

- Begun as part of the 1960s War on Poverty, **Head Start** is a child development program for low-income children. Head Start services include preschool, health, and nutrition programs.

Like many social work students, Emily questioned the value of studying social welfare history and the myriad government programs. After all, she just wanted to help people, and spending time reading about policies had nothing to do with helping people, or did it? One day at Oasis House, Emily and her social work supervisor, John, met with one of the shelter's residents, Tonya. Tonya's TANF and Medicaid benefits were about to be terminated because she was not employed full time. Instead, she was enrolled in a licensed practical nurse program and working part-time at a nursing home. She had only three months until graduation, and her only income was the public assistance she received. Since she and her two children fled from her violent husband, Tonya had tried to comply with the TANF work requirements. However, she had difficulty keeping a job because the LPN program is full time. In addition, she had to make frequent medical visits related to her older child's cerebral palsy. She had held several part-time jobs while she was in the LPN program, but she either had to quit each one or she was fired due to absenteeism because her child was hospitalized or had medical appointments.

In his role as an advocate, John telephoned Tonya's income-maintenance caseworker to request that Tonya be scheduled for a hearing at which she could request a work waiver to complete training. He also requested that the agency allow him to accompany Tonya to the hearing and present photographs verifying that she was a victim of domestic violence. As a result of John's knowledge of governmental benefits and Tonya's rights, Tonya obtained a waiver to allow her to finish training. John also helped Tonya apply for SSI for her disabled child. Through her experience with Tonya and John, Emily learned the importance of being knowledgeable about policies and programs if she intends to become an advocate for people in need.

This chapter has described key governmental programs that are available to the people with whom you will be working as a social worker. Remember that regardless of the area of social work in which you specialize, you are responsible for staying current with the myriad changes made to these programs every year.

CONCLUSION

The causes of poverty are multifaceted and complex, as are the solutions. The dynamics of political, social, and economic factors interact to create an economy and a culture in which poverty exists. Social welfare policy and, subsequently, programs change frequently related to the prevailing economy and society's views on the level of funding and how much of a safety net to provide.

Understanding the historical roots of contemporary social welfare philosophy and programs is essential for a practicing social worker. Social workers' knowledge, skills, and values give them valuable insights into the systemic impact of poverty on those with whom they work.

More policy changes are needed to address a growing number of people, especially children, living in poverty. To help people achieve economic stability, social workers can advocate for policy changes in such areas as TANF, health care and insurance, the minimum wage, tax structures, and educational benefits. But you cannot advocate for your position unless you know the varied positions of others involved. Social workers have long been on the forefront of advocacy efforts, and they will continue to use their knowledge of systems, organizations, and communities to advocate for and with others at the local, state, national, and international levels to alleviate poverty.

Another of Don Bakely's poems captures this sense of optimism and hope.

When I was a kid,
> *I looked to the day when*
>> *I would stop dreaming those wild hopes*
> *and*
>> *I'd be old enough*
>>> *to make real life*
>>>> *out of*
>>>>> *unreal dreams.*
But I still catch myself
> *hanging onto dreams—*
> *and I'm forty.*
Sometimes I catch myself thinking
> *maybe today*
>> *a big, beautiful car is going to pull up out front*
>>> *and*
>>>> *the rich man is going to get out*
>>>>> *and say,*
"I heard about you,
> *that*
>> *you are a good man*
>>> *and work hard*
>>>> *and love your kids*
>>>>> *and are down on your luck.*
Here's a check.
Come by the office. I've got a good job for a man like you.
By the way, keep the car.
>> *I see you need one.*
>> *I'll catch a cab back."*

Of course,
> *he never comes.*
I really know
> > *he*
> > > *never*
> > > > *will.*
But, see,
> *with poor folks*
> > *even wild hopes*
> > > *are*
> > > > *hopes worth thinking.*
> > > > > *Kind of fun, in fact.*
Then, too,
> *if we can't have some glimmer*
> > > > *in*
> > > > *tomorrow.*

> *even a*
> > *long-shot,*
> > *never-happen*
> > > *glimmer.*
Then each today
> > *is always*
> > > *only*
> > > > *darkness.*

Excerpt from The Family of Poor: Part Three,
From *If . . . A Big Word with the Poor*
By Don Bakely
Used by permission

MAIN POINTS

- Poverty is a complex political, economic, and social issue, but essentially is not having enough money to live adequately.

- The poor are not just the stereotype of the homeless man or woman sleeping in a doorway or pushing a shopping cart on the downtown streets of a city; those groups at highest risk for living in poverty are women, persons of color, older adults, and children (who cannot work).

- The causes of poverty continue to be hotly debated. Some people believe that the individual is responsible for her or his economic plight, while others believe that external factors (such as employment and economic conditions) place people at risk for living in poverty.

- Poverty can be transitional, or episodic; marginal, in which the individual is working but cannot earn enough money to move out of poverty; or residual (chronic), in which the individual's poverty is long term.

- Understanding both the literal meanings and societal connotations of terms such as welfare, public assistance, and social policy helps in understanding society's perception of poverty.

- A variety of federal, state, and local government agencies are involved in the administration of social welfare programs. Societal responses to poverty tend to reflect the current political climate, with conservative political administrations restricting social programs and more liberal administrations expanding social programs.

- Social welfare programs fall into two categories: universal (Social Security and Medicare) and selective (for example, TANF, SSI, and food stamps). Social workers are responsible for being familiar with these programs and staying current with the myriad changes made every year.

EXERCISES: PRACTICING SOCIAL WORK

Determining Benefits

As you have learned from the Sanchez family case scenario, the family has struggled financially throughout the years. Hector has prevented the family from utilizing many of the resources available to them. Complete the following two exercises:

1. Using the information and the Web sites provided in this chapter along with those from your state government, identify benefits that may be appropriate for various members of the Sanchez family.

From the Client Perspective

Reflect on the reasons that Hector may feel resistance to utilizing social services. Additionally, reflect on how you think Hector and the members of his family may feel in the client role.

Junior Sanchez

Using the Sanchez Family interactive case study, review the information regarding Junior Sanchez and answer Junior's Critical Thinking Questions.

EXERCISES: THE SOCIAL WORK LIBRARY

Everyone is Still on Welfare

After reading "Everyone is Still on Welfare: The Role of Redistribution in Social Policy" (Abramovitz, 2001), address the following issues:

1. Summarize the three welfare systems describe in the article.

2. Discuss the differences in welfare systems noted between Abramovitz and Titmuss.

3. Share your own reactions to the premise that fiscal and occupational welfare are forms of welfare.

Understanding the Safety Net

After reading "Welfare Use as a Life Course Event: Toward a New Understanding of the U.S. Safety Net" (Rank & Hirschl, 2002) in the Social Work Library, address the following issues:

1. Summarize Rank and Hirschl's description of current usage of welfare benefits in the U.S.

2. Describe the concept of a "safety net."

3. Discuss the implications of the findings in this article for the social work profession.

OTHER EXERCISES

Budgeting for a Family of Three

As you learned from this chapter, Tonya is a single mother with two children. Her son, William, is three years old and her daughter, Erica, is six years old. For the purpose of creating a budget, Tonya's current employment or welfare benefits are not to be considered. Develop a budget that would be required for Tonya and her two children to live for one month. You may want to have a calculator available to help you in this exercise.

This budget should not reflect a luxurious lifestyle or a life at bare minimum, but rather should show what you believe are essentials for living and their costs for one month. For each basic human need, enter an amount that you think is a true monthly cost regardless of who would pay for it. For example, the cost of food will be the same if the family receives Food Stamps or not. In actuality, the family may not have the resources to purchase that amount of food, but it is still a cost. As you are creating this budget, identify your reasons for deriving that particular amount.

Once you have developed a picture of Tonya's needs for one month, you can compare your amounts with the actual amounts required if this family lived in your state. As you progress with this exploration, consider the Tonya's situation from two different perspectives. First, assume that the Tonya and her children receive TANF benefits and compare your budget with the amounts of benefits that they will receive. Secondly, consider the scenario in which Tonya is employed full-time in a minimum wage job. Decide if she receives health/dental benefits for herself and/or her children. In order to make these comparisons, you will need information on living costs in your community.

Questions to consider as you complete this exercise:

1. What information do you need to know to be able to develop a monthly budget?

2. What categories of expenses would a single mother with two children have during the month?

3. What is the amount of TANF provided by your state for a mother and two children?

Identifying Attitudes toward "Welfare"

Interview friends, family members, co-workers, and/or others about their definitions and attitudes about "welfare." Reflect on the similarities and differences in their responses and the way in which their definitions and attitudes compare to the definitions described in this chapter.

CHAPTER 4

The Social Work Environment

T HE SOCIAL WORK PROFESSION HELPS INDIVIDUALS, FAMILIES, groups, organizations, and communities. The profession's helping mission places it in the center of people's lives and the societal issues that influence their lives. Therefore, social workers must be knowledgeable about the makeup of society in general and the populations who use social workers' services in particular.

In this chapter, you gain an understanding of the diversity of the U.S. population and then examine the challenges that confront social workers in the contemporary United States. Political, economic, and social issues that present obstacles for those persons served by social workers also provide opportunities for growth and social change. We will explore these issues from the perspectives of both challenges and opportunities for social work practice.

Recognizing that demographics are constantly undergoing shifts, let us first turn our attention to an overview of the current demographic profile. Within each category that creates the portrait of U.S. society are the links to the knowledge and skills that social workers will need to practice with that particular segment of the population.

AMERICA'S CHANGING PROFILE

According to the 2000 census, the United States is a country of 281,421,906 diverse people, but government policies are not always supportive of all segments of the population. Recent demographic shifts have made the population more diverse than at any previous time in history. Using data from four main sources—the 2000 census (U.S. Census Bureau, 2004), the 2002 Annual Demographic Supplement to the Current Population Survey, Population Projections (Day, 1996), *Women's Health USA 2002* (U.S. Department of Health and Human Services, 2002), and the 2000 Statistical Abstract of the United States—this chapter presents highlights of the diversity of the present population with projections for the future. The discussion focuses on five demographic characteristics: race and ethnicity, age, gender, income, and religion.

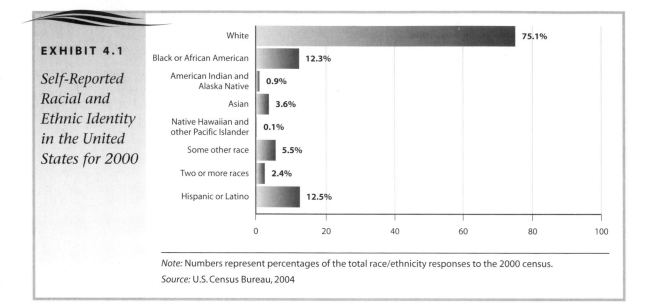

EXHIBIT 4.1

Self-Reported Racial and Ethnic Identity in the United States for 2000

Note: Numbers represent percentages of the total race/ethnicity responses to the 2000 census.

Source: U.S. Census Bureau, 2004

Changes in Race and Ethnicity

A racial profile of the United States, taken from the 2000 census, is shown in Exhibit 4.1. The United States experienced greater population growth between 1990 and 2000 (32.7 million people) than during any other 10-year period in history, with the largest growth occurring in the western states and metropolitan areas. Going further, from 1995 to 2050 the U.S. population is expected to increase by 50 percent, with the largest growth occurring within the Hispanic/ Latino and Asian populations, primarily due to immigration. Thus, racial and ethnic diversity clearly is increasing, particularly among older adults, in general, and older adults of color, in particular. One reason for this trend is that persons of color are gaining better access to health care and are therefore living longer. In addition, fertility is expected to remain constant while mortality declines.

One consequence of this increased diversity is that the U.S. population will include greater numbers of people whose first language is not English and who identify with more than one racial or ethnic group. For social workers, increased diversity requires that they have culturally competent skills to meet the needs of clients whose cultural heritage, language, values, and traditions are different from their own.

The Aging Population

Not only is the U.S. population becoming more diverse racially and ethnically, but it is also aging. Since 1990, the median age has increased from 32.9 to 35.3 years, and it is expected to increase to 38.7 years by 2035. Significantly, a greater percentage of the population of persons of color falls within the under-18 category, whereas whites make up the largest percentage of older adults.

Based on current demographic projections, by 2030 more than 40 percent of the total U.S. population will be either under age 17 (21 percent) or over age 65 (22 percent). As children and older adults tend to be the most vulnerable segments of the population, such increases will result in a greater need for social work competence in working with these groups.

Life expectancy is currently at 77.2 years for all groups. Men and persons of color have lower life expectancy (National Center for Health Statistics, 2003). However, longevity is on the increase for all groups; by 2050 life expectancy is projected to be as high as 83.9 years overall, although lower for persons of color and men. The fastest growing segment of the population will be those over 85—this group will double by 2025 and increase five times by 2050.

As the population gets older, social workers need skills to work with the entire continuum of ages, particularly in multigenerational family situations. More older adults are rearing grandchildren as a result of the children's parents being unavailable for a variety of reasons, including substance abuse, incarceration, and divorce. Current trends suggest that multigenerational families will reside together more often, and more older adults will live in congregate living situations such as retirement communities, assisted living facilities, and long-term care facilities. These arrangements will require social workers to be as skillful in working with older adults as with children and younger adults.

Gender Makeup of the Population

Today, women make up 51 percent of the U.S. population, although the male population experienced more growth between the 1990 and 2000 censuses. Men outnumber women until age 24, but for the 65-and-older segment, women make up 58 percent of the population. By age 85, women outnumber men by two to one. Male mortality begins to increase initially due to professional and recreational activities and later due to chronic fatal illnesses such as heart disease and cancer. These patterns are expected to continue, as the elderly proportion of the female population increases.

For social workers, links to gender are particularly significant in the area of aging. As the number of older women increases, social workers need to be aware of the issues that confront this population. Compared to older men, older women are more likely to live alone, to have lower incomes, to experience more chronic health problems, and to assume more care-giving responsibilities (for example, for spouses or grandchildren). With the changes that have occurred in recent decades regarding women's roles in society, women's aging will be changing as well due to increased participation in the workforce, and social workers need to be preparing proactively for the new generations of older women.

Income Levels and Poverty

From 2000 to 2001, overall median household incomes fell 2.2 percent, while median household incomes for African Americans, Asians, and Pacific Islanders fell 3.4 percent to 6.4 percent. The number of people living in poverty rose by 1.3 million. In a review of the past 30 years, the number of persons living in poverty has climbed steadily, although the percentage of the population living in poverty fluctuates. Overall, 12 percent of the U.S. population lived in poverty in 2002, with 13 percent of women and 10 percent of men living in poverty (U.S. Census Bureau, 2004).

High divorce rates and more single women heading households will also contribute to the "feminization" of poverty, as more women, making less money, will be heading households by themselves. Interestingly, overall incomes for women rose slightly (3.5 percent), bringing the female-to-male earnings ratio to an all-time high of .77 (women earn 77 cents per every dollar earned by men) (U.S. Census Bureau, 2004).

A startling fact is that the richest 20 percent of the population receive almost 50 percent of household incomes, while the poorest 20 percent receive 3.5 percent of overall household incomes. Poverty rates rose from 11.3 percent of the population to 11.7 percent, with non-Hispanic whites, Hispanics, urbanites, Southerners, and children being most affected. The poverty rate for the white population is approximately 8 percent, while the rates for African Americans and persons of Hispanic/Latino origin are approximately 24 percent and 21 percent, respectively (U.S. Census Bureau, 2004).

These demographic shifts have implications for social work practice. As poverty rates increase, more people will need assistance with finances, health, employment, food, housing, utilities, and child care. In addition, family crises and violence often increase when families are experiencing stresses. Therefore, social workers increasingly will need the necessary skills to work with diverse families in crisis.

Religious Affiliations

At the beginning of the 21st century, approximately 1,600 different religions and denominations were being practiced in the United States, almost half of which have been established in the past 40 years (Mindell, 2001). Exhibit 4.2 shows two ways of looking at religion that have implications for social workers. Although people who self-identify as Muslim are a small percentage, they and other religions are increasing. Increases reported include Islam—109 percent; Buddhism—170 percent; Hinduism—237 percent.

Despite the number of different religious affiliations, the United States is far from being free of religious segregation and discrimination. The events of September 11, 2001, for example, prompted a rash of discrimination directed

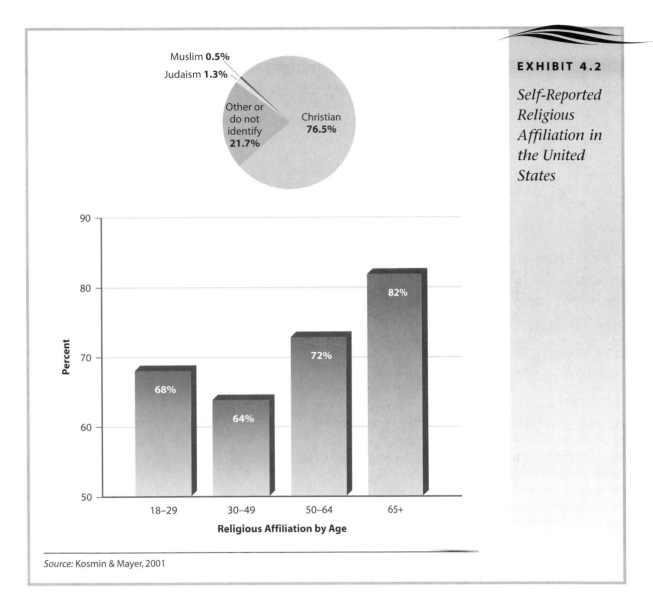

Source: Kosmin & Mayer, 2001

EXHIBIT 4.2

Self-Reported Religious Affiliation in the United States

toward Muslims. Muslims have been subjected to physical, verbal, and written assaults, threats against their lives, and damage to their businesses and homes.

For social workers, this means that they should be aware of their own religious and spiritual beliefs as well as those of others. They can then work to promote religious acceptance and understanding and to incorporate spirituality into their practice. Because the population is aging and religious affiliation increases with age, social workers will benefit from knowledge of religion and sensitivity to the role of religion and spirituality in the lives of older adults. For example, being aware of an older person's religious involvement can be a resource in the social work intervention.

CHALLENGES AND OPPORTUNITIES FACING SOCIAL WORKERS

Emily began to notice that the domestic violence shelter program where she worked was serving an increasing number of women whose first language was not English and who frequently had limited English-speaking skills. The women were being identified primarily as victims of domestic violence through hospital emergency rooms where they were seeking emergency medical treatment. The community in which Emily worked was experiencing an overall increase in the number of refugees and immigrants from Eastern Europe, Russia, African countries, and several Spanish-speaking countries; therefore, multiple languages were involved. The domestic violence program staff and volunteers only spoke English and therefore had to rely on the women's family members (often their children who were more proficient in English) or the on-call interpreters engaged by the hospitals. Emily and her co-workers also realized that their understanding of domestic violence within other cultures was limited. Providing services to non-English-speaking women in crisis without regular interpreters hampered Emily's ability to establish rapport, gather information, and develop supportive and helpful interventions with this client group. Consequently, Emily and her co-workers were growing increasingly concerned that their non-English-speaking clients were not being effectively served by their agency or other agencies that provided services to victims of domestic violence and their children.

As you have learned, social work practice is often shaped by current political, economic, and social philosophies and events. Although the political, social, and economic issues of today and tomorrow may be different from those that affected past generations, the social work profession must be prepared to influence and respond to the effects of such changes on the individuals, families, organizations, and communities that it serves. Changes will bring new and controversial issues for social workers, but it will be the profession's "values and mission that will anchor the profession in the sea of change" (Allen-Meares, 2000, p. 179).

A major issue that has long confronted social workers is the political, economic, and social oppression and discrimination faced by those groups with whom practitioners work. Although oppression and discrimination are closely related, they are distinct concepts. **Oppression** occurs when the actions or beliefs of individuals, groups, or institutions are controlled or repressed by other persons or groups within a society. Oppression can be formalized and overt, as in the case of the historical treatment of gay, lesbian, bisexual, and transgendered persons in society. However, it can also be informal and covert, such as the continued mistreatment of these groups following passage of hate crimes legislation. In contrast, **discrimination**, in a social context, is the behavior that results from possessing a bias toward an individual or group based on such characteristics as race, ethnicity, gender, religion, age, sexual orientation, mental and physical conditions, class, and lifestyle (Barker, 2003). Both concepts involve actions whereby an individual or group exerts power over a less-powerful group, often through force, violence, or restriction of resources (Wambach & Van Soest, 1997).

In spite of the fact that many people come to this country to escape oppression and discrimination in their homelands, the history of both the country and the social work profession has been fraught with devastating and long-standing examples of both oppression and discrimination. We can see this in the ways in which persons of color, women, homosexual, transsexual, or transgendered persons, persons living with a disability, and many immigrant, refugee, and religious groups historically have been mistreated. If such treatment goes unchallenged, both the oppressed and the oppressors can rationalize oppression and discrimination, which in turn perpetuates these behaviors. For example, such rationalizations often include beliefs by both the oppressed and the oppressors that those in power are superior to or protective of those being oppressed or have control of needed resources (Wambach & Van Soest, 1997).

To help understand how oppression is perpetuated, look at Exhibit 4.3. This framework illustrates how oppression is perpetuated because we are exposed and socialized to misinformation in our youth, which is reinforced by the people and entities within our individual environments. Continued socialization then becomes internalized as the person being oppressed begins to believe the stereotypes that the dominant culture has about the group, resulting in the inability to distinguish truth from misinformation. Feelings generated by this socialization process can include anger, guilt, confusion, and alienation. Each phase of the cycle of oppression can elicit a variety of reactions from the individual or group. Four responses are depicted in Exhibit 4.3:

- *Emotions:* Emotional reactions can range from anger to sadness.

- *Internalization:* Attitudes and behaviors can manifest at either the conscious or the unconscious levels.

EXHIBIT 4.3

*Cycle of
Oppression*

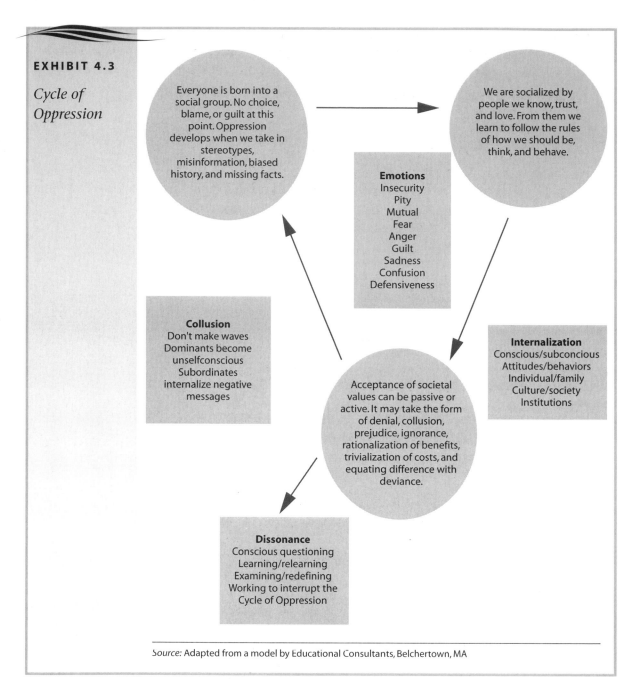

Everyone is born into a social group. No choice, blame, or guilt at this point. Oppression develops when we take in stereotypes, misinformation, biased history, and missing facts.

We are socialized by people we know, trust, and love. From them we learn to follow the rules of how we should be, think, and behave.

Emotions
Insecurity
Pity
Mutual
Fear
Anger
Guilt
Sadness
Confusion
Defensiveness

Collusion
Don't make waves
Dominants become unselfconscious
Subordinates internalize negative messages

Acceptance of societal values can be passive or active. It may take the form of denial, collusion, prejudice, ignorance, rationalization of benefits, trivialization of costs, and equating difference with deviance.

Internalization
Conscious/subconcious
Attitudes/behaviors
Individual/family
Culture/society
Institutions

Dissonance
Conscious questioning
Learning/relearning
Examining/redefining
Working to interrupt the Cycle of Oppression

Source: Adapted from a model by Educational Consultants, Belchertown, MA

- *Dissonance:* As a result of the emotions, attitudes, and behaviors that occur through socialization, individuals often respond by examining and exploring their feelings about the oppression they have observed.

- *Collusion:* Through nonaction, individuals may participate in the perpetuation of the cycle of oppression.

We all possess assumptions about others. These assumptions can lead to prejudicial or discriminatory attitudes and behaviors, but can also provide a basis for cultural insight. A sampling of such assumptions includes

- People are not born with prejudice.
- Prejudice and bias are learned.
- Devaluation and disempowerment are the preconditions for prejudice and oppression.
- Prejudice is learned and can be unlearned.
- Privilege, recognized or not, is a social and economic (or political) benefit.
- All people have prejudices, but not all people can enforce their attitudes through institutions and systems of power.
- Discrimination is a real problem.
- Guilt immobilizes. Our work here is about issues, not blaming.
- People need a safe place to work.

There will always be diversity and difference; unity is possible only through understanding, accepting, and valuing diversity. Throughout the history of the profession, social workers have played an active role in working to eliminate social injustices that lead to oppression and discrimination. For example, they have helped vulnerable groups band together, as in the case of welfare rights organizations, and they have advocated for change at the legislative level. Social workers have lobbied for justice for victims of domestic violence and hate crimes and have campaigned for access to housing and public facilities for older adults and persons with disabilities. Current changes in the demography of our country challenge social workers to maintain an awareness of the social forces that face society so that the profession can respond to the needs of diverse and changing client groups.

Now that you understand the role of social workers in combating oppression and advocating for social justice, let us consider some of the political, economic, and social challenges and opportunities that will confront society and, in particular, the social work profession in the coming years. We will also explore the knowledge and skills that social workers will need to acquire in order to competently practice in an ever-changing society.

Political Environment

Because funding for social services is often a volatile and controversial political issue, the political climate in the United States has always had a significant impact on the social work profession. As you saw in Chapter 2, the present political climate has shifted in a more conservative direction, resulting in decreased political and financial support for many social service programs and resources. Some observers have speculated that the beginning of the 21st century, much like the beginning of the 20th century, will be known as a "period of increasing political tension" with issues of race, culture, diversity, civil rights, immigration, religion, abortion, gun control, and nontraditional families on the forefront of the political scene (Austin, 1997, p. 398). Because the issues with which practitioners work have become "politicized," social workers cannot view their work as apolitical. Therefore, they assume responsibility for understanding and participating in the political process (Haynes, 1996).

Challenges in the Political Environment   Although social workers historically have maintained a "love/hate" relationship with the political system and the politicians who spearhead political change (or lack thereof), social workers can initiate change by working inside the political system as opposed to attempting to change the system from the outside (Reisch, 2000). As Reisch pointed out in a 1997 article:

> We have long operated under the illusion that compassion alone will produce change. Although compassion motivates some people to act and think differently, it is insufficient to transform the deep-rooted institutional indifference of our society. (p. 90)

The continuation of many social service programs, however, will likely require social workers to integrate "political action into a broader pro-social welfare strategy" (Reisch, 1997, p. 81). In other words, in order to continue to work with individuals, families, groups, organizations, and communities, social workers are active at the political level to ensure that adequate funding and resources continue to be available for those services.

The National Association of Social Workers has long been committed to helping social workers be involved in political activity. Through PACE (Political Action for Candidate Election), national, state, and local candidates from any party whose political platforms are consistent with the NASW agenda are endorsed and financially supported.

The conservative political times of this decade have created a transfer of policy making from the national to state level, thus creating widespread inequities in the way that individual states administer social policies and programs (Schneider, 2002). Moreover, in an effort to cut costs and transfer power to the states, the role of the federal government has shifted from one of a service provider to that of a monitor of services (Reisch & Jarman-Rohde, 2000). Given the increasing diversity of our population, such a shift means that social workers must become the advocates for social service programs that are socially just and equitably delivered.

Opportunities in the Political Environment   Strategies that social workers employ to affect political change include both an educational and participant focus. From an educational perspective, social workers raise the awareness of client systems, community residents, organizational staff, and policy makers regarding the inadequacies of the political and social service systems (Reisch, 1997). From a participant perspective, social workers can engage in the electoral advocacy and lobbying process by (1) becoming candidates for political office, (2) encouraging candidates to support issues that are important to the client systems served by social workers, (3) supporting candidates who may be excluded from political office due to the exorbitant costs of contemporary political campaigns, and (4) working to promote governmental monitoring of the social service delivery system (Reisch, 2000).

With much of the decision making for social services now occurring at the state level, the closer proximity to legislators allows social workers and client systems to provide input regarding contradictory policies and inefficiencies in service delivery (Jacobson, 2001). Social workers can embrace opportunities to influence political decision making through a variety of strategies. Strengthening the role of social work in the public sector can help social workers better understand the needs of client systems. Such understanding can contribute to the ability of social workers to advocate for policy changes that address the inequities of the service delivery system.

In a related area, determining the role for social work in managed health care, mental health care, and the political arena can promote equitable and effective treatment for all persons (Gibelman & Schervish, 1997). Gaining a better understanding of the impact of global influences on social work practice can enable social workers to better serve the increasingly diverse client systems.

Economic Environment

Inextricably linked to the political climate, the economy has a powerful influence on the social work profession. Social workers need to understand the U.S.

economy as it relates to daily work with client systems. For example, assisting persons with securing a job depends on overall employment opportunities in a community.

As with the political roller coaster of modern times, the economic status of life in the United States has its ups and downs. The effect of increased social and economic inequities (the rich becoming richer and the poor becoming poorer) creates increasing poverty rates for persons of color, women, and older adults. Due to economic downturns, many employers are laying off workers, consolidating jobs, using temporary workers who do not receive costly employee benefits, and moving companies out of the country to less-expensive work environments. Such employment instability has resulted in increased unemployment and underemployment (Reisch & Jarman-Rohde, 2000). For social workers, these trends mean more persons with greater economic needs.

Challenges in the Economic Environment   The implications of economic turbulence for social work practice can be pervasive and challenging because they seriously affect both the lives of client systems and the social worker's ability to provide services. For example, the economic impact of the billions spent on the war in Iraq and the rebuilding effort can affect areas ranging from social service funding to the availability of employment for returning service personnel. An unstable economy can generate greater financial, social, and emotional needs for client systems. Women and persons of color may present with greater needs, as these two groups often have the least stable employment histories and are the first to be laid off in times of economic hardship.

Social service workers whose agencies are experiencing downsizing as a result of decreased funding and private contributions can be faced with increased workloads. Larger caseloads can mean that the social worker has less time to devote to client systems. An increased emphasis on cost-effectiveness in social service delivery can result in fewer resources being allocated to client systems. Governmental downsizing often triggers decreased funding for social programs, a particularly devastating outcome for children, who are often pitted against older adults in terms of resource allocation (Reisch & Jarman-Rohde, 2000).

Opportunities in the Economic Environment   A first step in understanding and participating in the economic process is to develop a working knowledge of economics. Understanding economic trends and implications can improve the social worker's ability to serve and advocate for social service resources. Armed with knowledge of social work and economics, social workers can influence the economic system by advocating for increasing the number of jobs and for employers to pay a living wage to promote self-sufficiency that can, in turn, decrease the need for a number of social services (such as financial assistance, housing, and health care). **Living wage** is defined as the amount needed to ensure that the standard of living for a person/family does not fall below the poverty line. Community-based advocates across the country have equated that amount to be an hourly wage ranging from $6.25 to $12.00 an hour, with many advocating for $8.20 an hour. Living wage advocacy groups are also campaigning for the inclusion of benefits such as health care and vacation leave (Living Wage Resource Center, 2003).

Public welfare policies that embrace a true multicultural vision as opposed to those that work to separate and isolate ethnic groups, and the development of more equitable family and labor policies and job opportunities, will begin to address the underlying economic injustices (Reisch & Gorin, 2001). Educating others regarding the relationships among economic instability, decreased resources, and social stressors (such as chemical dependency and addiction, domestic violence, child/older-adult abuse and neglect, and mental illness) is another strategy for positively impacting the lives of the client systems served by social workers.

Social Environment

Although deeply embedded within the political and economic controversies that exist, several social issues emerge in their own right as themes for the future of social work practice. We look at some of them in this section, including inequities in health care access, the aging of the U.S. population, and the need for increased knowledge of multicultural issues.

Challenges in the Social Environment   As previously highlighted, the U.S. population is expected to experience considerable growth within the populations of persons of color and older adults over the next several decades. This has significance for the future of social work practice in the area of health care. Projections suggest that health care needs, particularly for persons of color and older adults, will increase, but the available resources will decrease. The number of older adults living in long-term residential care facilities will increase, requiring considerable increases in both financial support and staff trained in gerontological care areas.

In the workplace, downsizing and increasing use of temporary workers can lead to decreased social relationships, which in turn can result in increased isolation, morale problems, and reduced productivity. Increases in single-parent (mostly female and many persons of color) households will result in greater financial and social service needs. Related to increases in single-parent households, decreases in average household incomes will lead to more households, particularly those with children, being considered "poor." As the number of families living in poverty increases, so will the need for social services (Reisch & Jarman-Rohde, 2000).

The Social Work Library

Explore the issue of social reform versus individual treatment as debated by Haynes & Specht.

Opportunities in the Social Environment   Social workers have the knowledge, skills, values, and the vantage point for creating changes that occur as a result of social influences. Opportunities for change within both the profession itself and the social service system include

- Diversifying the makeup of the profession to include more persons of color and males (Gibelman & Schervish, 1997). The profession is largely white and female and does not and will not accurately reflect the overall populations served.

- Working toward expanded socioeconomic opportunities, particularly for children who grow up in poverty, persons of color, and immigrants, all of whom utilize social services more than other groups (Murdock & Michael, 1996).

The Social Work Library

Read Polack's article for a broader perspective on globalization.

- Becoming more globally sophisticated in order to intervene successfully with the increasing numbers of client systems who live in or have emigrated from other countries. Changes may include self-assessment and expansion of global awareness as well as developing knowledge and skills related to language, values, culture, and policy (Ramanathan & Link, 1999).

- Creating more ethnically sensitive social and health care programs that focus on localized community building. Such efforts can help to develop services for the diverse and changing client populations. Such enhancements can help reduce the lack of coordination and communication that currently exists among agencies in the social service delivery system. Client systems must often travel to multiple agencies in varying locations to complete applications for services.

- Developing programs and services that emphasize a multicultural perspective by ensuring that a consistent program ideology, culture, and practice are embraced by the agency (Gutiérrez & Nagda, 1996).

Although the future of the social service delivery system seems fraught with challenges, and social workers might have diminished resources with which to respond to these challenges, the profession can look to its strengths and to the practice of seeking change from an individual level to the larger society. Many aspects of the social service system may not work as efficiently or effectively as they could or should; however, the social work profession will work to build and strengthen the system for those who count—their clients and their communities. Social workers will be participants in shaping the future, but first, they must recognize that change is needed within both society and the social work profession (Raffoul, 1996). From that perspective, the profession can assess, intervene, and evaluate the change efforts—just as you will learn in generalist social work practice.

Emily's and her co-workers' concern about communicating effectively with the increasing number of women appearing in emergency rooms who did not speak English led them to face one of the challenges of the changing profile of U.S. society. They saw this situation as an opportunity to assess the need for interpreters, determine the availability of interpreting resources, and develop a network of interpreters who could supportively and accurately translate for this client population during times of crisis.

The staff conducted interviews with agencies that typically provided services to victims of domestic violence—public welfare, health care organizations, schools, mental health agencies, and housing programs—to determine their needs and resources for translation services. Following this assessment, Emily's agency contacted other agencies and organizations that had access to the ethnic communities that spoke the languages of the abused women. As a result, the staff were able to create a database of volunteer interpreters who spoke a variety of languages, and they sent the list to all the organizations that provided services to victims of domestic violence.

CONCLUSION

Social work is a profession that functions within the context of the larger society; therefore, social work practitioners must have a comprehensive set of knowledge and skills that enables them to understand the social environment in which the client systems live. In addition, social workers need to maintain current knowledge of the shifts in the general population and, in particular, the population being served by their agency. The projections related to shifts in the U.S. demographic profile included in this chapter give you insights into the knowledge and skills that you will need in order to practice social work in the coming decades. You have seen how understanding diverse racial and ethnic groups and their languages and cultures, the needs of older adults and their families and caregivers, and the impact of religious and spiritual beliefs on behavior will be critical in the coming years. These are just a sampling of those competencies needed for effective social work practice.

Social workers must also be vigilant in their efforts to maintain up-to-date knowledge of the political, economic, and social issues that impact their work and their clients' lives. Regardless of the path that you pursue in your social work career, being an advocate for social and economic justice is going to be a part of virtually every social worker's professional life.

MAIN POINTS

- The demographic profile of the United States is becoming more diverse. This country is now a multicultural, multiethnic, aging, and socially diverse society whose members have differing beliefs and value systems.

- The largest growth in U.S. history occurred between 1990 and 2000, with the largest increases being among the Hispanic/Latino and Asian populations.

- By 2030, nearly one-fourth of the U.S. population will be 65 years or older, with the fastest growing segment of the older-adult population being in the 85 and older group. Women make up the majority in this age group, and social workers will need to be aware of gender-related issues.

- Religious diversity is increasing and in some cases means increased religious discrimination.

- Demographic shifts require social workers to be aware of the trends and the needs of the changing society. To be effective social workers, professionals need knowledge and skills to work with diverse client systems.

- Both challenges and opportunities exist for the social work profession, specifically within the context of the political, economic, and social changes.

- Social workers remain advocates of social justice while working with individuals and groups that continue to experience discrimination and oppression.

EXERCISES: PRACTICING SOCIAL WORK

Beyond the Family

Using the Sanchez family interactive case study, respond to the following:

1. What are the political, economic, and social issues that are present in this case?

2. Identify the information from the case that helped you to determine the political, economic, and social issues.

Implications of Policy

Using the Sanchez family interactive case study, select one of the policy areas identified and examine the evolution of that issue. Identify the relevant societal, economic, political, or religious implications of the policy.

Layoffs Pending

In reviewing the information regarding Hector Sanchez, you learned that Hector may be laid off from his job at the construction company. Reflect on the implications for Hector and his family if he were to be laid off. What benefits will he/they be eligible to receive? What strengths does Hector possess that will enable him to obtain employment? What barriers exist that may present challenges for Hector in obtaining employment?

EXERCISES: THE SOCIAL WORK LIBRARY

The One Hundred-Year Debate

After reading "The One Hundred-Year Debate: Social Reform Versus Individual Treatment" (Haynes, 1998), respond to the following:

1. Synthesize the position held by each of the debaters, Haynes and Specht.

2. Based on your current perceptions of the social work profession, discuss your reactions to each of the state positions.

The Globalization of Social Justice

After reading "Social Justice and the Global Economy: New Challenges for Social Work in the 21st Century" (Polack, 2004), respond to the following:

1. Define social justice in the context of globalization.

2. Discuss the role that social workers can and should take in advocating for social justice within our world.

OTHER EXERCISES

Is There Protection for All?

In an effort to gain insight into the societal and legal protection for gay, lesbian, bisexual, and transgendered individuals, search the internet to identify a city or municipality in your state that includes sexual orientation in their city or municipal codes. Write a reflection on the number of communities that have included protection for sexual orientation. Are you surprised by your findings?

Social Work Issues in the Press

From a recent Sunday issue of your local newspaper, identify the key political, economic, and social issues. Reflect on your thoughts regarding whether these issues are consistent with social work concerns.

What "Class" Am I?

Describe the social class with which you identify and respond to the following:

1. Do you believe your class influences your attitudes toward others in society?

2. Do you believe your class influences your behaviors and life choices?

3. If so, how? If not, explain.

CHAPTER 5

Diversity in Social Work Practice

As a result of increased globalization, enhanced communication, and greater access to transportation, the world in which social workers function has expanded. The population of the United States has become more diverse in the areas of race, ethnicity, culture, age, and sexual orientation. Diversity is a concept that is woven throughout every facet of social work practice. Since practitioners work with the entire spectrum of society, they must be keenly aware of the social and cultural environments in which they work, and they must possess knowledge and skills to be effective in working with all people, whether they are similar to or different from themselves. Through the accreditation standards for social work education programs, the Council on Social Work Education (2001a) requires that students learn about diversity and use knowledge and skills that demonstrate their understanding of and appreciation for the diversity of those persons and groups they serve.

Working effectively with diverse populations is a lifelong learning and growing process, as social workers encounter diversity of all kinds throughout their careers. Competent practice requires social workers to continually learn about other cultures and aspects of a diverse society. The first step in becoming an effective social worker is to embrace **cultural competence** as a vital social work skill. Culturally competent social workers understand the need to address diversity and examine individual awareness and experiences. Achieving command of the language of diversity helps a social worker become culturally competent. Such workers are equipped to explore the meaning of their own life experiences and the impact of their personal beliefs on their ability to be effective practitioners. Understanding your own identity and experiences helps to understand the identities and experiences of others.

In this chapter, we explore the reasons that diversity is a key facet of the profession of social work, the theoretical concepts of oppression, and the roles that language plays, both negative and positive. We also review the areas of diversity that have presented challenges for social workers and the practice skills necessary for working effectively with diverse client systems.

DIVERSITY AS A COMPONENT OF THE EDUCATIONAL PROCESS

One of Emily's protective service cases provided her with a new perspective on the meaning of culture and family. Emily was assigned to investigate the alleged neglect of Shanté, a six-year-old African American child who lived with her mother, Jerilyn. Shanté had missed a number of days of school and often came to school unkempt and hungry. During her investigation, Emily learned that Jerilyn had sustained a head injury during a car accident several years earlier and was now living with a physical disability. Until recently, the two had lived with Jerilyn's mother, who had been the primary caregiver for both Jerilyn and Shanté, but the mother had recently died following a stroke. Recognizing that she was unable to care for Shanté, Jerilyn agreed to award custody to her sister, Roberta. Roberta lives in the house next door to them.

The case went to court to finalize the custody arrangement, and during Roberta's testimony, the fact emerged that she was not Jerilyn's biological sister. The two women had been lifelong friends and belonged to the same church, one whose members referred to one another with the honorifics of "sister" and "brother." Emily had assumed that sister *meant a familial connection because her cultural experiences had not included in-depth knowledge of the African American culture or the religion practiced by the two women. From this experience, Emily learned some valuable lessons related to making assumptions, particularly when working with persons whose cultures are different from her own. Ultimately Roberta was awarded custody of Shanté, who was well cared for and saw her mother on a daily basis.*

U.S. society is multicultural, and all citizens need an understanding of the cultures of others. In considering cultures, social workers learn about the history, beliefs, family structure, religion, dress, food, and lifestyles of a group. Although the specific issues related to diversity may be different today than they were during earlier periods of social work, the profession continues to advocate vigilance in regard to such issues of social justice as discrimination, oppression, and inequalities. Emily's experience demonstrates that attention to diversity and culture is as important as ever.

The National Association of Social Workers and the Council on Social Work Education, through their publications, mandate that social workers acquire the

BOX 5.1

Elements of Culturally Competent Social Work Practice

Ethics and values: Within the context of the client system's culture, the profession's values mandate that social workers respect the individual and her or his right to self-determination, and confront any ethical dilemmas that result from conflicts.

Self-awareness: Culturally competent social workers are responsible for being aware of their own cultural identities as well as "knowing and acknowledging how fears, ignorance, and the 'isms' have influenced their attitudes, beliefs, and feelings."

Cross-cultural knowledge: Baseline and ongoing knowledge of cultures other than one's own is an expected component of culturally competent practice.

Cross-cultural skills: Because culturally effective social workers intervene with a wide range of people who are different from them, they must remain open to learning new knowledge and skills.

Service delivery: Interacting with co-workers, agencies, and the community to maintain awareness of cultural diversity and to ensure the provision of culturally competent services is critical to effective practice.

Empowerment and advocacy: Within the context of the client system's culture, social workers advocate for and with client systems toward consciousness raising, development of personal power, and social change.

Diverse workforce: Social workers advocate for maintaining the diversity of the social service delivery system.

Professional education: Social workers advocate for cultural-focused education and training for the social work profession.

Language diversity: Social workers are obligated to ensure that services are provided in the language of the client systems through multilingual employees or interpreters.

Cross-cultural leadership: The profession is committed to sharing the profession's values and ethics training knowledge with others.

Source: NASW, 2001

knowledge and skills necessary for culturally competent practice. The NASW *Code of Ethics* (1999) calls for social workers to respect the inherent dignity and worth of a person, to be sensitive to cultural and ethnic diversity, and to work toward ending discrimination, oppression, poverty, and social injustice. It further charges social workers with the obligation to practice within and develop their areas of competence and directs social workers to understand human behavior within the context of culture and to use a strengths-based perspective when viewing all cultures. Finally, it binds all social workers to practice competently and without discrimination.

As an extension of the *Code of Ethics*, the NASW membership endorses the Standards for Cultural Competence in Social Work Practice, a set of 10 standards for culturally competent practice, shown in Box 5.1.

To practice social work with cultural competence, you need an extensive knowledge of persons different from yourself, an awareness and understanding of yourself, and skills that are appropriate for application with persons and groups different from yourself. In essence, cultural competence is the ability to differentiate between that which is unusual, cultural, and idiosyncratic and to adapt practice to the unique needs of all client systems. It is important to note that culturally competent knowledge, skills, and values extend beyond racial differences. Being culturally competent "can mean the difference between a person making it or falling through the cracks" (NASW, 2004b).

SELF-AWARENESS: AN EXPLORATION

Think of a time when you felt "different." What emotions does that memory evoke? Why did you feel different—was it race, gender, religion, sexual orientation, or maybe your dress or speech? What was the outcome of that situation? Getting in touch with the experience and feelings of being different can help you develop empathy for others and their experiences of difference. Raising your self-awareness about issues of diversity, oppression, discrimination, and social justice can be exhilarating and liberating as you learn more about your own culture. At the same time, however, delving into your own culture, your place in society, and the impact of your behavior on others can be a painful process, as you may discover biases about which you were unaware.

To understand the meaning of social justice, it is important to identify the ways in which you knowingly or unknowingly speak or act in ways that can result in the discrimination of other persons. You may come to terms with the fact that you have biases (we all do) or that you or others have engaged in or supported behaviors that have been hurtful to others. Recognizing these facts will likely be painful and difficult, but it is an important step toward achieving cultural awareness and sensitivity.

Another useful strategy to heighten your self-awareness is to examine your own diversity and its impact on your life. To identify issues related to your own culture and experiences, consider the questions posed in Exhibit 5.1. Compare your culture to other cultures by considering the similarities and differences in the ways in which you celebrate special occasions, interact with others, and use language to describe your group and other groups, for example.

Having strategies for broadening your awareness of other cultures is also useful in achieving cultural competence. You can use these strategies to acquire knowledge about the practices of other cultures, compare and contrast these practices with those of your own culture(s), and develop an understanding of the culturally competent skills that are needed to be an effective social worker

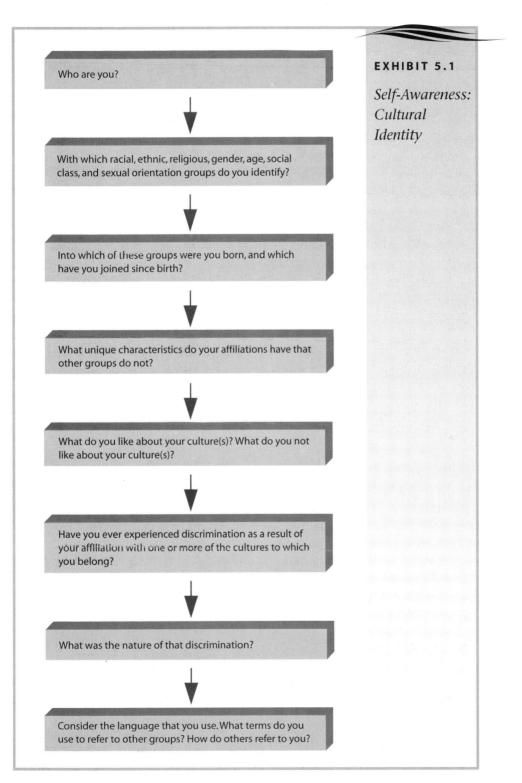

EXHIBIT 5.1

Self-Awareness: Cultural Identity

Who are you?

With which racial, ethnic, religious, gender, age, social class, and sexual orientation groups do you identify?

Into which of these groups were you born, and which have you joined since birth?

What unique characteristics do your affiliations have that other groups do not?

What do you like about your culture(s)? What do you not like about your culture(s)?

Have you ever experienced discrimination as a result of your affiliation with one or more of the cultures to which you belong?

What was the nature of that discrimination?

Consider the language that you use. What terms do you use to refer to other groups? How do others refer to you?

with specific groups. Some suggestions for exposing yourself to new experiences are listed here. Each of these experiences will be most educational and meaningful if you are with other people with whom you can compare observations and feelings.

- Seek out interactions with persons or groups who are different from you. For instance, engage someone you see on a regular basis but have never talked with.

- Attend international festivals, museums, or arts events, and ask questions about the culture.

- Read a magazine or newspaper targeted to a specific group with whom you are not familiar.

- Attend a service in a religious institution that is new to you. This experience will be even more meaningful if you attend the service with a member of that religious group.

- Read a book that portrays a culture with which you are not familiar.

- Watch a television show or movie in a language other than your first language or one that portrays a culture with which you are not familiar.

- Visit a restaurant or eat food that is new to you (or better yet, organize a potluck gathering in which people bring food of their culture).

- Identify a controversial issue that is currently plaguing society or your community and identify your thoughts and feelings about the issues. Talk with others, seek out information from credible sources on the issues, and reflect on strategies for resolving the dilemma on the individual, community, or societal level.

- Observe the conversations of others: Do they use discriminatory language, make inappropriate jokes, or engage in offensive behaviors? If so, what is your response (or lack of response)? Are you silent and, if so, why?

- Volunteer with an age or a cultural group with whom you have little experience. Senior centers, nursing homes, child day care centers, and programs for the developmentally disabled are all good choices.

Moving out of your "comfort zone" and having new experiences is a positive step toward understanding more about yourself and your cultural origins. It also serves to expand your comfort zone so that you can be effective with others who are different from you.

THEORY THAT HELPS US UNDERSTAND DIVERSITY

In order to practice competently with diverse populations, social workers understand issues related to diversity from multiple perspectives. Having explored these issues from the historical and demographical perspectives in earlier chapters, we will now consider working with diverse populations from a theoretical perspective. We will focus on two theoretical frameworks that can help social workers understand, assess, and intervene with clients from different cultures: the ecological perspective and the strengths perspective. By using an appropriate theoretical approach, social workers are already sensitized to the need to include cultural information. Culturally competent knowledge and skills are essential for the application of theoretical frameworks to social work practice.

The ecological and strengths perspectives are strategies that can guide social workers in conducting an assessment, intervention, and evaluation with all client systems, but they are particularly helpful in working with client systems whose cultural experiences are different from their own. When working with persons with diverse backgrounds, social workers should note differing home environments and family cultures so that identifying culturally related strengths becomes key to the assessment process. As you come to appreciate how theory can help in understanding diversity, you can focus on the language and challenges of multicultural social work practice.

Ecological Perspective

A theoretical approach to social work practice that views the client system within the context of the environment in which the client lives is known as the **ecological perspective** (Germain & Gitterman, 1980). The concept of "environment" includes family, work, religion, culture, and life events (for example, developmental issues and life milestones and transitions). This perspective directs the social worker to consider each aspect of the client system's life when establishing rapport, conducting an assessment, and developing an intervention plan with the client system. Moreover, it emphasizes the fact that clients' beliefs, emotions, behaviors, and interactions are influenced by their past and present life experiences. Within each client system encounter, the social worker must be aware of the influence of such cultural factors as race, ethnicity, place of origin, age, gender, social class, religion, and sexual orientation.

Another fundamental component of the ecological perspective is recognition of the impact of oppression on the client system's life experiences. As an example, consider a scenario in which you are a social worker working with a client who is Native American and you are not Native American yourself. Native Americans have long been oppressed by society in such areas as resource allocation, education, and employment. They have been victims of exploitation, abuse, segregation, open hostilities, and violence. In working with the client, you would be remiss if you did not consider the historical, political, and societal issues related to Native Americans, in general, and to individual tribes, in particular. Client systems that have experienced institutionalized oppression are likely to feel powerlessness and a lack of trust, particularly regarding members of the oppressing group.

In building rapport, the effective social worker will gain knowledge of the client system's history of oppression and experiences of discrimination, while not promoting either. At the same time, the social worker is responsible for knowing about the client system's values, beliefs, and cultural practices. Such sensitivity to issues of diversity takes into consideration multiple aspects of the client system's environment and conveys to the client the worker's respect for the client's cultural heritage. For example, the social worker assigned to work with a Native American family can be more effective if armed with knowledge about that client system's tribal affiliation, history, traditions, and current issues.

Strengths Perspective

A concept embedded within the ecological perspective is the **strengths perspective.** Viewing the client's cultural experiences and beliefs as strengths on which to build an intervention is an extension of the ecological model of social work practice. Too often in the past, practitioners have seen culture, ethnicity, religion, and sexual orientation as irrelevant, different (a deficit), or an area for change, rather than as an asset or resource in problem solving. Incorporating the client's cultural characteristics into the social work strategy as a strength is consistent with the social work value of respecting each individual's uniqueness and worth. Applying the knowledge and skills of the strengths-based perspective along with those of culturally competent practice, social workers can promote a multicultural environment.

The strengths-based perspective is particularly important for practicing social work with cultural competence at all levels (Saleebey, 1992). Using a strengths perspective, the social work relationship is built around the experience and life of the client system, thus demonstrating respect for culture, lifestyle, and client right to self-determination. Framing cultural diversity issues as part of the client system environment provides the social worker with additional resources for understanding the stressors being experienced by the client system, aids in building rapport and trust, and contributes to culturally appropriate intervention plans.

Consider a scenario in which you are a social worker working with an older Jewish woman who immigrated to this country from Europe following World War II. She is a widow and a retired teacher who lives alone and has no immediate family nearby. Since the death of her husband, she has become more withdrawn, and you are concerned that she is depressed. While conducting an assessment, you learn that she is a survivor of the Holocaust and the concentration camps. You help her to see her life experiences as a resource for educating others about the atrocities committed during the Holocaust, and you arrange for her to join a speaker's bureau for the local Jewish Community Center. She travels to schools to share her story with children, most of whom have never met a Holocaust survivor. Her depression dissipates; she is now feeling useful because she is using her skills as a teacher and her life experiences as a survivor.

THE LANGUAGE OF DIVERSITY

Social workers must not only become familiar with the language of diversity if they wish to be effective practitioners and advocates for marginalized and oppressed populations, but also understand, use, and advocate for language that is respectful and nondiscriminatory. Language is a powerful tool and can be used to encourage as well as demean individuals or groups. Social workers are mindful not to use negative language that can perpetuate stereotypes and to use and promote the use of **person first language.** Person first language is referring first to the person and then to the situation (for example, "person with a disability" instead of "disabled person").

Throughout history, society has developed, used, and misused a variety of terms to describe groups that are different from one another. Because of differences of opinion, changing perceptions, and the dynamics of language, the meanings of terms—particularly terms related to race and ethnicity—have become inconsistent. Box 5.2 presents many of the terms and their meanings, which are necessary to understand in order to practice social work ethically and responsibly. These are not the only terms you may find in the social work literature, but are an inclusive and appropriate sampling.

THE "ISMS"

The following statement by Martin Luther King Jr. speaks to pervasiveness of discrimination: "Injustice anywhere is a threat to justice everywhere" (King, 1963). Throughout history, social workers have been on the forefront of challenging the ever-present **isms**—doctrines, causes, or theories, which within the social work profession, typically imply negative attitudes or beliefs regarding a specific population of people, although they can connote positive belief systems as well.

Once a person has been identified as a member of a group that is targeted as a vulnerable group, society tends to view that person only by her or his membership in that group. For example, a person with a physical disability is

BOX 5.2

Terminology for Culturally Competent Social Work Practice

Accommodation/acculturation/assimilation: Used interchangeably, these terms are, in fact, distinct concepts regarding a majority group's treatment toward a minority group within a society. **Accommodation** refers to the efforts of one group to make changes to enable another group to live within society. For example, offering printed materials in multiple languages to enable persons whose first language is not English is a form of accommodation. **Acculturation** is the socialization of one culture into the ways (that is, values, beliefs, and behaviors) of another culture. In contrast, **assimilation** is adoption of one group's cultural practices (for example, values, norms, and behaviors) by another group. For example, refugees become "Westernized" when they immigrate to the United States. Assimilation can be viewed as a form of oppression when the traditions of the assimilated group are ignored or its members are forced to give up those traditions and values.

Despite the fact that the United States has always been a diverse society, considerable inconsistency exists in the ways in which the majority culture has interacted with persons of color. At various points in history, the majority group has attempted to achieve acculturation, assimilation, and accommodation, while only recently recognizing that each racial, ethnic, and religious group can retain its own culture without being "changed." Although members of the majority culture often recognize that minority groups could retain their cultures, some question whether such ties to their origins would hamper their ability to become truly American.

Bias/prejudice: Positive or negative prejudgments or attitudes toward a person, group, or idea. Not typically based on fact or evidence, **bias**, or **prejudice,** grows out of misperceptions.

Color: Despite the political, social, and emotional connotations that this word conveys, remember that *color* literally refers only to the pigmentation of a person's skin.

Culture: One of the terms that has been defined differently at different times and in different sources, **culture** can be considered as the way a group of people perceive the world around them and structure their interactions within and outside their unique group (Schlesinger & Devore, 1995). Specifically, a culture is defined by the many characteristics and components possessed by a group, such as values, beliefs, religious and political tenets, and behaviors. Culture is an *overall* social construct encompassing such issues as race, ethnicity, and group membership that individuals and groups use in interacting, communicating, and interpreting information (Okun, Fried, & Okun, 1999).

Ethnicity: Determined by the cultural group with which an individual identifies, **ethnicity** can be characterized by national origin, race, language, and/or religious beliefs and practices. Depending on the culture, country, region, and religion into which a person is born, she or he can self-identify with multiple ethnicities.

Ethnocentrism: Group members who practice **ethnocentrism** believe that their culture is the norm and that other cultures with different practices or beliefs are therefore outside the norm (Okun et al., 1999). Ethnocentric attitudes and behaviors generally result when members of a group perceive themselves as superior to other groups.

Integration: Just as segregation has been institutionalized (formalized) within our society, so too has **integration**, in which diverse groups such as those in public schools, the military, and the workplace have been brought together as equals.

Marginalization: The subordination of individuals or groups who possess less power, **marginalization** occurs as a result of the perpetuation of stereotypes and oppression.

Multicultural competence: The practice of multicultural competence, or **multiculturalism,** is the practice of understanding, recognizing, and respecting the cultural values, beliefs, and behaviors of others.

Pluralism: Aimed at increasing inclusiveness, **pluralism** values all groups and provides a basis for understanding the way members of a society interact with one another and the environments in which they live (Logan, 2003).

Race: The term **race** refers to human characteristics that can be determined by physical traits (such as skin color or hair texture); geography (for example, place of origin); or culture. The U.S. Census Bureau (2004) separates race from Hispanic/Latino origin and uses five categories:

- White—origins in Europe, the Middle East, or North Africa.
- Black or African American—origins in any of the black racial groups of Africa.
- American Indian or Alaska Native—origins in any of the original peoples of North, Central, or South America.
- Asian—origins in any of the original peoples of the Far East, Southeast Asia, or the Indian subcontinent.
- Native Hawaiian or Other Pacific Islander—origins in any of the original peoples of Hawaii, Guam, Samoa, or other Pacific Islands.

Besides having a physical meaning, race has assumed a meaning that carries intensely emotional and personal implications.

Segregation: Racial and religious **segregation**—the separation of one group from other groups—are two forms of institutionalized segregation that our society has deemed unlawful. In contrast, informal segregation, which can be just as devastating, cannot be legislated.

Social class: An individual or group may be categorized in a **social class** depending on characteristics such as income, social status, education, and religious affiliation.

Stereotyping: Similar to bias and prejudice, **stereotyping** occurs when someone assumes a person possesses the same characteristics as all other individuals within his or her group.

BOX 5.2
continued

OLC **The Social Work Library**

Fellin's work will expand your knowledge of multiculturalism and its importance for social workers.

often viewed only as a person with a disability and not in light of father, mother, teacher, or other possible roles and memberships. As you read the following sections, keep in mind that each group comprises individuals who are also members of other groups. We are more than our race, gender, sexual orientation, age, abilities, or religious affiliations.

The following discussion is not intended to be an all-inclusive list but rather a sampling of those areas that social workers encounter on a routine basis. Awareness and knowledge of these isms are part of becoming a culturally competent social worker. Because the demographic characteristics of the United States are changing, social workers are also responsible for acquiring and maintaining cutting-edge skills in order to serve the changing population and also to advocate for oppressed and marginalized groups.

Racism

Probably the most common ism challenging modern-day society, racism results from the categorization and stereotyping of groups by racial characteristics or ethnic origins. Whether on a personal or societal level, racism is defined as the belief that one group is superior to another group(s) based solely on race. Racism in its most extreme form is typically perpetrated by a majority or dominant culture and serves to segregate, isolate, and disempower a minority or less powerful group of people. In the United States, the Caucasian population has historically held the majority position due to population composition, but as demographic trends indicate, the population ratios are changing.

Racism has permeated essentially every aspect of U.S. society. Racism exists on two levels: institutional racism and individual racism. **Institutional racism** refers to discrimination against persons of color in accessing such resources as employment, education, financial assistance and credit, organizational membership, and home ownership. In contrast, individual racism is abuse or mistreatment propagated by a person or group. For example, the uttering of a racial slur by one person to another is individual racism.

Over the past 50 years, U.S. society has dramatically modified its definitions of and approaches to race-related issues. During the mid-20th century, a "melting pot" approach in which sameness among the races was emphasized aimed at creating a society in which all cultures become blended into a single culture without the distinctions of diversity. Not all segments of society embraced such an approach; for example, a forced segregation approach was the dominant philosophy in most southern U.S. states. Then, during the late 1950s and 1960s, support grew for an approach that embraced a "world of difference" philosophy that focused on racial uniqueness. However, others within the civil rights movement advocated for total racial integration.

The decades of the 1970s and 1980s began to emphasize a multiculturalist perspective that valued individual ethnicities. This perspective met with intense intellectual and political opposition from persons and groups that wanted to maintain racial separateness. For some, this view again shifted during the 1990s to a pluralistic conceptualization in which people exist within a society of groups that are distinctive in ethnic origin, cultural patterns, and relationships.

For most people, racial issues can evoke intense emotional reactions. Most people have been either a victim or perpetrator of racist thoughts or behaviors, and many people have been both at one time or another. As students and instructors, we all bring our life experiences to the social work classroom. As long as we remain open to expanding our cultural awareness and sensitivity, the social work classroom can be an excellent environment in which to learn and grow. Some students, both white students and students of color, report being uncomfortable in a classroom in which racism is discussed because of feelings of discomfort regarding the behaviors of their racial group, anger regarding the treatment of persons of color, or resentment toward students who have not experienced discrimination. However, when students agree to create a safe environment in which issues, and not people, are confronted, they can initiate stimulating and meaningful discussions.

Social workers can confront racism in many ways. The most obvious strategies include advocacy, education, and, sometimes, mediation (for example, serving as an agent to promote effective communication). To be effective in any of these areas, social workers engage in self-awareness, particularly the willingness to recognize areas in which their own knowledge and skills are lacking. Social workers confront racial injustices at any and all levels.

The status of racial justice at the beginning of the 21st century remains controversial and is, as yet, undetermined. Think about your own knowledge and skills and, more importantly, what your role is in promoting justice.

Ageism

When most people hear the term *ageism*, they immediately think of the mistreatment of older adults. In fact, ageism refers to discrimination based on *any* age. The two groups most at risk for age bias and discrimination are children and older adults. Being on the two ends of the age spectrum places these groups in vulnerable positions regarding access to resources. Moreover—and perhaps even worse—the two groups are pitted against each other when resources are allocated. As the sheer number of older persons has risen dramatically, their collective "voices" are increasingly being heard, in part because they have become highly organized and are diligent advocates for their own rights and benefits. Even so, older adults continue to need support from social workers and others who will advocate on their behalf. Children have a difficult time being heard by policy makers and funders and must depend on adults to champion their causes.

Dealing effectively with ageism begins on a personal level. Conduct an inventory of your ageist experiences. Have you ever purchased a greeting card that lamented the fact the person was over the hill? Have you ever been dismissed by someone because you were too young (or too old) to understand something? Have you heard or made stereotypical remarks about the driving abilities of either young or old people? Have you ever referred to a person's age in a derogatory manner—"geezer" or "baby," for instance? As a part of any diversity self-awareness campaign, checking ourselves and our society on ageism issues is our obligation as social workers. In social work specifically, all practitioners are ethically bound to acquire knowledge and skills that will enable them to be effective in working with persons of any age.

Sexism

A part of U.S. history and still pervasive today, sexism has been defined as the belief that men are superior to women as a result of gender. Sexism occurs when women are discriminated against because they are women. Consider just a few of the institutionally enforced examples of sexism that were in place for most of the history of this country: Women could not own property, vote, run for public office, or divorce their husbands, and they were prevented from being trained in many professions. Although our nation has made considerable strides toward improving the status of women, significant gender-based inequities remain. As you read earlier in this book, women's earnings continue to be lower than men's for the same positions. Women are still in the minority in most traditionally male-dominated professions (such as medicine, engineering, and politics), and when women achieve a major presence within a professional discipline, the salaries of both men and women tend to decrease.

Although equal employment and sexual harassment policies have eradicated institutional sexism, other forms of sexism continue to exist but appear to have gone "underground." For example, both genders continue to make sexist remarks, particularly in the areas of domestic and sexual violence, clothing, and behaviors. When women engage in traditionally male activities, they may be criticized, particularly when the women excel in the activity. Women continue to function as the primary caregivers for the family, even when they work full time outside the home.

Social workers have an ethical responsibility to address issues of gender equality for all women. Social workers can work at the prevention level by dispelling stereotypes and myths about women's rights and abilities. Social workers can also empower women by informing them that they do not have to let a sexual assault go unreported or remain in a violent relationship. Social workers can work at the policy level to ensure that policies are crafted to guarantee gender equity. Every social worker can write letters to the media when women are portrayed unfairly, stereotypically, or as inferior to men. You might take a minute to consider other types of activities that you can do to combat sexism.

Classism

Based on social class (for example, economic and social status), classism can occur as a result of occupational status (for example, blue collar or white collar) or income (for example, lower socioeconomic class, lower-middle class, owning/ ruling classes). Although some philosophers have claimed that the United States can and should be a classless society, the reality is that our society has distinct classes that have evolved over time to include categorized values, expectations, beliefs, and lifestyles (Okun et al., 1999). In fact, the distinctions between the richest and the poorest in our society are at an all-time high (Yeskel & Leondar-Wright, 1997). Moreover, based on recent census data, the economic gap between the richest and the poorest is widening (U.S. Census, 2004).

Most often defined as socioeconomic status, social class is used prejudicially as a mechanism for labeling people in formal and informal ways. Classism, thus, is the discrimination that occurs as a result of this compartmentalization by income and wealth. Some people believe that membership in a particular social/economic class is based on the person's willingness to work hard—the philosophy of pulling yourself up by your bootstraps, discussed in earlier chapters. Because of this, people on the low end of the economic continuum are characterized as simply lacking ambition, without consideration for such factors as race, ethnicity, gender, disability, and access to resources and opportunities.

Your experiences with and views on socioeconomic class are yet another issue to consider as you conduct your diversity self-assessment. Consider the following messages that you have received throughout your life regarding social class and income:

- Have you ever thought about the socioeconomic class into which you were born? If not, in which class does your family of origin belong?

- Do you continue to be a member of that class? If you have changed socioeconomic class, how did that occur?

- What does membership in your socioeconomic class, or any other socioeconomic class, mean in terms of your education, resources, opportunities, place of residence, and employment?

- Have you been a victim of classist remarks, or (be honest here) have you made classist remarks?

- Do you perceive a difference between those students whose parents pay for college and those students who must take out loans?

As with all the isms, the social worker's role in combating classism is often one of advocacy and education. Countering the "bootstrap" myth, empowering people to reach their optimal functioning and quality of life, and confronting classist language are just three anticlassism activities in which social workers can engage proactively.

Ableism

A recent addition to the language of diversity, *ableism* is defined as "discrimination and exclusion that oppresses people who have mental, emotional, and physical disabilities" (Rauscher & McClintock, 1997, p. 198). Disabilities can be perceptual, illness related, physical, developmental, psychiatric, psychological, mobility related, or environmental (for example, allergies). Unfortunately, U.S. society again has a long and shameful history of discrimination against persons with disabilities. From the language used to refer to a person with a disability, to the restriction of access to schools and buildings, and to the penchant for "warehousing" people with disabilities in institutions and separate schools, the United States has oppressed this population for centuries.

Only in recent years has ableism been considered in such areas as policy making, funding, and public sensitivity. In particular, two legislative mandates, the Rehabilitation Act of 1973 and the Americans with Disabilities Act of 1990, established institutional support for assuring the civil rights of, and providing supportive accommodations and services for, persons with a wide range of disabilities. Think for a moment of all the disability-related terms you have heard or used throughout your lifetime. Box 5.3 lists some common terms and provides alternative language, known as "words with dignity," that is more likely to preserve the dignity of people with different abilities.

In striving to eradicate ableism, the social work profession has long championed equity, respect, and physical accommodation. Although our society has made strides in many areas—particularly education, accessibility, employment, and benefits—the professional challenge is to continue to draw attention to the abilities and strengths of persons with different abilities. As with other isms, social workers are obligated to be on the cutting edge of services and resources for persons with disabilities. They must also combat both the use of inappropriate language and discrimination in the provision of services. Finally, they should fight to ensure the rights of any person with a disability. The following are principles of practice to keep in mind when working with persons with disabilities:

- All people are capable or potentially capable.
- Persons with disabilities do not need to be "fixed" in order to function in society.
- Disabilities are a social construct, and interventions therefore must target the political realm.
- Persons with disabilities have more common characteristics than differences.
- Disability does not imply dysfunction.
- Persons with disabilities have a right to self-determination. (Mackelprang & Salsgiver, 1999, pp. 241–243)

WORDS TO AVOID	WORDS WITH DIGNITY
Cripple/handicapped/invalid	Person with a disability/disabled
Victim/afflicted	Person who has/person with (disability)
Restricted/confined to a wheelchair/wheelchair bound	Uses a wheelchair
Deaf mute/deaf and dumb/hearing impaired	Deaf/does not voice for themselves/nonvocal
Birth defect	Disabled since birth/born with
Crazy/insane/lunatic/mental patient/wacko	Psychiatric history/psychiatric disability/emotional disorder/mental illness
Fits	Epilepsy/seizures
Slow/retard/lazy/stupid/underachiever/ high functioning/low functioning	Learning disability/mental retardation/developmental delay/ADD/ADHD
Hypochondriac/imagination/it's in your head	Multiple chemical sensitivity/ environmental illness

Source: Paraquad, 2002

BOX 5.3

Substitutes for Ableist Terms

Heterosexism

Heterosexism, the belief that heterosexuality is the only acceptable form of sexual orientation, exists at all levels of our society and is perpetuated formally and informally. Linked to religion, morality, and deviance, a nonheterosexual orientation has been and continues to be considered by many people to be a choice, a defect, or a perversion and therefore "curable." As a result of such homophobia, gays, lesbians, bisexuals, and transgendered persons (persons whose gender identity is counter to traditional definitions of heterosexual or homosexual) have been prohibited from employment in many areas, from legally marrying, adopting children as a couple, receiving partner benefits, serving in the military if they disclose their sexual orientation, and making legal and medical decisions for their partners. These groups have often been the victims of homophobic hate crimes that range from verbal harassment, to physical assaults, or "gay bashing," to murder. As a result of the overwhelming biases that have prevailed in our society, these groups have historically been highly reluctant to disclose their sexual orientation in any but the safest places, often not even "coming out" to their families, co-workers, or some friends.

Recent years have seen significant progress in the area of gay rights as a result of the mobilization of the gay population and their supporters. The recognition of same-sex partners and marriages by some states and employers is one example of the progress made.

More than with most of the other isms, talking about homosexuality makes many people uncomfortable. Talking about sexuality, in general, is awkward for many of us, but a lack of knowledge, fear of offending the person, deep-rooted religious beliefs, or even fears about our own sexuality make talking about homosexuality particularly difficult for some of us. In fact, for some students, their first social work course might also be the first time that they engage in a discussion in which homosexuality is not framed as deviant. Social work classrooms can be a safe place to share thoughts and feelings about working with sexual orientation issues.

To become culturally competent to intervene successfully with gays, lesbians, bisexuals, and transgendered persons, social workers must be mindful of the historical issues that surround the oppression of this population. They should also learn and use appropriate language, be open to understanding differences, and see beyond the person's sexual orientation. Finally, as with all the other areas, social workers can advocate for equality and respect in legislation, policies, service delivery, and practices for these groups.

Religious Discrimination

Religious oppression and discrimination have existed for thousands of years. People have been persecuted for practicing a variety of religions by being physically separated, denied employment, and even tortured and killed. Even in recent times in the history of this country, religious discrimination has taken the form of restrictions on educational and employment opportunities, holding public office, and joining social clubs.

Although religion has always been a part of the lives of the people served by social workers, religion has not always been included in social work education and practice in the mainstream of the profession. In recent years social workers have recognized the important role that religion and spirituality play in their clients' lives. Consequently, they have begun to incorporate these issues into their assessments and intervention plans. Along with knowledge of biological, sociological, cultural, and psychological development across the life span, spirituality is now required content in human behavior and the social environment courses for CSWE-accredited programs.

Despite these developments, the profession is still divided on how these issues should be incorporated into the social worker–client relationship. For instance, should social workers pray with clients, use religion as a part of the intervention strategy, or agree to work with clients based on religious preference? As the profession continues to struggle with these questions, social workers are exploring issues of religion and spirituality on both personal and professional levels. Although social workers cannot possibly be knowledgeable about all of the world's religions, they are professionally bound to consider each client's religious and spiritual life as part of the client's environment and to learn the influence of religion and spirituality on the client system's life.

The Social Work Library

Learn more about spirituality and religious diversity in social work through the writing of Dr. Canda.

THE CULTURALLY COMPETENT SOCIAL WORKER

During the time Emily worked in the domestic violence program, she encountered a particularly challenging cultural dilemma that involved ethnicity, religion, and gender issues. Emily was called to the emergency room to see a woman who was Muslim who had been brought in by the police after being severely beaten by her husband. The woman had moved to the United States from a country in the Mideast five years earlier with her husband and three children. A neighbor called the police when she heard the screams. Despite her severe injuries, the woman, who did not speak English, was extremely reluctant to seek medical help. In fact, she refused to press charges and insisted that she be taken home. Through an interpreter, Emily learned that based on her religious convictions, the woman considered herself to be her husband's property, and the Koran dictates that men have a right to beat their wives if they commit a wrongdoing. In her case, the evening meal was not prepared on time.

Emily's responsibilities in this situation were to conduct an assessment, offer the services of the domestic violence program, explore options for safety, and develop an intervention plan if the woman would agree to it.

Consider for a moment the cultural competency skills that Emily was required to demonstrate in this situation:

- Knowledge of the Muslim religion, traditions, and values, particularly as they relate to women, marriage, and domestic violence.

- Ability to communicate with a reluctant person in crisis through an interpreter.

- Ability to relate to a woman whose values and religious beliefs differed dramatically from Emily's views on women, marriage, and violence.

- Willingness to affirm the woman's right to self-determination when she opted to return to the violent situation.

As Emily's experience depicts, culturally competent practice comprises skills at multiple levels: cognitive (knowledge of diversity history and issues), affective (emotional), and behavioral (language and communication skills) (Schlesinger & Devore, 1995). An effective practitioner possesses a high level of awareness in each area as well as a commitment to the idea that cultural competence is a lifelong learning process that can be both challenging and rewarding.

The following discussion is intended to heighten your sensitivity regarding the basic practice skills in awareness, language, and communication that are critical for cultural competence. The skills offered here are not specific to any particular group, because it is important to recognize the diversity within client populations and refrain from practicing social work with a "cookbook" approach (Dunn, 2002).

Cultural Awareness

Increased self-awareness and knowledge of your own identity are the first steps in cultural awareness. Key skill areas include

- Every social worker–client system relationship is a cross-cultural experience in that everyone has distinct cultures and backgrounds.

- Stay in touch with your own beliefs at all times—your biases and lack of knowledge as well as feelings of comfort.

- Before you encounter a client system or situation, identify the knowledge and skills that you may need. For instance, do you need to arrange for an interpreter, do you need information on religious practices, or do you need to ensure that the meeting location is accessible for the client(s)?

- Know that you will make mistakes, and be open to the possibility that the client system can teach you about diversity and help you learn from your mistakes. When you make a mistake, do not attempt to cover it up. Rather, acknowledge the mistake, and take the opportunity to learn a better way to interact.

- Recognize that characteristics and differences can be a resource in the helping process.

- Recognize that the client system with whom you work may be uncomfortable with your cultural differences.

- Monitor your communication style and the ways in which your verbal and nonverbal behaviors could be interpreted. For example, do you speak too quickly to be clearly understood by a person who is just learning English? Are you uncomfortable when people you do not know well get too physically close to you?

Your level of awareness may be different in different areas, such as sexual orientation, age, or class. Use the Action Continuum, shown in Exhibit 5.2, as a tool for determining your level of awareness. As you review the continuum, ask yourself these questions: (1) Where are you on the continuum? (2) Where would you like to be? (3) What will help you move to the next place on your journey?

Language and Communication Skills for Cultural Competence

As you have observed throughout this chapter, language is a particularly challenging area of culturally competent practice. Language is intricately tied to the culture of any group. It is a powerful mechanism for imparting positive and negative messages, and for this reason it can serve both to perpetuate oppression and discrimination and to demonstrate respect and sensitivity. Therefore, social workers are responsible for using appropriate and culturally sensitive language whenever they refer or speak to any group. Although slang may be acceptable in certain settings, social workers are always mindful of using language that is the most respectful and empowering and that is preferred by the group being addressed. Using culturally appropriate language and communication skills helps to create a safe environment for the client system that will foster trust and build rapport. Society and, in particular, social workers often struggle with being appropriate in the language of diversity. Terms change, they have regional connotations, and they are heard differently depending on the speaker.

Although learning, understanding, and using language correctly are essential components of culturally competent social work practice, effective multicultural practitioners also possess practice skills that enable them to communicate sensitively with diverse groups. When in doubt regarding the most appropriate language, you have several options for obtaining more information. You can ask other professionals who work with the population or persons who are members of the cultural group with whom you are working to serve as your cultural guide. In cases in which you have established a rapport with the client system, you may ask the client system for help in understanding appropriate language. In addition, pay particular attention to the opening of any

EXHIBIT 5.2

Action Continuum for Increasing Cultural Awareness

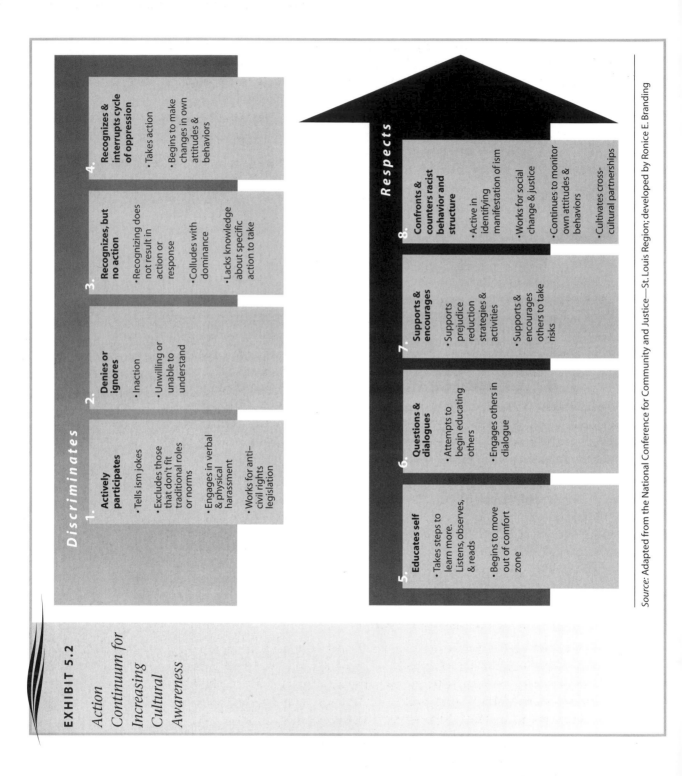

Discriminates

1. Actively participates
- Tells ism jokes
- Excludes those that don't fit traditional roles or norms
- Engages in verbal & physical harassment
- Works for anti–civil rights legislation

2. Denies or ignores
- Inaction
- Unwilling or unable to understand

3. Recognizes, but no action
- Recognizing does not result in action or response
- Colludes with dominance
- Lacks knowledge about specific action to take

4. Recognizes & interrupts cycle of oppression
- Takes action
- Begins to make changes in own attitudes & behaviors

Respects

5. Educates self
- Takes steps to learn more. Listens, observes, & reads
- Begins to move out of comfort zone

6. Questions & dialogues
- Attempts to begin educating others
- Engages others in dialogue

7. Supports & encourages
- Supports prejudice reduction strategies & activities
- Supports & encourages others to take risks

8. Confronts & counters racist behavior and structure
- Active in identifying manifestation of ism
- Works for social change & justice
- Continues to monitor own attitudes & behaviors
- Cultivates cross-cultural partnerships

Source: Adapted from the National Conference for Community and Justice—St. Louis Region; developed by Ronice E. Branding encounter with a client system by introducing yourself by name and title, referring to an adult client using an honorific that is respectful and culturally appropriate (for example, Mr., Mrs., or Ms.), and clarifying the pronunciation of the person's name and desired address. Then inquire about the person's culture, specifically the preferred name of the group in which the person is a member (for example, Cherokee versus Native American).

Here are further suggestions for communicating sensitively:

- Balance the use of professional language and language that is familiar to the client system. Client systems may misunderstand or be offended by professional jargon (particularly medical terminology or acronyms), slang, or colloquialisms.

- Be genuine in your use of language and style of communication, particularly avoiding words or behaviors with which you are not familiar.

- Be aware of the meanings that different cultures attach to certain nonverbal behaviors. These meanings may be assigned or interpreted based on traditions, thus resulting in a misunderstanding (Okun et al., 1999). For example, eye contact is interpreted many different ways: as an invitation to continue speaking, as a sign of sexual interest, aggression, respect, or disrespect. Similarly, silence and facial and physical expressions convey different messages depending on the individual's culture, ranging from discomfort to anger to respect. Finally, space and physical touch can be interpreted as intimacy, aggression, or dominance based on cultural definitions.

- Be sensitive and aware of a person's culture, but do not discuss it unless it is relevant to the situation. For example, a disability or sexual orientation may not be pertinent to the reason for your encounter. Therefore, there is no need to focus the professional relationship on that aspect of the person's life. In referring to persons who have a disability or experience homelessness, use person first language to avoid labeling. Referring accurately to the client system's cultural background may include, for example, Asian American (citizen or born in the United States) or Asian (international person or non-U.S. citizen).

- Check regularly with a person whose culture is different from your own to ensure that she or he has understood what you have said or meant. Ask the person to repeat her or his understanding of the content of the conversation. This strategy will prevent you from assuming that you are being understood simply because the person nods in assent.

- If you are unsure of the meaning of a word, phrase, or behavior used by the client, ask the client in a nonjudgmental, nonpatronizing way to explain the meaning.

CONCLUSION

We have explored a range of issues related to diversity and culturally competent social work practice. Like other aspects of social work practice, striving to be a culturally competent practitioner requires that you continually seek out knowledge, skills, and self-insights. Being an expert in all areas of diversity is impossible, but social workers are obligated to acquire as much information as possible about the populations that are living in their communities and to whom they are providing services. Culturally competent practice means being proactive and assertive in your efforts to understand other cultures. Clients bring a rich and inspirational history of diversity and can serve as teachers for the social worker who views that diversity as a strength.

Let us end this chapter with William M. Chace's 1989 perspective on diversity:

> *Diversity,*
> Generally understood and embraced, is not casual liberal tolerance of anything and everything not yourself. It is not polite accommodation. Instead, diversity is, in action, the sometimes painful awareness that other people, other races, other voices, other habits of mind, have as much integrity of being, as much claim upon the world, as you do. No one has an obligation greater than your own to change, or yield, or to assimilate into the mass. The irreconcilable is as much a part of social life as the congenial. Being strong in life is being strong amid differences while accepting the fact that your own self can be a considerable imposition upon everyone you meet. I urge you to consider your own oddity before you are troubled or offended by that of others. And I urge you, amid all the differences present to the eye and mind to reach out and create the bonds that will sustain the commonwealth that will protect us all. We are meant to be together.

MAIN POINTS

- Culturally competent social work practice is the ability to work respectfully and effectively with all persons. A key element is developing insights into your own beliefs and values regarding culture—your own and that of others—and continually learning about others.

- Social workers must routinely conduct a "reality check" regarding their beliefs and actions related to working with persons different from themselves as well as persons from similar backgrounds as themselves.

- Two theoretical frameworks, the ecological and strengths perspectives, help social workers understand and work with client systems that are different from themselves.

- Language plays a major role in both oppression and building respect for diverse groups. Social workers should understand the various ways certain terminology, such as race, ethnicity, and assimilation, have been used throughout history.

- Understanding the isms faced by many cultures in our society helps social workers to be more sensitive to people of different races, ages, and abilities.

EXERCISES: PRACTICING SOCIAL WORK

Vicki Sanchez

Using the Sanchez family interactive case study, review the information regarding Vicki Sanchez and answer Vicki's Critical Thinking Questions.

Hector Sanchez

Using the Sanchez family interactive case study, review the information regarding Hector Sanchez and answer Hector's Critical Thinking Questions.

Culturally Competent Social Work Practice

Using the Sanchez family interactive case study, imagine that you are a social worker newly assigned to work with Hector and Celia on the adoption of their grandson, Joey. Based on your own cultural heritage, select a description from the general list below:

- You are not of Hispanic or Latino origin and have had little experience with this population.

- You are not of Hispanic or Latino origin, but have had some experience with the Hispanic population and have limited Spanish-speaking skills.

- Your ethnic background is of Latino origin, but you have not lived in or near a Latino community.

- Your ethnic and cultural background is Latino. You speak fluent Spanish and your upbringing is similar to that of the Sanchez children.

   Having identified your personal characteristics as they relate to the Sanchez family, consider the following social work skill issues:

- What are the differences that you may encounter?

- What are the similarities that you may encounter?

- What are your feelings about working with the Sanchez family, including stereotypes, biases, feelings of familiarity, or anxiety?

- Given your knowledge of the Latino culture (or lack of), what information, knowledge, or skills do you need to acquire before meeting with the Sanchez family?

- How might you respond if you make a cultural mistake (speak or behave in such a way that you offend the person(s))?

- What might you ask the Sanchez family to help you in establishing a rapport?

- Who or what resource can be helpful to you in preparing for your meeting with the Sanchez family?

- If you do not speak Spanish, how will you communicate with Celia? If you are bilingual, will you speak in Spanish or English? How will you determine which is appropriate?

Although your responses to the above questions are speculative at this point, you have engaged in an exercise that is critical to becoming an effective and culturally competent social worker.

EXERCISES: THE SOCIAL WORK LIBRARY

Spirituality, Religious Diversity, and Social Work Practice

After reading "Spirituality, Religious Diversity, and Social Work Practice" (Canda, 1988), write a brief description of the ways in which you believe:

1. Spirituality and religious beliefs can and should be integrated into social work practice.

2. Your own spiritual and religious belief system will influence your professional life.

OTHER EXERCISES

Self-Awareness: An Exploration

THINGS I LEARNED GROWING UP . . .

In order to better understand the origins of your thoughts, feelings, and stereotypes about the diverse range of persons in our society, consider each of the following social groups and the sources of your information about each group. List the specific information you gained from each of the sources in the two categories on the right of the table.

SOCIAL GROUPS	FROM FAMILY, TEACHERS, AND FRIENDS	FROM TELEVISION
People with Disabilities		
African Americans		
Asian Americans		
Latino Americans		
American Indians		
Americans of European Descent		
Persons with Dual Racial Heritage		
Women		
Men		
Gays, Lesbians, Bisexuals, and Transgendered Persons		
Low-Income People		
Rich People		
Older Adults		
Persons who practice religions different from my own		

Adapted from the National Conference for Community and Justice–St. Louis Region

Self-Awareness: Continuing the Exploration

Consider an experience that you have had with diversity at any point in your life. This experience may be one in which you were the recipient or perpetrator of discrimination or oppression, or an experience in which you uncomfortable due to your lack of familiarity with the situation or person(s). After you have identified the experience, write a narrative that includes the following:

- A description of the experience

- What was uncomfortable, awkward, or painful about this situation?

- Which of the "isms" is relevant to this situation? Why?

- How did you respond to the experience?

- If you were to encounter this situation again, would you respond differently? Why? How?

- How might this experience influence your future professional life?

Now that you have completed this portion of the exercise, stop and read the narrative that you have written and answer these questions:

- Did you learn anything new about yourself?

- Have you changed since this experience? How?

- What would you say to someone else who has had this experience?

- What culturally competent skills did you use? If you were to encounter this situation again, which culturally competent skills would you use?

You have begun a lifelong journey of self-reflection that is essential for culturally competent social work practice. You can continue to use this exercise as you encounter future issues of diversity.

Being Honest with Yourself

Respond to the following:

- When you see an older adult in a wheelchair, what are your thoughts?

- When you see someone who is cognitively impaired, what is your reaction?

- When you are on public transportation and you are sitting next to a person with a developmental disability or a possible mental illness, how to do react? What are your feelings in this situation?

- When you see a person with Down Syndrome, what is your reaction?

- When you see two persons of the same gender walking down the street holding hands, what is your reaction?

- Can you think of other situations in which you have had a reaction?

Once you have considered your responses to the above questions, identify the culturally competent skills that you feel you possess. How did you gain these skills? What skills do you lack?

Journal Entry #2—A Diversity Challenge

Identify an area of diversity (racial, ethnic, religious, economic, gender, age, sexual orientation, etc.) that has challenged you. Describe your response, how you might respond differently in the future, and how this experience may impact your professional work.

CHAPTER 6

Values and Ethics in Social Work Practice

Emily faced a difficult situation while completing the community service require-ment for her introductory social work course at Oasis House, a shelter for persons who are homeless. She was in the recreation room of the shelter talking with one of the residents, Lorinda, a single mother with two young children. Emily had talked with Lorinda on several previous occasions and felt a special bond with her. Lorinda and Emily were the same age and had many similar interests. They had both been on their high school track teams and had competed in the same events. During one conversation, Lorinda asked Emily for money. Lorinda told Emily that she needed the money to help her boyfriend get bus money to get back home. He had gone to another city to look for work so he could earn money and send for Lorinda and the children. He had not found a job and had no money for the trip back. Lorinda assured Emily that she would repay the money as soon as she and her boyfriend had jobs.

Emily did not know what to do. She liked Lorinda and wanted to help her, but was not sure that she should give Lorinda her own money. What would you do in this situation?

The situation that Emily encountered is considered an **ethical dilemma**, a commonplace occurrence in the social work profession. An ethical dilemma exists when the social worker "must choose between two or more relevant, but contradictory, ethical directives, or when every alternative results in an unde-sirable outcome for one or more persons" (Loewenberg, Dolgoff, & Harrington, 2000, p. 9). A dilemma can occur when a social worker's ethical principles and standards conflict with those of the client, agency, or society. Areas of challenge can include the birth of a child, loss of a loved one, natural disasters, child or older-adult abuse, neglect, or exploitation; mental or physical illness; financial or housing needs; discrimination; and domestic violence. Such value-laden issues create the potential for an ethical dilemma to occur because the social worker may have to involve authorities, challenge the client system's choices, or confront an injustice.

When a social worker intervenes in a situation, several value systems and ethical practices are already in place. Specifically, the values and ethics of the social worker, client system, agency, and society are all present, and they impact the social work intervention and outcome. In this chapter, we focus on values and ethics and the ways in which they relate to social work practice. We will begin our exploration of this topic by defining the terms and highlighting the reasons that values and ethics are central to competent social work practice. As part of this process we will consider the NASW *Code of Ethics* (1999). You will have an opportunity to examine your own values and to apply social work values and ethics to challenging social work practice.

SOCIAL WORK'S COMMITMENT TO VALUES AND ETHICS

*National events determine our ideals, as much as
our ideals determine national events.*
—JANE ADDAMS

Values can be defined as a society's system of beliefs, principles, and traditions that guide behaviors and practices. You might also think of values as the ideals by which we live. To rephrase the quotation from Jane Addams, our values are shaped by society and society is shaped by our values. For example, the social work profession believes that all people have a right to access the resources needed to optimize their quality of life.

The definition of **ethics** is somewhat different: "a system of moral principles and perceptions about right versus wrong and the resulting philosophy of conduct that is practiced by an individual, group, profession, or culture" (Barker, 2003, p. 147). You can see that values and ethics are closely related. As one example, the social work profession has turned the value regarding access to resources into a professional ethic by advocating with policy makers for groups marginalized by society (for example, advocating for low-income families to gain better access to resources).

With this understanding of the interconnections between values and ethics, let us examine some issues that students in the introductory social work course frequently ask about. You will see that value conflicts and ethical dilemmas can be an everyday occurrence in the life of a social worker, but they take place on several different levels. An ethical code, such as NASW's *Code of Ethics,* provides guidelines for professional conduct in six key areas: clients, colleagues, practice setting, professionalism, the profession, and the broader society.

The Social Work Library

Written during the 100th anniversary of social work, Reamer's article on the evolution of social work ethics provides an overview of the development of social work ethics and the Code of Ethics.

Why Values and Ethics Are Important in Social Work

Value and ethical issues are present in every encounter that a social worker has with a client system, but because the client systems with which practitioners often work are persons or groups who have experienced some form of discrimination or oppression, and may not have adequate resources, their "voices" are often not heard by society. The role of the social worker may be to advocate for a client system's rights, to help the client system access information and resources, or to assist the client in enhancing her or his quality of life. Therefore, at this level, a competent social work practitioner is aware of value and ethical issues and the implications of those values and ethics on the social work intervention.

Having an awareness and understanding of their own value system as well as the value systems of their clients, the agency of employment, and the larger society can help to ensure that social workers do not unknowingly discriminate against a client system through inappropriate language or behavior. Although social workers are not expected to *share* these value systems, they are ethically bound to *respect* the value systems of others. Moreover, having insight into the client's value system can help the social worker to understand the client's decision-making processes, choices and behaviors, and patterns of dysfunction. In order to approach an ethical dilemma, the social worker needs to understand the value systems of all involved. This is the first step toward a resolution to the ethical challenge. The social worker does not attempt to change the client system by imposing her or his values on the client system, but instead strives to understand and respect the client's values.

Values and Ethics Issues in Social Work

Every client with whom a social worker interacts is different, and each conflicted situation is unique. Therefore, in order to maintain an individualistic perspective, a social worker cannot formulate blanket responses to ethical dilemmas. Instead, social workers are mindful of the client system's values as well as any ethical implications that may result from the social worker–client system relationship.

Due to the complex nature of social work, the values of the social work profession operate at multiple levels. That is, social workers are knowledgeable about values at the personal, professional, and societal levels. One popular model delineates values by level of involvement (Loewenberg et al., 2000):

- *Individual or personal values:* the values of one person.

- *Group values:* the values of groups within society (for example, religious and ethnic groups).

- *Societal values:* the primary values of the larger social system.

- *Professional values:* the values of a specific discipline or professional group.

An alternative framework for exploring individual, group, and societal values categorizes these values by type and outcome (Reamer, 1995):

- Ultimate values are those broad-based, societal values that guide a group's long-term aims. Our society's rules against discrimination and oppression are examples of ultimate values. For social workers, ultimate values are a consistent extension of societal values, including respect for people, equality, and nondiscrimination.

- Proximate values are specific, short-term values that relate to policies and rights. In the social work profession, for example, proximate values include the right to have access to services.

- Instrumental values are directed toward the process of attaining a desirable end through desirable means. Within a social work context, instrumental values refer to the client's right to confidentiality, self-determination, and informed consent.

Having a conceptual basis for understanding your own, your client's, and societal values can help you to interpret the inevitable value conflicts that you will encounter as a social worker. Let's continue this examination of values and ethics by considering another situation in which Emily finds herself.

After Emily graduated with her BSW degree, she secured her first social work position. Finally, she was going to be in a position to really help people. Her first social work job was in the adult social service unit of a multiservice community agency. When she interviewed for this position, she was told she would be working as a case manager with older adults to help them maintain their independent living situations. Emily enjoyed this position for three years, at which time the agency overhauled the structure of its social services, and all workers became "generic" workers, handling both child and adult services. Emily found herself being assigned child protection cases, in which she investigated charges of abuse and neglect, testified in court, and often recommended that the child be removed from the home and placed in foster care. For the first time in her career, Emily felt conflicted regarding her role as a social worker. She felt her lack of knowledge about and interest in working with children and their parents would hamper her ability to serve the best interests of the clients.

Emily experienced a **value conflict**—a situation in which a social worker's values (or "shoulds") clash with the value system of a client, agency, co-worker, or society in general. Value conflicts present themselves in many different forms. You cannot possibly anticipate all the potential conflicts that await you, but you can anticipate that such conflicts *will* arise, and you can prepare yourself by developing a set of skills to respond to them when they do. The following sections describe some value conflicts that you may encounter as a social work professional.

Job-Related Value Conflicts   Emily's conflict is one example of a situation in which the social worker's value system comes into conflict with the duties that she or he has been hired to perform. Because social workers intervene in settings in which they assume a position of authority over the client system, such conflicts are not uncommon. Possible settings for value conflicts include the public welfare system, the criminal justice system (for example, an incarceration facility), a residential care facility, or an agency to which client systems are mandated by the judicial system.

Value conflicts can also arise when social workers find themselves in the role of an authority or "pseudo-cop" (Baldino, 2000, p. 25). Pseudo-cop social workers may be torn, for example, between their duty to comply with the court's directives and their obligation to support their client. For social workers that find themselves in such a dilemma, observing and seeking the wisdom of other experienced workers in similar settings can be an effective strategy for gaining perspective and competence in this role.

Unethical or impaired behavior on the part of a co-worker may also create value conflicts. Consider a scenario in which you learn that a co-worker's drug or alcohol use is beginning to impair his ability to perform his job duties. Consider also the co-worker who defames or discriminates against clients and co-workers. What is your personal and professional obligation in these situations? Is it acceptable for you to look the other way? Do you confront the co-worker or report your suspicions to a supervisor? As a social work professional, you consider the potential conflict between your personal loyalty to a co-worker and the profession in the area of unethical or dangerous behavior (Wilshere, 1997).

Value Conflicts Related to Religion and Belief   Many people are drawn to the social work profession out of a sense of religious calling or obligation or as a result of experiences related to their religious beliefs. A number of social work practitioners are employed by faith-based organizations that espouse a religious mission and philosophy. Ideally, social workers in these situations will work with client systems and colleagues who share their religious beliefs. Although many social workers find that practicing social work and their religion go hand-in-hand, others experience conflicts between the two. In reality, religious differences are common, even in situations in which the client or colleague is of the same faith as the social worker. A value conflict can occur when the religious beliefs of the client and the social worker impede their ability to work together effectively or when the religious beliefs of the social worker and the agency conflict. For example, consider a situation in which the worker's position on abortion is pro-life and the client is seeking an abortion.

Although social workers are trained to maintain emotional objectivity, issues related to religious beliefs and practices are areas in which the social worker's experiences may be an asset for effective practice. For example, consider a situation in which a client appears to be uncooperative with the physician's plan for a medical procedure. Because the social worker is familiar with the client's religious beliefs, she recognizes that the client's resistance is not resistance at all, but rather an expression of the client's religious beliefs, which make it impossible for the client to consent to the medical procedure (Senkowsky, 1996a).

Value Conflicts over Limited Resources   The social work profession values each person's right to have access to resources to optimize her or his quality of life. Although society as a whole supports this value, heated debates occur at the personal and policy levels regarding the distribution of those resources, most of which are limited. One example is the value held by many people that persons living in poverty do not deserve a "handout" but instead should have to work "like the rest of us" for their living. This value can be translated into an anti-poor attitude and further into supporting political candidates who oppose welfare. Social work students may struggle with this particular issue, which actually may be a conflict between values to which they have been exposed and different value systems that they are encountering in social work classes.

The Social Worker's Values

Although social work training emphasizes being nonjudgmental, the reality is that you cannot "check your values at the door." Your value system reflects the influences of the family who reared you; your educational, religious, spiritual, social, and professional experiences; and your formal social work training. You bring your value system into each and every social work situation. Before you can begin to determine strategies for understanding and working with the value systems of clients, agencies, or society, you must consider your own value system, its origins, and the implications of your values for your life and your future practice.

Throughout the history of social work, some social workers have espoused the views that social work practice should be value free and that values do not affect social work practice (Loewenberg et al., 2000). Over time, however, most social workers have recognized that personal, group, and societal values do influence their work. The challenge for the profession then becomes to enable social work students and practitioners to clarify their values, understand the profession's values, and acquire skills for ethical social work practice.

An important step in understanding values and their impact on ethical behavior is to clarify your own values. **Values clarification** is the process of exploring your values and comparing them to others for the purpose of developing an appreciation and respect for your values and the values of others (Barker, 2003). Clarifying your values does not mean that you automatically change them. In fact, taking the risk to learn other perspectives may confirm your commitment to your values. Sometimes, however, values do change as a result of efforts to clarify them. As you are exposed to new and different ideas or provided with different information, your previous perspective can be altered. The key is your willingness to risk change by exposing yourself to other views and value systems that may differ from your own.

Some people might go so far as to argue that attaining a social work degree is, in fact, an ongoing exercise in values clarification. As a social work student, you will find that your value system will constantly be challenged through your discussions with faculty and fellow students, readings, assignments, and field experiences. You can begin the process of clarifying your values by starting with casual conversations or issues that arise in your classes. Part of the process of understanding your own values is taking the risk of hearing ideas that are different from your own. Although that may not be a comfortable situation, it is an important process to engage in during your training so that you will be more comfortable and aware once you become a practitioner. Although you will continually encounter new situations throughout your career, you will eventually develop a strategy and a comfort level for these situations.

When you are involved in a conversation regarding ethics, you can initiate the process of clarifying your values by asking yourself these questions:

- What do I think about this issue?
- What are the origins of my values on this issue?

- What are the other person's values on this issue? Are our values similar or different? If they are different, does this difference create a dilemma for me? For the two of us?

How the Social Work Profession Defines Ethics

Action indeed is the sole medium of expression for ethics.
—JANE ADDAMS

Many professions have developed a standardized approach to guide their members in establishing a competent and effective practice. As the quote from Jane Addams implies, ethics is defined by action. By definition, a **code of ethics** is a document, created by the members of the profession, that provides specific guidelines for appropriate and expected professional behaviors. These behavioral expectations are rooted in the values and ethical standards deemed acceptable by the profession.

The social work profession has several codes aimed at promoting ethical practice. The NASW *Code of Ethics,* referred to many times in this book, was developed to clearly specify expected professional conduct for the members of the association. Other social work organizations have developed codes of ethics that are similar in intent to the NASW's but are specific to their organizational mission and membership.

The NASW Delegate Assembly, a body of NASW members elected by their state chapters, meets once every three years to debate and vote on NASW policies, including the *Code of Ethics.* Recognizing that social work changes as society changes, the NASW has revised the *Code* several times since its inception in 1960, most recently in 1996 and 1999.

Although the *Code of Ethics* is intended as a guide, it also serves as a mechanism for monitoring social workers' practice competency and ethics. Violations can be reported to a state chapter or the national office. A committee of NASW members then reviews the complaint and can recommend any number of actions if the complaint is substantiated. Such actions may include corrective action (such as suspension from the organization, mandated consultation, or censure), informing the regulatory board of the state in which the social worker practices, or public sanction through publication of the individual's name in the *NASW News* "Sanctions in Force" section. Social work licensure or certification, which exists in every state, requires practice adherence to the *Code of Ethics.* Moreover, social workers can risk being sued for malpractice in civil court if ethical practice is violated.

The initial NASW *Code of Ethics,* accepted by the membership in 1960, emphasized the primacy of professional responsibility over personal interests, the client's right to privacy, obligations for service during public emergencies, and a duty to contribute to the knowledge of the profession (Reamer, 1995). The current version mirrors the earlier documents, despite its increased length and proliferation of legal terms. It consists of four sections: preamble, purpose, ethical principles, and ethical standards.

The preamble outlines the mission and core values of the social work profession. As stated in the 1999 *Code of Ethics,* the mission of the social work profession is

> to enhance human well-being and help meet the basic human needs of all people, with particular attention to the needs and empowerment of people who are vulnerable, oppressed, and living in poverty. A historic and defining feature of social work is the profession's focus on individual well-being in a social context and the well-being of society. Fundamental to social work is attention to the environmental forces that create, contribute to, and address problems in living. Social workers promote social justice and social change with and on behalf of clients. "Clients" is used inclusively to refer to individuals, families, groups, organizations, and communities. Social workers are sensitive to cultural and ethnic diversity and strive to end discrimination, oppression, poverty, and other forms of social injustice. These activities may be in the form of direct practice, community organizing, supervision, consultation, administration, advocacy, social and political action, policy development and implementation, education, research, and evaluation. Social workers seek to enhance the capacity of people to address their own needs. Social workers also seek to promote the responsiveness of organizations, communities, and other social institutions to individuals' needs and social problems.

From the profession's mission, we can derive the core values of the social work profession: service, social justice, dignity and worth of the person, importance of human relationships, integrity, and competence.

Following the preamble, the second section outlines the six purposes of the *Code:*

- Identify core values on which social work's mission is based.

- Summarize broad ethical principles that reflect the profession's core values and serve as the basis for a set of specific ethical standards to guide social work practice.

- Help social workers identify relevant considerations when professional obligations conflict or ethical uncertainties arise.

- Provide ethical standards to which the general public can hold the social work profession accountable.

- Socialize practitioners new to the field to social work's mission, values, ethical principles, and ethical standards.

	CORE SOCIAL WORK VALUES	SOCIAL WORK ETHICAL PRINCIPLES
TABLE 6.1 *Ethical Principles Based on Core Social Work Values*	Service	Help people in need and address social conditions and concerns.
	Social justice	Challenge social injustice.
	Dignity and worth of the person	Respect the inherent dignity and worth of the person.
	Importance of human relationships	Recognize the central importance of human relationships.
	Integrity	Behave in a trustworthy manner.
	Competence	Practice within areas of competence, and develop and enhance professional expertise.

- Articulate standards that the social work profession itself can use to assess whether social workers have engaged in unethical conduct.

The statement of ethical principles—highlighted in Table 6.1—is based on the six core values identified in the preamble. These ethical principles are the "ideals to which all social workers should aspire" (NASW, 1999, p. 5). These help provide a guide for social work practice in challenging ethically laden situations.

The final part of the *Code* includes six sections that list ethical standards or categories of ethical responsibilities: (1) clients, (2) colleagues, (3) practice settings, (4) professionalism, (5) the social work profession, and (6) the larger society. Considered to be the substance of the *Code,* these six standards include 155 specific items that stipulate social workers' ethical responsibilities within each standard. The standards are intended to guide the conduct of social work professionals and serve as the basis for evaluating violations of the *Code of Ethics.* Box 6.1 discusses these ethical standards in detail.

The NASW *Code of Ethics* addresses a range of broad but important—and sometimes controversial—behaviors and practices. A number of themes recur throughout the standards encompassed by the *Code.* Possibly the most important theme is respect for the client, as reflected in such standards as the social worker's commitment to clients and client self-determination. Another underlying theme is responsibility for the profession, as evidenced by those standards that address colleagues with impairments and unethical colleague behaviors. The *Code* also articulates the responsibility of the social work profession for society, which is attained through such efforts as advocacy, education, and political action.

1. *Clients:* This grouping of ethical standards addresses the responsibilities to clients, including the topics of:

commitment to clients	client's right to self-determination
informed consent	competence and diversity
conflicts of interest	privacy and confidentiality
access to records	sexual relationships and harassment
physical contact	derogatory language
payment for services	interruption/termination of services
clients who lack decision-making capacity	

2. *Colleagues:* Ethical responsibilities in this standard relate to collegial behaviors, including guidelines for:

respect	confidentiality
interdisciplinary collaboration	disputes involving colleagues
consultation	referral for services
sexual relationships	sexual harassment
impairment of colleagues	incompetence of colleagues
unethical conduct of colleagues	

3. *Practice settings:* This set of ethical standards encompasses the social worker's responsibilities to the setting in which she or he practices, including employers, co-workers, supervisors, and supervisees:

supervision and consultation	education and training
performance evaluation	client records
billing	client transfer
administration	continuing education
commitments to employers	labor-management disputes

4. *Professionalism:* The NASW defines professionalism as the "degree to which an individual possesses and uses the knowledge, skills, and qualifications of a profession and adheres to its values and ethics when serving the client" (Barker, 1999, p. 380). Professionalism requires the social worker to practice ethically, competently, fairly, and honestly, and prevent such unethical behaviors as:

interference of private conduct	dishonesty, fraud, and deception
impairment of ability	misrepresentation
solicitations	failure to acknowledge credit
discrimination	

BOX 6.1
continued

5. *The social work profession:* This section of the *Code* addresses social workers' commitments to the entirety of the social work community in the areas of maintaining:

    integrity of the profession   evaluation and research

6. *The broader society:* Social workers are responsible to society (for example, the community in which they live and the community at large) in the areas of:

    social welfare   public participation

    public emergencies   social and political action

The application of social work ethics evolves over time as social problems and issues evolve. For example, mandated reporting of suspected child abuse, neglect, and exploitation is an ethical practice issue that emerged in response to the changing social climate. Until the 1970s, social workers were not legally required to report incidents of suspected abuse. However, as society focused attention on this issue, the social work profession followed suit by supporting mandated reporting.

Why Have a Code of Ethics?

As you read this book, I hope that you have questioned why the social work profession needs any codes to dictate appropriate professional behavior. After all, don't we all become social workers because we are altruistic and giving persons? If this is true, then why should we require a formal document to guide our practice? Critics of the *Code of Ethics* argue that to be ethical, social workers need only "practice wisdom" (the knowledge, skills, and values that a social worker collects over the course of a career), instincts, and virtuosity and that being governed by a code is time consuming, coercive, and a wasted effort (Loewenberg et al., 2000, pp. 34–36). Now that you have reviewed the *Code of Ethics,* what do you think?

The profession's interest in values and ethical practice has been formalized largely since the 1970s. This emphasis on ethical practice may be due, in part, to societal changes that have affected the clients served by social workers. Advances in such areas as medicine (for example, treatments, technology, and disease awareness), computer technology, global awareness, resource management, and nuclear power prompted social workers to consider the impact of these developments on their clients (Reamer, 1995).

As the complexity of the social worker's job has increased, so has the potential for ethical dilemmas. When faced with multiple alternatives, directions, or potential contradictions of ethical principles, social workers can use a set of guidelines in establishing an ethical intervention that serves the best interests of the client and the system in a manner that is consistent with present-day cultural demands (Loewenberg et al., 2000).

Another issue that may occur to you as you read this book is the way the social work profession uses the various ethical codes. Most social workers view the codes as guides for their professional behavior, but many practitioners also recognize that even a well-developed, professionally binding code has its limitations. As you reviewed the standards in Box 6.1, you undoubtedly noticed that the items are broad in nature and leave particular situations open to interpretation. Nevertheless, despite its general approach to ethics, the *Code* remains the best resource to consult when you are faced with an ethical dilemma.

APPLYING VALUES AND ETHICS AT WORK

The potential for a value conflict or an ethical dilemma is something that social work practitioners keep in mind at all times. No matter how clear, simplistic, or mundane a situation may seem on the surface, social workers do not trivialize the situation or routinize the interpretation or the response. Instead, social workers keep in mind the value base that has long guided social work practice. The knowledge and skills developed by social work professionals are deeply rooted in this set of values, which have changed little since they were first introduced.

Although the core social work values and ethical principles are widely accepted by the profession, their meanings and the implications of those meanings are routinely open to interpretation and often result in disagreements (Dunlap & Strom-Gottfried, 1998a). To help in the application of ethical principles, social work theorists have developed tools for making ethical decisions. One is known as the Enhanced Ethical Decision-Making Matrix (D'Aprix, Boynton, Carver, & Urso, 2001). The model is based on the premise that the social worker (1) explores all options before taking action, (2) recognizes her or his personal values and biases, and (3) evaluates the effectiveness of the action. The first step in applying this model is to identify the ethical issues using the *Code of Ethics*. Table 6.2 presents a set of questions and the basis for those questions that can aid in the identification process.

Using a decision-making framework does not ensure "easy answers to the tough questions," but it does provide an approach for analyzing the situation and devising an ethical and thoughtful response. The model prompts the social worker to ask the questions that are relevant to the ethical dilemma, to compartmentalize the information, to establish priorities, and to consider the impact of the outcome on all the parties involved.

Although social work training places the utmost importance on respecting the client system's values, determining the client's values or understanding the

TABLE 6.2

Ethical Decision Making: Identifying the Issues

QUESTIONS TO IDENTIFY ETHICAL ISSUES	BASIS FOR QUESTION
1. What are the interventions and ethical issues that make it difficult to choose a course of action?	Worker is able to address all potential ethical issues. Worker determines if any *Code of Ethics* standards or laws are involved.
2. What are my viewpoints about these issues?	Worker is able to recognize her/his personal biases and determine any impact of the biases on client system outcomes.
3. Which actions (interventions) might address the practice and ethical issues listed in number 1?	Worker is able to consider all potential alternatives for intervention.
4. What are the potential consequences/outcomes of these actions?	Worker can conduct a cost-benefit analysis of the potential intervention.
5. How would I prioritize the intervention and ethical issues using the Ethical Principles Screen (EPS)?	Using the EPS, the worker can rank-order priorities.
6. Based on this prioritization, which issues will I address first, and which action will address this issue?	After prioritizing the ethical issues, the worker can prioritize the proposed interventions.
7. Throughout this process, have I consulted with colleagues for their professional opinions?	Worker can benefit from the practice wisdom of other social work professionals.
8. How will I monitor and evaluate the effectiveness of this plan of action?	Ongoing monitoring enables the worker to know when to proceed to the next priority and to assess the status of the dilemma.

Source: D'Aprix, Boynton, Carver & Urso, 2001

implications of those values may not always be easy. For example, could you be an effective social work practitioner when the person with whom you are working has a history of abusing children? Would you be able to see the client as someone other than an abuser? Could you acknowledge the client's strengths and potential for change given that she or he has abused another person? These and most value-laden questions can be answered only when social workers review their own value system and the values of the profession. Emily was confronted with just such a situation.

ETHICAL DILEMMAS: WHEN THE PERSONAL AND THE PROFESSIONAL CONFLICT

During one of her practicum experiences, Emily was invited by her field instructor at a mental health center to co-lead a male batterers' group with a male colleague. You will recall from Chapter 1 that Emily was a victim of domestic violence several years earlier. She did not share that reality with her field instructor or her co-workers at the practicum site because she was afraid they would view her as inept. After all, if she were a competent individual, would she have allowed herself to become involved in a violent relationship? Nevertheless, Emily agreed to participate in the group, feeling that she would disappoint her supervisor if she rejected the invitation. She also believed that she had put the experience behind her and that because of her personal experience and social work training, she would bring a valuable perspective.

Unfortunately, Emily's experience was less than successful, to say the least. She was extremely uncomfortable as she listened to the men rationalize their violence against their female partners. Based on her value system, Emily viewed violence as reprehensible, and she was now solidly entrenched in that belief because of her own experience. Emily's belief system had evolved to believing that batterers could not be rehabilitated. She soon realized that she probably had not "put the experience behind her," and she was faced with ethical dilemmas:

- *In her current state of discomfort, she was not fulfilling her commitment to be a co-facilitator.*

- *If she left the group, she would be leaving her colleague without a co-facilitator. The agency was strongly committed to having a male/female team for this group.*

Because she had not told her supervisor or her colleagues of her past, Emily was fearful they would think she was hiding this information. This belief might lead them to question her ethical behavior. She questioned whether her personal values were impeding her practice obligations. She was especially fearful of her reactions if she continued in the group: Would she "lose it" during a group session, or would she continue to be immobilized? What would you do in Emily's situation: leave, stay, or seek help?

An ethical dilemma is most challenging when personal values and professional ethical obligations conflict. Most practitioners agree that the "best interests" of the client system should take precedence, but your personal values may override your professional duty in some situations. Consider Emily's dilemma, for example. Her experience with domestic violence made it difficult for her to work with male batterers at this early point in her career. Nevertheless, when she was given the opportunity to co-lead a batterers' group, she felt she could maintain enough emotional objectivity to be an effective co-leader. Clearly, her personal experiences and values clouded her objectivity. It was important for her to learn that putting personal values aside is not always an easy task. The negative group experience enabled her to confront her fears during supervisory sessions. With her supervisor's support and challenges, Emily was able to come to terms with her feelings and shift her belief to consider that treatment of violent behavior could be successful. As a result, she ultimately was able to co-facilitate the group.

Although the ethical dilemmas that you are likely to encounter in your practice will all have unique characteristics, some common areas that challenge social workers can be identified. The ethical dilemmas presented in the following sections, when linked to the social values and ethical principles discussed earlier, can provide a context in which to consider appropriate responses to the situation. As you review these situations, consider your own value system, your potential responses, and the intersection of the two. You may find that these situations prompt more questions than answers, but keep asking the questions.

Right to Privacy and Confidentiality

The social worker–client relationship is based on trust. When that trust is threatened or violated, an ethical dilemma may occur. A key to establishing a trusting relationship is for the social worker to respect the client's confidentiality. Defined as the disclosure of client-related information only with the permission of the client, **confidentiality** can be categorized as either absolute or relative. Absolute confidentiality means that all information is to be held in confidence; relative confidentiality means that some information can be disclosed. In cases of relative confidentiality, social workers frequently share information with colleagues or law enforcement officials, but only with client consent (Barker, 2003).

Standard 1.07(a–r) of the NASW *Code of Ethics* addresses privacy and confidentiality in great detail because social workers are privy to considerable and intimate client information. The standard, derived from the social work value of viewing each person with dignity and worth, provides guidelines for protecting information related to the client's reasons for receiving services, her or his legal and financial status, and other personal life details.

Legally, social workers must share information in two situations. In cases of suspected abuse of children, older adults, and persons with disabilities, social workers are mandated to report the suspected abuse to the state agency. Secondly, in cases in which a person threatens harm to self or others, the social worker must report to the designated authority in that state.

Social workers can also share information when the client has granted **informed consent** through a signed release of information. Such consent is needed for the practitioner to share information regarding the content of the professional relationship, client information/statements, professional assessments, and information from client records (Burkemper, 2004; Dunlap & Strom-Gottfried, 1998b). In order to grant a valid informed consent, the client or the client's guardian must give written permission and be told what information is to be shared and the reasons for sharing it, with whom the information will be shared, and the date of expiration for the information. Most agencies have a standardized consent form.

Additional protection of client information is included in the Health Insurance Portability and Accountability Act of 1996 (HIPAA) (U.S. Department of Health and Human Services, 2004). The HIPAA legislation is designed to protect and enhance the rights of consumers of health care services without compromising the access to or effectiveness of the provision of services. The law mandates that consumers of health care services have the following rights: to see and obtain copies of their health care records; to be informed in writing about the ways in which health information is used by the health care provider; and to have assurance that their identifiable health information is protected.

Privacy and confidentiality do, however, have limits. When the limitations of the social worker's ability to maintain privacy or confidentiality are challenged, an ethical dilemma can arise. For example, the social worker strives to maintain the client's confidentiality (and trust) but may have a legal or societal duty to divulge the information, as in the case of suspected abuse or harm to self or others (Loewenberg et al., 2000). In such situations, the social worker may face a conflict between maintaining the client's trust and recognizing the mandate to violate confidentiality.

For beginning social workers, the responsibility to maintain a client's privacy and confidentiality can become overwhelming. When do you share or not share client information? What can you write or not write in a client record? What if you accidentally breach a confidence? These are all questions that you should be vigilant about. Here are recommended practices to maintain your client's privacy and confidentiality (Dunlap & Strom-Gottfried, 1998b):

- Be vigilant. Make confidentiality foremost in your mind as you practice.
- Protect records by keeping them in a locked receptacle, and safeguard computer files with a firewall, password, or short-delay screen saver.

- Monitor your ongoing client-related activities by gathering only the information that is relevant to the services being provided.

- Learn and understand laws and agency policies and practices regarding the protection of information.

- Monitor yourself. Use your supervisor and colleagues for consultation, not the clients or your friends or family.

- Picture yourself as a consumer of your services—how would you like to be treated?

Right to Self-Determination

The right to **self-determination** is also derived from the social work value and ethical principle related to dignity and worth of the person. Standard 1.02 specifies that the social worker is obligated to respect the client system's right to make decisions and choices and to determine her or his own goals. As with confidentiality, situations can arise that limit the social worker's ability to fully comply with this obligation. As mentioned earlier, when a person has threatened physical harm to herself or himself or to others, the social worker is ethically obligated to protect the person and override the right to self-determination (Reamer, 1998).

Ethical dilemmas can also occur in non-life-threatening situations in which the social worker feels the client is making a decision that may have a negative or harmful outcome. Consider, for example, the person who resumes drinking or using drugs, who returns to a violent relationship, or who is mandated for services but refuses to participate even though noncompliance will result in a return to prison. In these situations, the social worker must balance the issue of respecting the client's right to self-determination with the competing obligation to help the client achieve a positive outcome (Loewenberg et al., 2000).

A useful guideline to follow in these difficult situations is to remember that the person's right to self-determination takes precedence whenever possible. Even the client who has not voluntarily come to the social worker for services has the "right" to choose nonparticipation. The social worker's responsibility is to offer or provide the opportunity to identify and examine the consequences of that choice. Maintaining this stance can be challenging, but it is necessary if social workers are to truly respect and value their client systems. The reality is that all people have the right to make poor decisions about their lives.

Boundaries

The lines that define your relationship with the client system as professional rather than social are called **boundaries.** Boundaries can be difficult to delineate and maintain because clients often share intimate details of their lives with their social worker, making the relationship appear to be personal and intimate. The social worker–client relationship can involve sharing, cooperation, and even liking each other, but it is not a friendship, romance, or business partnership (Strom-Gottfried & Dunlap, 1998). Having a personal as well as a professional relationship with a client is considered to be a dual relationship. For example, dating is a dual relationship and is considered unethical. Similarly, conflicts of interest are addressed in Standard 1.06 of the *Code of Ethics,* which states that a social worker must maintain separateness in personal, religious, political, or business areas. An example of an ethical violation would be to enter into a business venture with a client.

Becoming familiar with the profession's ethical standards as well as agency policies and practices will help you to avoid committing ethical infractions related to client-worker boundaries. Conducting periodic reality checks with colleagues and supervisors in cases of ambiguity can also help social workers maintain appropriate boundaries. Despite the best precautions, boundaries are not always possible to maintain. You could encounter a client somewhere outside the social work setting, for example. In those instances, allow the client to acknowledge you first, and if you engage with the client, ensure that you do not discuss the professional relationship during the encounter. Be prepared for the possibility that the client may not choose to acknowledge you at all, or that she or he may openly acknowledge you and discuss the reasons why you know each other. In either case, it is the social worker's responsibility to maintain professional boundaries.

Self-Disclosure

Related to boundaries is the issue of **self-disclosure**, the sharing of personal information with a client. The *Code of Ethics* states that social workers should not allow their personal issues to interfere with the best interests of the client. Although this does not specifically address the issue of self-disclosure, it implies that social workers should approach self-disclosure with caution. Sharing personal information with clients may be done with the best of intentions. For example, substance abuse treatment programs may hire workers who are recovering from chemical dependency or addiction and encourage them to disclose their history of abuse to their clients to establish a rapport. The social worker may believe that if the client knows that the worker has had similar experiences, the client will be better able to work through the challenge. In fact, the social worker's self-disclosure may achieve that goal. The client may see the social worker as more credible or trustworthy, feel that her or his experience was normal, or feel more confident and inspired to change (Reamer, 2001).

In other cases, however, self-disclosure can sabotage the social work intervention. The client may become confused by the worker's disclosure, may try to mirror the worker's recovery, or may shift attention to the worker's life (Strom-Gottfried & Dunlap, 1999; Reamer, 2001). For example, consider Emily's experiences related to self-disclosure. In the case of the client at Oasis House, her self-disclosure prompted the client to feel comfortable asking Emily for money. In the situation with the batterers' group, would Emily have wanted to share with the batterers her history as a victim of domestic violence?

Social workers monitor themselves closely regarding the disclosure of personal information. Here are some strategies for self-monitoring:

- Learn the agency policy and practice regarding self-disclosure.

- Determine the appropriateness, benefits, and costs of sharing the information and the client's ability to use the information (Strom-Gottfried & Dunlap, 1999).

- Consult with colleagues and supervisors regarding their experiences with self-disclosure.

Allocation of Resources

Social workers are often faced with the dilemma of too few resources for too many client systems. They may have to deny an application for assistance because the funding has been exhausted or there are no beds in a shelter or food in the pantry. As social workers are often the first contact for the clients, they typically must shoulder the burden of informing them that there are no resources to meet a request.

Resources are typically allocated on the basis of equal-sized proportions, a lottery system, or on a competitive basis using financial need or past oppression as the criteria (Reamer, 2001). Ethical dilemmas involving resource allocations can be particularly challenging because there may be little that the social worker can do to influence the outcome. Nevertheless, social workers have an ethical obligation to play a role in the allocation of resources. Social workers who work directly with client systems can be the voice for these clients. Similarly, social workers who occupy supervisory, administrative, and policy positions can advocate for equitable allocation of resources.

CASE STUDY: CARLA'S RIGHT TO PRIVACY AND CONFIDENTIALITY

We have explored a number of issues related to social work values and ethics. It is now time to apply the concepts and framework to an ethical dilemma. The dilemma is followed by the questions that might arise from the situation, and the issues are applied to the decision-making matrix presented in Table 6.2. A tool for using the decision-making matrix is the Ethical Principles Screen (D'Aprix, Boynton, Carver, & Urso, 2001). When presented with an ethical dilemma, the social worker can rank-order the issues using the seven ethical principles: (1) protection of human life, (2) equality and inequality, (3) autonomy and freedom, (4) least harm, (5) quality of life, (6) privacy and confidentiality, and (7) truthfulness and full disclosure. Using these seven principles prioritizes the ethical questions and enables the social worker to determine the issues that are most important to address.

Here is the ethical dilemma: You are a social worker at Oasis House, where your supervisor asks you to talk with a new resident, Carla. Carla told shelter workers that she is 18 and homeless. During your talks with Carla, however, she admits that she is really 15 and has run away from home. She further divulges that she does not want to go home because her mother's live-in boyfriend sexually abused her. She begs you not to share the information about the sexual abuse with anyone or to contact her mother.

The questions that might arise include the following:

- Does the adolescent have a legal right to make decisions about her life without parental consent?

- Would it be appropriate for you to discuss Carla's situation with her mother without Carla's informed consent?

- If Carla is being sexually abused, does she have a right to privacy after she has shared her secret with you?

- What is your responsibility to Carla's parents?

- Was Carla informed that you might not be able to maintain complete confidentiality *before* she confided in you?

- What are the agency's policies and procedures related to sexual abuse and Carla's status as a minor and a runaway?

You can analyze this practice situation by using the decision-making matrix in Table 6.2 as a guide. Table 6.3 uses that table's general categories in presenting possible ways of breaking down the problem to reach a satisfactory solution.

As you can see, this ethical dilemma poignantly addresses the client's right to protection, self-determination, privacy, and confidentiality. At the heart of the NASW *Code*'s first ethical standard, Social Workers' Ethical Responsibilities to Clients, is respect for the client. Having respect for the client is based on the core social work value of "dignity and worth of the person" and the ethical principle of "respect the inherent dignity and worth of the person." Respecting Carla's right to self-determination, privacy, and confidentiality is key to upholding her dignity and worth. You are ethically bound to respect her dignity

TABLE 6.3

Ethical Decision Making in the Case Study: Carla's Right to Privacy and Confidentiality

PRACTICE/ ETHICAL ISSUES	ETHICAL PRINCIPLE(S)	PERSONAL BIASES	ACTION(S) OPTIONS	POTENTIAL CONSEQUENCES/ OUTCOMES	ACTION(S) TAKEN	MONITOR/ EVALUATE EFFECTIVENESS
Client's request not to report the sexual abuse.	Protection of human life. Privacy and confidentiality.	I think the mother is at fault.	(a) Report the abuse to the public agency despite her opposition. (b) Work with client to make the report together.	(a) Report is made, but client's trust is lost. (b) Build trust with client so report can be made.	Jointly work with client to make report.	Check with client at each step to determine her sexual safety.
Client's request not to contact her mother.	Privacy and confidentiality. Self-determination. Commitment to client.	I think her mother must be contacted.	(a) By reporting to the public agency, the mother is contacted despite Carla's opposition. (b) Trust is built and mother is contacted.	(a) Mother is contacted, but client's trust is lost. (b) Trust is built and mother is contacted.	Jointly work with client to contact her mother.	Check with client at each step to determine her comfort levels with contacting mother.

Source: Adapted from D'Aprix, Boynton, Carver, & Urso, 2001 and worth, behave in a trustworthy manner, and practice with competence. By asking you to keep the alleged abuse in confidence and help her with emancipation, Carla is attempting to exercise her right to self-determination, privacy, and confidentiality. However, although you want to maintain her trust, as a social worker you are ethically and legally bound to report the abuse. The ethical dilemma here clearly is between client confidentiality and mandated reporting of suspected abuse. Even having determined that, to best serve Carla, you must report the suspected sexual abuse to the child welfare agency. Moreover, you continue to respect her right to self-determination and privacy.

The challenge is to help Carla without losing her trust. Exploring her options and the pros and cons associated with the various options could help her to feel positive about reporting the abuse. Helping Carla to understand that reporting the abuse is part of the helping process can serve to maintain her trust.

CONCLUSION

To maintain a professional perspective and avoid feelings of being overwhelmed, remember that clarifying your own values and practicing social work in an ethical manner is a lifelong endeavor for social workers. As social workers interact with people in a changing society, new ethical challenges will continue to emerge. The effective practice of social work means that social workers approach each situation with questions regarding the ethical implications of their actions. I hope this chapter encourages you to begin to explore your own values and ethics and their origins, and that such an exploration will become an ingrained part of your social work practice.

The Social Work Library

For insight into future ethical challenges for social workers in the international arena, read Polack's article.

MAIN POINTS

- Social work values are defined as the beliefs that we hold for ourselves and others in our communities. Ethics are the behavioral manifestations of the values that we hold about the way we and others should behave toward one another.

- Ethical dilemmas can occur in every aspect of social work practice. Social workers face ethical dilemmas in the areas of legal and health care issues, client rights and responsibilities, allocation of resources, and maintaining privacy and confidentiality.

- To practice social work in an ethical manner, awareness of your own values and of the profession's code is key.

- Understanding values and ethics is a personal thought process that is difficult to measure, seldom has obvious or concrete solutions, may evolve and change over time as a result of culture, contemporary norms, and events, and is applicable at all levels of social work practice.

- The NASW *Code of Ethics* serves as the guide for ethical practice. Taking advantage of the practice wisdom of your social work colleagues, consulting the *Code of Ethics*, and familiarizing yourself with the laws, policies, and practices related to your position are three "musts" for being an ethical practitioner.

EXERCISES: PRACTICING SOCIAL WORK

A Values Inventory for Social Workers

To prepare yourself for working through the exercises in this chapter, click on Assessment and complete Task #3, A Values Inventory for Social Workers.

Carmen Sanchez

Using the Sanchez family interactive case study, review the information regarding Junior Sanchez and answer Carmen's Critical Thinking Questions.

Joey Sanchez

Using the Sanchez family interactive case study, review the information regarding Junior Sanchez and answer Joey's Critical Thinking Questions.

Case Study: Emilia's Rights to Confidentiality

The best method for clarifying your values and developing responses to the inevitable ethical dilemmas that will arise is to practice. In this exercise, you can explore the values, ask the questions, and apply the ethical principles highlighted in this chapter. When you have read the following scenario, use the modified version of the Enhanced Ethical Decision-Making Model (D'Aprix et al., 2000) to complete the matrix. When you have completed the matrix, you can compare your analysis with mine to see how we compare. There are seldom "absolute" right or wrong answers in an ethical dilemma, just lots of questions and possibilities.

The Ethical Dilemma

Using the Sanchez family interactive case study, imagine that you are a social worker in a not-for-profit agency that provides crisis services over the telephone and to walk-in clients. Emilia Sanchez, a 24-year-old who is two months pregnant has telephoned several times. In her last telephone call, she confided to you that she uses crack cocaine and drinks alcohol several times a week. You have expressed your concern that her drug use may be dangerous for her unborn child, but she does not seem worried. She has also stated that she is unable or unwilling to give up the drugs. In this telephone conversation, she told you that she is unsure if she wants to keep "it." You suspect that she has traded sex for drugs and she is not working or attending school. Emilia tells you that her Catholic parents do not know about the pregnancy and she does not want them to know anything because they will insist she have the baby. Her mother already cares for Emilia's son, Joey, and has two younger children still living at home, and Emilia's father works long hours. They have little money and she does not want to burden them with another mouth to feed.

Your Analysis:

MODIFIED VERSION OF ENHANCED ETHICAL DECISION-MAKING MODEL						
CLINICAL/ ETHICAL ISSUE	ETHICAL PRINCIPLE(S)	PERSONAL BIASES	ACTIONS/ OPTIONS	POTENTIAL CONSEQUENCES/ OUTCOMES	ACTION(S) TAKEN	MONITOR/ EVALUATE EFFECTIVENESS
1.						
2.						
3.						

Consider this question: If your best friend was in Emilia's situation, would your analysis change? If so, in what way?

EXERCISES: THE SOCIAL WORK LIBRARY

Understanding Social Work Values and Ethics

Utilizing the knowledge that you have gained from reading this chapter and Reamer's (1998) article, "The Evolution of Social Work Ethics," respond to the following:

1. Define the concepts, values, and ethics as they each relate to the social work profession.

2. Describe your understanding the intent and scope of the NASW *Code of Ethics*.

3. Provide a comparison of recent versions of the NASW *Code of Ethics* and the 1998 version.

OTHER EXERCISES

Ethics in Everyday Social Work Practice

Using *Ethics in Introductory Social Work and Social Welfare: A Primer* (Strom-Gottfried, 2005), select one of the ethical challenges described in Chapters 4–8 and, before reading the author's analysis, respond to the following:

1. Identify the social work ethical dilemmas that exist.

2. Identify the social work values that are relevant in this scenario.

3. Identify the presence of any personal value conflicts.

4. Develop a list of options that you, as a social worker, might consider in this situation.

Upon completion of this exercise, return to Dr. Strom-Gottfried's chapter and review her analysis and compare it with your own.

Where Do Your Values Come From?

In this exercise you will (1) identify five values that are important in your life, (2) consider the origins of those values, and (3) compare those values to those of the social work profession. You can then think about the ways in which you act on each value. Do you engage in activities or behaviors that enable other people to discern your value on that particular issue, or would other people have no idea about your value? Finally, consider whether this value has ever created a dilemma for you. If so, what was the dilemma, and how did you re-solve it? To help you compare your values with those of the social work profession, the six social work values are listed below:

Service

Social justice

Dignity and worth of the person

Importance of human relationships

Integrity

Competence

PERSONAL VALUE	ORIGINS OF VALUE	BEHAVIOR
1.		
2.		
3.		
4.		
5.		

After you have completed this exercise, reflect on your work and consider these questions:

- Did you learn anything new about yourself?

- Did you learn anything new about anyone else?

- Are you satisfied with the ways in which you act on your value system? If not, what changes can you make?

- If any of your values created an ethical dilemma for you, were you satisfied with the way in which you handled the dilemma? If not, what could you have done differently?

- Do you feel your value system is consistent with the values of the social work profession?

- Which of the social work values is the most important to you?

- How do you currently see that you may be exercising this value in your life?

Journal Entry #3—A Personal Ethical Dilemma

Identify a value conflict or ethical question you have encountered in your life. Include your thoughts and feelings, response to the dilemma, and what you might do in the future with a similar situation. Discuss how your values related to this issue may impact your profession.

CHAPTER 7

Social Work Perspectives and Methods

Emily's BSW provided her with the knowledge and skills to work with individuals, families, groups, and communities. In her first job as an adult services worker in a small multiservice community service agency, she intervened on all these levels. On the individual level, she worked with the older adults through the home-maker/chore program as well as with visually impaired persons and female wel-fare recipients who were seeking employment. In each of these programs, she also worked with the clients' families. On the group level, Emily facilitated a sup-port group for persons who had recently lost their vision. Finally, at the commu-nity level, Emily helped a community group develop a telephone reassurance program in which volunteers from the Senior Center telephoned homebound older adults each day to ensure their safety and well-being. Emily helped the Center committee oversee this program and set policy. As a result of her involve-ment with the Senior Center group, Emily became part of a community task force that included community agencies and older adults to create an annual community-wide resource and wellness fair. Emily performed all these levels of social work in just one job. Her varied activities are an example of generalist social work practice.

Both the 1999 NASW *Code of Ethics* and the Council on Social Work Educa-tion (CSWE) describe bachelor-level social work practice in terms of the frame-work known as **generalist social work practice.** At this level, social workers have a broad-based set of knowledge and skills that they can use for assessing and intervening with competence at multiple levels. One of the six values included in the *Code of Ethics*, Importance of Human Relationships, calls on social workers to ". . . strengthen relationships among people in a purposeful effort to promote, restore, maintain, and enhance the well-being of individuals, families, social groups, organizations, and communities." In the 2001 version of the CSWE *Educational Policy and Accreditation Standards*, CSWE-accredited BSW programs are required to include content on working with individuals, families, groups, organizations, and communities. In this chapter, we define and explore the generalist area of social work education and practice from both theoretical and practice perspectives.

HISTORY OF GENERALIST SOCIAL WORK PRACTICE

Although the idea of providing services to individuals, groups, and communities is rooted in the origins of the profession, the generalist practice is a relatively recent development in the profession. Historically, two movements that shaped contemporary social work practice helped both to separate and to unite the profession around the concept of generalist practice. Specifically, the Charity Organization Society, which emphasized the individual, and the settlement house movement, with an emphasis on groups and communities, paved the way for three distinct theoretical and service paths: individual casework, group work, and community organization (Landon, 1995). However, the social turmoil of the 1960s prompted the profession to consider an approach to social work practice that would integrate these three modalities in an effort to provide more comprehensive services (Landon, 1995). This shift of philosophy led to the emergence of the generalist perspective.

Interest in a universal approach to social work practice resulted in the emergence of the baccalaureate in social work. Beginning in the 1960s and 1970s, BSW programs emerged as a strategy for promoting the generalist social work practice model. Before this period, the only social work degrees granted were at the master's level. Social work scholars and practitioners agreed that practitioners with BSWs, trained in the generalist perspective, could best fulfill the needs for professional services, particularly in inner-city and rural areas and the public sector. The generalist practice model provides a solid preparation for the graduate social work degree, which focuses on a specialty area of concentration. The BSW curriculum prepares generalist practitioners, and the MSW curriculum begins with a generalist perspective, but offers specialization through concentration in particular areas of study.

- Listen to others with understanding and purpose using such strategies as attending, paraphrasing, empathy and reflecting feeling, focusing, and summarizing.
- Elicit information and assemble relevant facts to prepare a social history, assessment, and report through exploring (open and closed responses), asking and reflecting meaning, and critical thinking.
- Create and maintain professional helping relationships.
- Observe and interpret verbal and nonverbal behavior, and use knowledge of personality theory and diagnostic methods.
- Engage clients (including individuals, families, groups, and communities) to resolve their own problems and gain trust.
- Discuss sensitive emotional subjects supportively and without being threatening.
- Create innovative solutions to clients' needs.
- Determine the need to terminate the therapeutic relationship.
- Conduct research or interpret findings of research and professional literature.
- Mediate and negotiate between conflicting parties.
- Provide interorganizational liaison services.
- Interpret and communicate social needs to funding sources, public, or legislators.

Source: Barker, 2003, pp. 409–10

LEVELS OF GENERALIST SOCIAL WORK PRACTICE

Perhaps the greatest strength of the generalist approach is that social work skills can be transferred to different types of situations that allow for influencing social change on a structural as well as personal level. As you know, social workers work with client systems at the individual, family, group, and community levels. Within generalist practice, the nature of the intervention is determined by the "size" of the client system. Generalist social work practice takes place at three levels: the individual and family level, the group level, and the organization and community level. In 1982, NASW proposed 12 essential skills for social work practice. These skills, shown in Box 7.1, are intentionally generic, thus making them applicable for all levels and phases of social work practice.

- *Individual and family level:* The most basic level of generalist social work practice is intervention with individuals and families. Interventions on this level can include working one-on-one with an elder and her or his family toward developing a post–hospital discharge plan or with a victim of sexual assault and her or his significant others. Consider the social worker who conducts the home study for a couple seeking to adopt a child. The worker interviews the couple to determine their motivation and qualifications for adoption, compiles a written assessment, and guides them through the legal adoption process. Working with individuals and families can sometimes provide insight into the gaps and concerns of the larger service delivery system.

- *Group level:* While engaged in the process of working with groups, the social worker may discover that social work practice on the group level demands many of the skills developed for working with individuals. Group-level practice can include assisting a group of families seeking family therapy, instituting a support group for persons with eating disorders, and providing guidance to a group seeking to eradicate the drug problems of young people in their neighborhood. Returning to the example of the couple seeking to adopt a child, the social worker may work at the group level by participating with the couple in a support group for adoptive parents.

- *Organization and community level:* At this level social work practice involves interventions with large groups, organizations, and communities of all sizes. The practitioner can be engaged in such varied activities as locality development (intervention targeted at enhancing a specific geographic area or region); analysis and implementation of policy; advocacy activities (for example, lobbying, letter writing, and public speaking); and administration (for example, personnel, supervision, budgeting, and grant writing). At the organization and community level, the adoption social worker may promote legislation that will open adoption records for adult adoptees, or create a community task force to address a need for improved economic stability.

Training in generalist practice enables the social worker to practice ethically and competently at all three levels. Moreover, most social work positions require the social worker to function at all three levels at some point. Most generalist practitioners develop a preference for one or two of the areas, although these preferences frequently change over the years of practice. For example, you might begin your career working with individuals in direct service but find later that you have a desire to move into social work administration. This is a major benefit of being a social worker: Your knowledge, skills, and values provide you with mobility.

GENERALIST SOCIAL WORK SKILLS AND ROLES

Regardless of where or with whom a beginning social worker intervenes, she or he must acquire a basic set of skills. Recently, one NASW chapter compiled a list, "100 Skills of the Professional Social Worker." Reproduced in Box 7.2, the

BOX 7.2

100 Skills of the Professional Social Worker

Activism	Financial counseling	Political action
Administration	Fund-raising	Post-discharge follow-up
Adoption	Gestalt therapy	Prevention
Advocacy	Goal setting	Problem evaluation
Applied research	Grant writing	Problem-focused therapy
Assessment	Grass-roots organizing	Problem resolution
Basic skills training	Group therapy	Program administration
Behavior therapy	Health education	Program planning
Brief therapy	Health planning	Psychosocial assessment
Career counseling	Home studies	Public relations
Case management	Independent practice	Qualitative research
Child advocacy	Information and referral	Quantitative research
Client and family conferences	Intake	Rational-emotive therapy
Client and family education	Interagency collaboration	Reality therapy
Client screening	Interdisciplinary collaboration	Recording
Coaching	Intervention	Referring
Coalition building	Interviewing	Residential treatment
Cognitive therapy	Legislative advocacy	Resource allocation
Community organization	Life skills education	Role playing
Conflict resolution	Lobbying	Service contracting
Conjoint therapy	Mandated reporting	Service coordination
Consultation	Marital therapy	Short-term therapy
Continuity of care	Mediation	Social action
Coping skills	Milieu therapy	Social work education
Counseling	Needs assessment	Staff development
Crisis intervention	Negotiation	Supervision
Data collection	Networking	Support group
Direct practice	Outcome evaluation	Task-centered casework
Discharge planning	Outreach	Teach coping skills
Divorce therapy	Parent training	Team player
Empowerment	Placement	Termination
Expert witness	Planning	Treatment planning
Family therapy	Policy analysis	Utilization review
	Policy development	

Source: Akin, 1998

list is a testament to the wide variety of skills that are part of the social work repertoire. This array of skills enables generalist social workers to function in a number of different and varied roles and in a variety of situations. Roles of generalist social workers who perform at the individual, family, group, organization, and community levels can be categorized as

- Broker
- Teacher/educator
- Enabler
- Advocate
- Mobilizer
- Mediator
- Caseworker

In functioning as a **broker**, the social worker facilitates a client system's access to needed resources. Broker activities could include helping an elderly client apply for assistance with his heating bill, assisting a group of parents of children with attention deficit disorder to arrange a meeting with the school board to improve school-based services, or working with another social service agency to streamline their application process for their clients.

In the role of **educator**, the generalist practitioner might teach job skills to a person with a developmental disability, help a group of adolescents with behavioral disorders to develop anger management skills, or train a group of social workers in a new therapeutic intervention modality.

Working with client systems to facilitate a planned change, the **enabler** intervenes with individuals, families, and groups in therapeutic situations and with organizations and communities to facilitate social change. As an enabler or facilitator, the social worker's role is to help the client system mobilize itself to meet an agreed-upon goal. A facilitator can work one-on-one with individuals and families, with small-scale therapeutic or self-help groups, as well as with larger groups seeking social and political change.

In the role of **advocate**, the social worker voices the needs of a client group to a larger group or the entire society for the purpose of achieving social justice. For example, the social worker can advocate on behalf of a client at the adoption hearing, or she or he can lobby the state legislature to enact laws to address the needs of foster children.

In the role of **mobilizer**, generalists help individuals and groups to organize and carry out activities designed to identify and meet their needs. On the individual and family level, the social worker may mobilize the friends and family of a person newly diagnosed with a brain tumor to provide food, support, and transportation. When working with groups and communities, the social worker may mobilize a group to protest the exclusion of gays, lesbians, bisexuals, and transgendered persons from a city's marriage registry.

Finding a common ground among conflicting groups with the aim of meeting a mutual goal is the role of the **mediator.** For example, social workers can conduct mediation with divorcing couples, landlords and tenants, and political parties.

A frequently sought-after job for social workers with BSWs, **caseworkers** are on the front lines of social service delivery, where they coordinate the services and resources needed by clients. For example, a caseworker for a person with severe and persistent mental illness may coordinate housing, mental health, financial, employment, and transportation services for the client. Social work practice at the group, organization, and community levels is built on a working knowledge of case management skills that enables the social worker to understand individual group members' needs.

THEORY IN GENERALIST SOCIAL WORK PRACTICE

The knowledge and skills of the competent generalist are based on a framework that is known to be effective for the client system. Theoretical frameworks that are empirically tested through research can provide the practicing social worker with a foundation for determining the type and direction of the assessment, intervention, and evaluation of the client relationship.

For our purposes, a **theory** is defined as an empirically tested concept used to explain a behavior, process, or phenomenon and develop a plan for intervention (Turner, 1995). A theoretically and empirically based practice approach is one that has been tested in controlled situations so that social workers have evidence that a particular approach is appropriate for specific populations. Their practice methods are not speculative or performed by trial and error. Such practice, known as **evidence-based practice,** uses research to guide the social worker in developing knowledge and skills for client system interventions. The ability to link theory with practice and articulate the who, what, when, where, why, and how of all interactions and activities in which social workers engage to influence or facilitate change differentiates the professional from the nonprofessional or the paraprofessional worker.

In the following sections, we explore several of the theoretical frameworks that have become hallmarks of the social work profession, particularly generalist social work practice. Social work theories are generated from actual practice and tested by research. Remember too that although the integration of theory with practice is critical to effective interventions, applying theory in practice situations can be challenging. Therefore, social workers must be well trained in a variety of perspectives so that the application of theory becomes a natural part of the delivery of services.

You have already been introduced to two of these theories in earlier chapters—the ecological and strengths perspectives, for example. We will look at these in more detail here, along with systems theory and the solution-focused perspective. These frameworks can be helpful in practicing at all levels. A final note will point out the way that social work draws on theory from other disciplines.

Person-in-Environment and Ecological Perspectives

In Emily's work with the senior homemaker/chore program, she came to appreciate the importance of viewing clients within the context of their social and physical environment. The homemaker/chore service provides in-home services to older adults who are unable to perform those tasks needed to maintain independent living. The typical homemaker/chore service client is an older adult with physical health problems who lives alone. Without the support of this program, the individual would likely have to enter a residential long-term care facility.

Marietta, a 78-year-old, widowed, African American woman living alone in a rental house, taught Emily the importance of seeing the "big picture." Marietta was referred to Emily's agency by her family physician, Dr. Stephens, who was concerned about Marietta's ability to care for herself. In her initial assessment of Marietta's situation, Emily was ready to recommend that Marietta be placed in a nursing home due to her physical frailty, vision problems, lack of ability to cook or maintain her house, limited income, and apparent lack of social support.

Through her assessment, Emily learned that Marietta's only son had recently died and she was estranged from her daughter-in-law and adult grandchildren because she believed they had not provided her son with adequate care during his illness. Marietta's daughter lived nearby, but they were frequently in conflict because Marietta believed her daughter should leave her husband because he was abusive to her when he was drinking. Marietta's only living sister suffered from Alzheimer's disease and was no longer able to care for herself. Marietta told Emily that she did not believe her children or sister would help her, and she refused to consider moving in with any of them.

Upon conducting a more thorough assessment, Emily learned that Marietta had close ties with her neighbors, church, and several of her nieces and nephews. Although she did need in-home services to continue living independently, she was part of a large, close, and supportive network of caregivers.

We begin our journey through the theoretical frameworks used in generalist social work practice by first examining two key perspectives: the person-in-environment and ecological perspectives. The profession has a long history of emphasizing the **person-in-environment perspective**, which perceives each individual as an interactive participant in a larger physical and social environmental system (Barker, 2003). The person-in-environment perspective enables social workers to understand the complexities of clients' lives by emphasizing the impact of the physical and social environment on the person. Had Emily not used this approach with Marietta, she would not have recognized that Marietta was only one part of a larger, supportive system.

As early as the 1950s, social work scholars were urging practitioners to consider the interaction between the individual and the larger world. This transition began in the 1960s, when interest in the social environment was heightened (Germain & Gitterman, 1995). A landmark event in this movement occurred in 1973, when social work scholar Carel Germain introduced the ecological perspective for social work. This perspective is based on the premise that the relationship between the individual and her or his social environment determines the individual's life situation. Examining the interaction between the client system and the larger social and physical environment is the focus for understanding human behavior, rather than looking to the cause of the interaction. For example, understanding the impact of a child's relationships with her family on her ability to perform well academically is more important than explaining the cause of the parent-child interactions.

The original ecological model encompassed 10 conceptual components, with 6 concepts added later (Germain & Gitterman, 1995). The 16 concepts are described in Table 7.1. The model provides a strategy for identifying the client system; assessing the client's dilemma in terms of strengths, supports, resources, and previous coping and adaptive skills; and intervening with the client with a number of possibilities. The generalist social worker can intervene with the person and use different facets of the person's system (for example, family, employer, or church) to address the client's needs. The practitioner can then use an ecological perspective at the individual, family, group, organization, and community levels. For example, Emily identified existing family and community resources and mobilized those resources to enable Marietta to continue living in her own home.

ECOLOGICAL CONCEPTS	DESCRIPTION
ORIGINAL MODEL	
Person-environment fit	The ability of client system to positively engage with the environment—a positive fit suggests the client system has adapted successfully.
Adaptations	To maintain a stable person-environment fit, systems constantly adapt to changing environment.
Life stressors	The person-environment fit may be compromised if the client system is unable to adapt to life crises.
Stress	The individual's response to a life stressor.
Coping measures	To maintain a desired person-environment fit, systems develop methods for adapting to life stresses.
Relatedness	Connections that people make with others in their environment; they serve as resources for adaptations.
Competence	Systems must have the resources to function effectively.
Self-esteem	The person's self-perception influences her/his ability to feel competence.
Self-direction	The client system's ability to feel control over itself impacts self-esteem, competence, and ability to adapt to life stresses.
Habitat and niche	Referring to clients' physical space and place within that space, habitat and niche can determine the client system's well-being.
ADDED CONCEPTS	
Coercive power	Poverty, isms, and homelessness are examples of "social pollutions" that inhibit the client system's ability to adapt and fit with the environment.
Exploitative power	Another stressor, exploitative power is the oppression of one group over another.
Life course	Ecologically, the path of a client's life is fluid, changing, and unique.
Individual time	The meaning that the client system attaches to life experiences.
Historical time	The impact of historical and social change on the client system.
Social time	The client system's transitions and life events are a product of social, biological, economic, demographic, and culture factors.

Source: Germain & Gitterman, 1995

TABLE 7.1

Basic Concepts of the Ecological Perspective

The Social Work Library

Review the works by Germain and Gitterman written in 1976, 1980, and 1996 to gain an awareness of the development of this important social work framework.

Systems Theory

An important theoretical framework that incorporates certain aspects of the environmental perspectives is **systems theory**. Strongly influenced by biological theory, systems theory evolves, logically enough, from the concept of a system, which comprises multiple components that interact with one another to create an entire entity. From a social work perspective, a **system** can be a physical and/or social entity that includes individuals, families, groups, organizations, communities, and even nations. You have no doubt noticed from your reading so far that the persons or groups served by social workers are considered **client systems**, but the term is used interchangeably with **clients**.

Every system is made up of elements, which can be any physical, social, or personal entity that is orderly, interactive, and functional. For example, a person may be part of a system that is composed of physical elements such as the individual's household, neighborhood, community, city, country, and world. Social elements can include the client system's relationships with persons that make up the environment in which the client lives. A system is composed of the various parts that interact with one another to contribute to the overall functioning of the system. A change in one element affects all of the other elements.

Systems Theory Concepts   The systems theory framework helps social workers view client systems within the context of their interactions within a larger environment and explains human behavior in terms of the reciprocal relationships among the elements in the system. Whereas the ecological model illuminates the relationship between a client system and the environment, systems theory provides a way of understanding the change process that the client system undergoes.

To understand change from a systemic perspective, consider that when one part of a system changes, the entire system must change. For example, when a family member is added or removed from a family system for any reason, the system must change because the addition or loss creates a different configuration of people, relationships, required tasks, and available resources. Just as natural change can modify a system, a social work intervention can prompt a system to change. In fact, the mere presence of a social worker as a "change agent" means that the worker becomes part of the system, thus producing a change. To function, a system must be dynamic and flexible.

Viewing the person, family, group, or community as a part of a larger system has numerous implications for generalist social work practice. For example, a systems approach enables the generalist practitioner to consider the client system within the larger context of the environment in which the client lives. Such a framing enables the social worker to understand relationships and factors that affect the client system as a result of interactions between the client and the environment. Defining the client within a larger context further provides the social worker an opportunity to target multiple components of the system for intervention. Lastly, viewing the client system from a systemic perspective incorporates the unique qualities of the client and emphasizes the dynamic nature of human interactions.

Systems Theory in Generalist Practice   Now that you are familiar with the systems framework, let us apply this framework to generalist social work practice. Due to the universality of systems theory, the concepts can be applied to virtually every level and type of social work relationship. In order to apply systems concepts, social workers use tools to systemically assess and intervene in client situations.

One such tool is the **ecomap.** Developed by Ann Hartman in 1975 as a strategy for systemically assessing individuals and families, the ecomap depicts the type and quality of relationships along with the dynamic nature of those relationships (Hartman, 1978). The ecomap can be used at all levels of social work practice.

Using Emily's experience with Marietta, described earlier in this chapter, an ecomap is presented in Exhibit 7.1. As you can see, each component of the client system is identified within a circle. The quality of the relationships can then be coded using the various types of lines. In addition to identifying the quality of the relationship by drawing lines, arrows indicate the flow of energy and resources that are invested in and derived from that relationship. After lines and arrows are drawn from the individual to each part of the sub- or suprasystems, the social worker and the client can review the ecomap together to identify strengths, stressors, and areas for change. An imbalance of energy either flowing into or out of a relationship may indicate an area for change.

By placing the client and her or his household members in the center circle and other persons and resources in the circles that surround the client, the ecomap heightens a client's awareness of the strengths and patterns of current relationships in her or his life. In addition, it serves as a strategy to identify changes the client would like to make in those relationships. Specifically, if the client would like to change a part of her or his life, the resources and specific areas that would have to be changed in order to achieve that goal are laid out on the ecomap. The ecomap is useful with larger systems (for example, neighborhoods) to identify links within and outside the system. This tool can be used to establish a social work relationship at multiple levels, monitor change, and evaluate progress at the termination of the professional relationship.

Looking at the ecomap to assess Marietta's social environment, you can see that the relationships in her life are sources of both support and stress, and

EXHIBIT 7.1

Ecomap

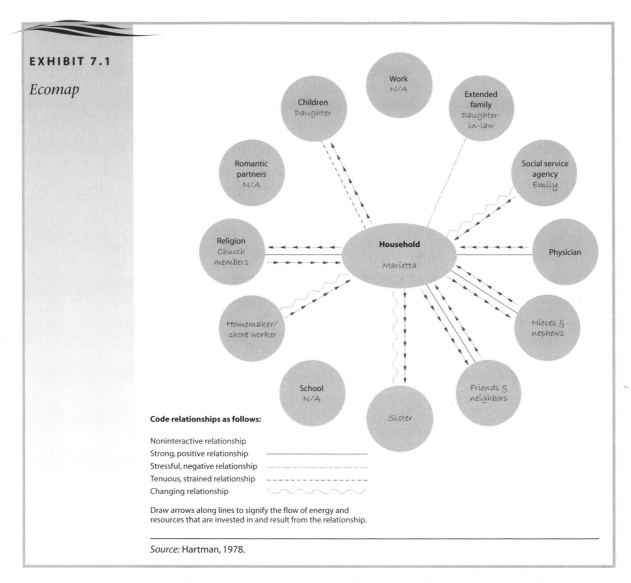

Code relationships as follows:

Noninteractive relationship
Strong, positive relationship
Stressful, negative relationship
Tenuous, strained relationship
Changing relationship

Draw arrows along lines to signify the flow of energy and
resources that are invested in and result from the relationship.

Source: Hartman, 1978.

several are in a state of change. The relationships that Marietta has with her
nieces and nephews, her neighbors, the members of her church, and her physician serve as strengths for her. Marietta's relationship with her sister is changing, as her sister's memory is deteriorating due to Alzheimer's disease. Stressors
in Marietta's life include the relationships with her estranged daughter-in-law
and her daughter. The new relationships that Marietta is developing with Emily
and, later, the homemaker/chore worker have the potential to be sources of social support, but they are still being stabilized. Having the ecomap as a tool for
assessment in Marietta's situation enabled Emily to identify existing resources
and strengths and target areas for intervention.

Strengths-Based and Empowerment Perspectives

While working at the public welfare agency, Emily was taking her turn at "intake"—seeing walk-in or call-in clients who were in crisis. Sarah, a 16-year-old, walked into the office and explained that she found the agency address in the telephone directory. She had her one-day-old daughter with her, and she told Emily that she delivered the baby at her girlfriend's house (in the bathroom with only her friend present). Neither Sarah's nor her friend's parents were aware of the birth. The friend's parents were out of town. By Sarah's calculations, the baby was near full-term. Neither Sarah nor the baby had seen a health care provider. Sarah was nursing the baby, and from Emily's quick assessment, the baby appeared to be healthy. Sarah refused to identify the father, but Emily suspected the father might be her 19-year-old stepbrother. Her verbal and nonverbal cues raised Emily's suspicions.

Sarah appeared extremely distraught, asserting that she "had to do something with this baby now." However, she was also adamant that she would not involve her parents, or anyone else, in her situation. She reported that she was an above-average student, she was active in a service organization, and she worked part-time at a fast-food restaurant. She claimed to have dated casually, but denied that she was currently involved in any serious relationship. She informed Emily that her family belonged to a conservative fundamentalist religion, and she feared severe consequences if they discovered that she had become pregnant.

Initially, this case may seem overwhelming, as Emily is faced with multiple challenges: Sarah, a minor who may have been sexually assaulted by a family member, delivers her own child without benefit of health care and is fearful of being discovered by her family. What strengths can there be in a situation such as this one? Let us look at this case more closely to determine the strengths that exist. First, Sarah was courageous and resourceful enough to deliver the baby safely (seemingly), nurse the baby, and come to Emily's agency for help. She has a supportive friend, attends school and performs well academically, has a job, and is involved in community service. Despite all the challenges Emily will face in working with Sarah's situation, there are strengths on which to build: Sarah has a history of being responsible, she is concerned for the child, and she is asking for help. Seeing Sarah through the eyes of her strengths as opposed to her deficits is the essence of strengths-based social work practice.

Focusing the client-worker relationship on client strengths has been a recent revolution in the social work profession. Historically, social workers were trained in the problem, or pathology, model of assessment and intervention. In this model, the social worker focuses first and foremost on the problems, weaknesses, and inadequacies of the client system. The shift to the strengths-based perspective occurred within the social work community during the 1990s (Saleebey, 1997). Conceived originally as a strategy for working with persons with severe and persistent mental illness, the strengths approach is now used with an array of client populations, in large part because emphasizing client strengths is consistent with the values and ethical code of the social work profession. For example, the social work value of recognizing client uniqueness and self-worth is inherently a strengths perspective.

The Social Work Library

Read Saleebey's article to better understand the extensions and cautions of the strengths-based perspective.

Strengths-Based and Empowerment Concepts "Problems versus possibilities" is the basis of the strengths-based perspective. Being a strengths-based social worker means that "*everything* you do as a social worker will be predicated, in some way, on helping to discover and embellish, explore, and exploit clients' strengths and resources in the service of assisting them to achieve their goals, realize their dreams, and shed the irons of their own inhibitions and misgivings" (Saleebey, 1997, p. 3). Although the strengths approach is relatively simple to comprehend, it can be challenging to put into practice for both the client system and the social worker. Client systems in crisis, or who have multiple challenges, may have difficulty perceiving any strengths in either themselves or their situations. Social workers will work with clients who can be hostile, resistant, or who have a history of inappropriate or illegal behavior. Assessing strengths in these situations is just as important to building a collaborative working relationship. Change occurs best when working with clients' strengths and assets.

Considered the key to the implementation of the strengths-based perspective, **empowerment** is the process of enabling individuals, groups, and communities to enhance their ability (power) in order to bring about desired changes (Gutiérrez, 1994). Using a systems framework to understand the environment in which the client system functions and then building on the existing and available strengths, assets, and resources, empowerment becomes the process used by the social worker and the client system to facilitate the change process. Identifying and understanding the social environment and its strengths are the first steps in helping the client(s) feel empowered to make a change.

The strengths-based framework assumes that building on a client's strengths can serve to empower the client to change, a process that can be collaborative, dynamic, and evolving. This theory is based on five principles, as follows (Saleebey, 1997):

- *Every individual, group, family, and community has strengths:* To discern client system strengths, the social worker must respect and value the client's "story" and knowledge of their situation. For example, the strength of a client suffering from severe clinical depression may be that she or he was able to get out of bed three days this week as opposed to only one day last week.

- *Trauma and abuse, illness, and struggle may be injurious, but they may also be sources of challenge and opportunity:* Without minimizing the emotional and physical scars that come from a painful or traumatic experience, the social worker helps the client to see that she or he can use the experience to learn and grow in order to move beyond the self-defeating perception of her- or himself as victim or failure. Think of the example of a neighborhood in which the older-adult residents are afraid to leave their homes. Mobilized by the social worker, the residents are empowered to rally together and organize a community center where they can go and participate in safety.

- *Assume that you do not know the upper limits of the capacity to grow and change, and take individual, group, and community aspirations seriously:* The social worker can empower client systems to think beyond negative life experiences, disabilities, or challenges, with the aim of expanding the client's self-vision of capacities and possibilities. Consider, for example, a middle-aged mother who dropped out of high school and collects public assistance but who goes on to finish high school, community college, and college to become a social worker.

- *We best serve clients by collaborating with them:* Respecting clients' knowledge and expertise in their own lives or communities is the first step in developing a collaborative relationship. Collaborating with the client system creates the opportunity to use the worker's and client's strengths and resources—a strategy that diminishes the prospect for further victimization of the client. For example, consider a situation in which the social worker facilitates a meeting between police and a group of immigrants whose neighborhood is the target of hate crimes to discuss strategies for addressing the problem.

- *Every environment is full of resources:* Regardless of the level of chaos or the sparseness of obvious strengths, the strengths-based social worker can identify resources on which to build an intervention plan with the client system. For example, a person who is homeless, addicted to drugs, and estranged from his family comes to a program for homeless military veterans. The very fact that the man has come for help constitutes a strength in this situation.

Strengths-Based and Empowerment Perspectives in Generalist Practice

Do things with people, not for people.
—JANE ADDAMS

Working *with* people is to empower them. Approaching every social work situation with the five principles of the strengths-based perspective just described sets the stage for an empowering and liberating social work encounter. To further understand the strengths and empowerment perspectives, a social worker needs skills to act on the principles. A useful strategy is to compare the client–social worker relationship from both a strengths and a deficit perspective. Table 7.2 depicts a comparison of the two models (Saleebey, 1996, p. 298).

A next step in becoming a strengths- and empowerment-based social worker is to develop the ability to identify strengths that will enable the

TABLE 7.2

Comparison of Deficits and Strengths Models

THE ISSUE	FROM THE DEFICITS PERSPECTIVE	FROM THE STRENGTHS-BASED PERSPECTIVE
The person is . . .	the case, symptoms, and the diagnosis	unique, and her/his traits are strengths
The intervention is . . .	problem focused	possibility focused
The client's "stories" are . . .	reinterpreted by the expert	a way to know and appreciate the client
The social worker's viewpoint is . . .	skepticism of the client's "stories" and rationalizations	knowledge of the person from the inside out
Childhood trauma can . . .	predict adult pathology	either weaken or strengthen the client in adulthood
The expert on the client's life is . . .	the social worker	the client
The intervention is determined by . . .	the social worker	the client's aspirations
Possibilities and development are . . .	limited by the client's pathology	opened by the client's possibilities and development
Resources and skills are . . .	possessed by the social worker	possessed by the client and the social worker
The focus of the relationship is . . .	symptom reduction	moving, affirming, and strengthening

Source: Adapted from Saleebey, 1996

client system to think and respond with a sense of empowerment. The following is a list of possibilities that a social worker might be able to identify in a given intervention (Saleebey, 1997). Can you think of other areas for developing questions to add to this list—from your own life experiences or those of others?

- Lessons learned about self, others, and the environment around the client system.

- Personal qualities, traits, and virtues.

- Knowledge of the world that surrounds the client system.

- Talents possessed by the client system.

- Cultural and personal stories.

- Resources found within the client system's community.

Social workers who use strengths-based empowerment strategies should keep in mind that for many clients, this may be the first time a helping professional has prompted them to consider their life stories in terms of what's right instead of what's wrong with them. In this sense, an empowerment-based approach can serve as a valuable learning experience for both the social worker and the client.

Returning to Emily's experience in working with Sarah, consider the strategies she could use to empower Sarah to take action in her situation. Building on Sarah's strengths of being responsible, having concern for the well-being of the baby, and the fact that she sought help for herself and the infant, Emily may begin by commending Sarah for these actions. Acknowledging the client's strengths is a step toward establishing rapport and building trust so that the client views the social worker as a partner in resolving a crisis. Emily can then explore with Sarah the options that are desired, realistic, and necessary.

From a legal and ethical perspective, it is unrealistic for Sarah's parents not to be informed about the birth and possible sexual assault by the stepbrother. Working from an empowerment approach, Emily can help Sarah develop a strategy with which she can feel safe to talk with them. For instance, Emily can offer to be with Sarah when she talks to her parents. In addition, let us assume Sarah and Emily are in one of the 42 states that have "safe haven" laws that protect parents from prosecution if they take their newborn child to a designated site (for example, a hospital, police station, or child welfare agency) within a specified amount of time. If they are in one of these states, Emily can assure Sarah that she will have legal protection because she brought her child to a designated safe place. Can you think of additional strategies that Emily can use to help Sarah feel empowered?

Solution-Focused Perspective

While working as a social worker for a home health agency, Emily was assigned to work with Charlie, a 30-year-old man recently discharged from the hospital after experiencing a gunshot wound. The gunshot resulted in a spinal cord injury, leaving Charlie a paraplegic (paralyzed from the waist down). When Emily first visited Charlie, he was hostile and refused to discuss any further rehabilitation. Emily suspected that Charlie was frightened and depressed, so she began to talk with him about the aspirations he had as a child. Charlie wanted to be a minister in his church, but he strayed from that goal when he dropped out of college.

Through their conversations, Emily helped Charlie to realize that his disability need not prohibit him from returning to college and becoming a minister. Over time, Emily and Charlie reconstructed his misconceptions of his abilities, and they developed a plan for working with the occupational and physical therapists so that Charlie could reapply to college and achieve his goal of joining the ministry.

Solution-Focused Concepts   The **solution-focused perspective** is an approach in which the social worker helps the client to construct or reconstruct her or his reality in regard to a challenging life situation. Solution-focused practice, based on the assumption that people are competent and have the solution, is directed toward identifying client system strengths and using those strengths to encourage the client's self-perception in a more functional light. Together, the client system and social worker then create an intervention plan that encompasses specific behavioral tasks aimed at the goal. The social worker's role is to help clients modify the ways they perceive the situation and interact with others. Typically, the client system has a previously successful experience on which to build for this situation.

In her work with Charlie, Emily employed a solution-focused approach. She first helped him identify his goals and recognize strengths he was not even aware he possessed. She and Charlie then collaborated to create behavioral strategies to accomplish his goals.

Solution-Focused Perspective in Generalist Practice   Solution-focused practice has been used primarily as a tool for working with individuals and families in clinical settings because of its emphasis on establishing individual goals and behavior change. Nevertheless, it can be used at all levels of generalist practice. At the group, organization, and community levels, the solution-focused social worker can help the group recognize its collective strengths and assets. In fact, the members can discover group strengths that do not exist on an individual level. The social worker can then help the group to agree on specific goals and mobilize to achieve those goals.

As an example, consider the case of a student who presents because of failing grades in academic work. The social worker asks if this is a recent situation, and the student responds that it is. The social worker uses a strengths-based, solution-focused approach and asks the student to describe a time when he was making better grades. Notice that instead of focusing on things that are not going well, the social worker builds on the student's strengths. The social worker continues by asking the student to speculate as to why he was previously getting better grades. Upon hearing the student respond that his grades were better when he did his homework, asked for help from the teacher, and played fewer video games, the social worker may say, "So, you made better grades when you completed your homework, asked for help, and played fewer video games." Therein lies the solution. Box 7.3 lists some possible types of questions that can be used in a solution-focused approach.

Integration of Social Work Theory

In this chapter we have discussed each theory separately, but keep in mind that these theoretical perspectives are not mutually exclusive. Just the opposite, they can frequently complement one another. For example, the person-in-environment perspective provides the foundation for identifying strengths and seeing the client system as part of a larger environment, while the ecological and systems frameworks influence each other and enable the social worker to compartmentalize the distinctive environmental influences that impact the client's life experiences. Similarly, thinking systemically helps the social worker to focus on the client's relationships with other elements within the system. The strengths-based and empowerment perspectives emanate from the ecological and systems models, while solution-focused practice is one application of these influences. These frameworks can also be integrated with other theoretical approaches to develop interventions for specific situations. Exhibit 7.2 depicts the way in which the theories and frameworks discussed in this chapter interrelate and guide one another.

Information integrated from other disciplines has also been instrumental in the development of social workers' knowledge and skills. **Eclecticism** is the process of using knowledge and skills derived from multiple theoretical concepts that are most appropriate to the client system, population, or situation at

BOX 7.3

Questions for a Solution-Focused Approach

PAST SUCCESS QUESTIONS

- It must not have been easy to grow up with cerebral palsy. How were you able to do so well in school?
- What skills did you learn in your last job?

EXCEPTION FINDING QUESTIONS (WHAT WAS IT LIKE WHEN PROBLEMS DID NOT OCCUR)

- What was your family life like when your parents were not fighting?
- What is it like for the rest of you in the group when Joe is not angry and hostile?

MIRACLE QUESTIONS

- What would your life be like if you were able to reach your goal of graduating from college?
- What do you need to accomplish the goal of graduating from college, and how can I help you?

SCALING QUESTIONS (USING A NUMERIC SCALE TO RATE PAST, PRESENT, AND FUTURE STATUS)

- On a scale of 1 to 10, how motivated are you to quit smoking? Where do you need to be to actually quit smoking? What do you need to do to get from 5 to 8?

COPING QUESTIONS

- When you feel like drinking again, what do you do to stop yourself?
- You and your children were homeless last year. What did you do to change that?
- How will you know when things are going well in your life? What will you be doing, who will you be with, and how will you be feeling, thinking, and acting?

Source: Berg, 1994, pp. 84–119

hand. The following is a sampling of the theoretical influences that social work has gained from other professional disciplines:

- Theory from the field of sociology has aided the social work profession in understanding relationships between people and their environments, particularly with regard to class, culture, and inequality issues.

- Anthropological theory has helped social workers understand the origins and relationships of the wide diversity of groups served by social workers.

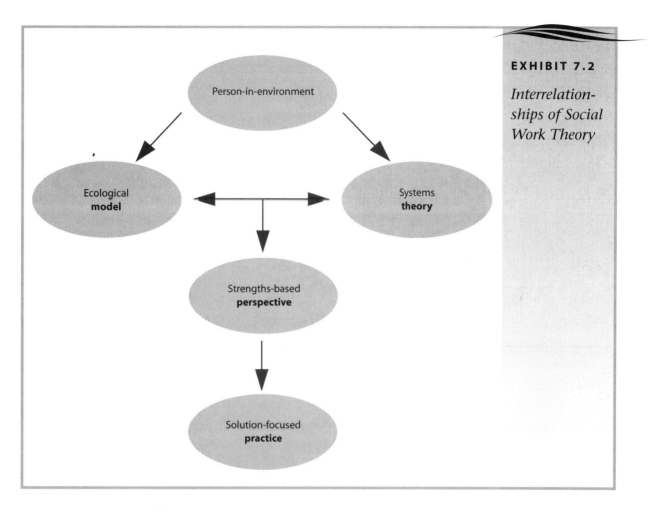

EXHIBIT 7.2

*Interrelation-
ships of Social
Work Theory*

- Psychological theories have been invaluable for enhancing social workers' insights into human behavior and for developing therapeutic treatment approaches.

- Political science theories have been helpful in understanding issues related to government, the political process and environment, and power and control.

- Economic theory has helped the profession understand the ways in which the economy impacts the economic conditions in which client systems live and in the development of strategies for effecting change in the economic lives of persons living in poverty.

- Biological theory has been influential in several areas of social work, including human biological functioning and health and disease issues.

Theories from other disciplines and schools of thought have enhanced the development of effective intervention strategies for working with client and system issues that span the spectrum of our society. As social workers serve such a diverse and wide-ranging spectrum of society, multiple approaches are needed for use across populations, situations, and levels of practice. To adopt an eclectic approach, the social worker clearly must be well versed in a number of theoretical perspectives and processes.

CONCLUSION

This chapter has explored the role of the generalist social worker and the theoretical frameworks that guide and inform generalist social work practice. Applying these theoretical concepts to your practice can feel like an overwhelming challenge, particularly because there are so many theories from which to choose. Nevertheless, these constructs provide a basis on which to build your knowledge of effective and ethical social work practice.

Only a small number of the many available theoretical approaches are included in this chapter. As you continue the lifelong process of social work education, you will add other theoretical constructs to your repertoire of conceptual frameworks. For additional information on the social work profession and generalist practice, resources that may be helpful include the Council on Social Work Education's *Educational Policy and Accreditation Standards* and the National Association of Social Workers *Code of Ethics*.

MAIN POINTS

- Generalist social work practice provides for assessment and intervention at three levels: individuals and families, groups, and organizations and communities. The generalist social worker employs a variety of skills and plays many roles, including educator, advocate, and mediator.

- The person-in-environment perspective views the individual within the context of the environment in which she or he lives. This perspective is the foundation of social work theoretical approaches.

- The ecological perspective is used to understand the meaning of the interactions between client systems and the environment in which they exist.

- Building on the ecological model, systems theory is a framework that helps social workers understand and facilitate the change process that occurs for client systems within the context of the larger physical and social environment.

- Strengths-based and empowerment perspectives help the social worker identify the client system's strengths and use those strengths to frame goals that will build on those strengths and empower the client system to make changes.

- The solution-focused perspective has implications for practice at all levels because it enables the social worker to help clients reconstruct the ways in which they view their situation.

- At all three levels of generalist practice, these theoretical approaches can be combined to develop an intervention strategy that includes engagement and assessment of the client system, planning and implementation of the social work intervention, and evaluation of the social work intervention.

EXERCISES: PRACTICING SOCIAL WORK

We have explored theoretical frameworks to provide you with a basis for beginning your social work practice. Now it is your turn to apply your new knowledge in two exercises with the Sanchez family.

Identifying the Strengths

Review the following case scenario and identify the strengths that you perceive exist within the client situation. Link each of those strengths to one or more of the Principles of Strength perspectives described below. Lastly, re-review the scenario to describe the client situation from a deficits perspective.

Principles of Strength:

- *Every individual, group, family, and community has strengths.*

- *Trauma and abuse, illness, and struggle may be injurious but they may also be sources of challenge and opportunity.*

- *Assume that you do not know the upper limits of the capacity to grow and change and take individual, group, and community aspirations seriously.*

- *We best serve clients by collaborating with them.*

- *Every environment is full of resources.*

You are the social worker at Our Lady of Guadalupe Church where the Sanchez family has attended for years. During a recent church event, you noticed Gloria Sanchez wearing a long-sleeved turtleneck sweater on a particularly warm day. You speculate the reason for her attire is that she covering up bruises. On numerous occasions, you have observed her husband, Leo, speaking to her in an extremely disrespectful manner and being demanding of her. The next time you see her you ask how things are going and she bursts into tears. She discloses to you that Leo has abused her throughout much of their marriage; she wants to leave him, but knows the teachings of the church oppose divorce. She shares that her sister, Carmen, is aware of the abuse but, for the present, has agreed not to tell the rest of the family. Carmen is very supportive, but is pushing her to "get help or get out." Gloria is terrified that her parents will learn about the abuse and blame her as they love Leo "like one of their own." Gloria has always felt close to her family and is saddened that she does not see them as often as she would like to. She visits less often out of fear that the family will suspect something is wrong.

CLIENT STRENGTHS	PRINCIPLE(S) OF STRENGTH PERSPECTIVE	CLIENT SITUATION FROM THE DEFICITS PERSPECTIVE

Applying Solution-Focused Principles

In the previous exercise, you identified the strengths in Gloria's situation. Now, you will have the opportunity to consider Gloria's situation using a solution-focused approach. With your help, Gloria has identified the following areas of concern: being battered by her husband; thoughts of divorce; ensuring that the rest of her family does not learn about the violence; and concern that her relationship with her family is becoming distant. From a solution-focused perspective, consider each of these areas in terms of the strengths and resources possessed by Gloria or could be attained for or by her, her goals and a behavioral strategy to help her achieve the goal.

CONCERN	STRENGTH/RESOURCE POSSESSED	GLORIA'S GOAL	RESOURCES NEEDED	BEHAVIORAL STRATEGY
Violent spouse				
Desire for divorce				
Family learning about the violence				
Losing her relationship with her family				

Cecilia Sanchez

Using the Sanchez Family interactive case study, review the information regarding Junior Sanchez and answer Celia's Critical Thinking Questions.

Alejandro Sanchez

Using the Sanchez family interactive case study, review the information regarding Junior Sanchez and answer Alejandro's Critical Thinking Questions.

Building an Ecomap

Using the Sanchez family interactive case study to guide this exercise, click on the Ecomap icon. Review the ecomap for the Sanchez family. Using the tool, create an ecomap for yourself. Provide a narrative analysis of your own ecomap, focusing on the strengths, areas for growth and change, and a future perspective on your life.

EXERCISES: THE SOCIAL WORK LIBRARY

The Strengths Perspective in Social Work Practice

After reading "The Strengths Perspective in Social Work Practice: Extensions and Cautions" (Saleebey, 1996), address the following:

1. Identify the basic principles of the strengths perspective.

2. Identify the basic criticism of the strengths perspective offered by Saleebey.

3. Share your own perceptions of the pros and cons of applying the strengths perspective in social work practice.

Ecological Perspective: The Debate

Utilizing the Wakefield series as a reference point, review the debate between Wakefield ("Does Social Work Need the Ecological Perspective? Reply to Alex Gitterman") and Gitterman ("Ecological Perspective: Response to Professor Jerry Wakefield"). Respond to the following:

1. Synthesize the positions held by each of the debaters, Wakefield and Gitterman.

2. Based on your current perceptions of the social work profession, discuss your reactions to each of the stated positions.

CHAPTER 8

Fields of Social Work Practice

Like many students considering a career in social work, Emily was captivated with the range and diversity of employment possibilities. Through her social work classes, Emily learned that a BSW prepares her for generalist social work practice with a variety of persons and settings. The challenge for Emily then became narrowing her practice focus. Emily decided she needed to explore in depth the many and varied opportunities available to her as a BSW generalist social worker.

In her investigation of the fields of social work practice, Emily used a number of strategies. She began by reading about fields of practice, using the Internet to learn about social work organizations and opportunities, talking to fellow students and faculty at her program, interviewing practicing social workers, and volunteering in a social service setting that provided her with a range of different experiences. Even as she progressed through this exploration, Emily could still see herself working in a number of different areas, but she felt confident that she was more aware of the breadth of opportunities that lie ahead for her.

Can you relate to Emily's dilemma? Social work is a profession that offers the potential to work in an array of fields. Many social workers are drawn to a particular field of practice as a result of life experiences or a strong interest in a particular setting or population. Have you considered the field or fields of practice that interest you? To get started in your investigation, Table 8.1 provides a sampling of the many fields of practice from which to choose.

For further insights into the realities of working in the field, in this chapter, eight social workers share their perspectives on the area of social work in which they practice. These "voices from the field" provide a window into the field of practice, the training and education required to work in that area, the rewards gained, challenges faced, and a perspective on the future of that field of social work practice. Written by the social workers themselves, these

FIELD OF PRACTICE	SETTINGS
Mental health services	Community-based mental health centers
	In-patient-based psychiatric facilities
	Disaster relief programs
	Employee assistance programs
	Private practice
	Hospitals and rehabilitation programs
	Residential facilities
Medical social work	Hospitals and rehabilitation programs
	Community-based health care programs
	Community-based health education programs
Gerontological social work	Community-based service programs
	Hospitals and rehabilitation programs
	Residential facilities
	Adult day care programs
Chemical dependency and addiction treatment	Community-based treatment programs
	Hospital-based treatment programs
	Prevention and education programs
Child welfare services	Family service agencies
	Adoption programs
	Elementary and secondary schools
	Public child welfare agencies
School social work	Elementary and secondary schools
	Alternative school programs
International social work	U.S.-based immigrant and refugee programs
	Non-U.S.-based programs
	Disaster relief programs
	U.S.-based international programs
	Advocacy organizations
Domestic and family violence	Shelter-based programs
	Hospitals
	Legal system programs
	Community-based mental health programs
Criminal justice	Corrections settings
	Legal system programs
Crisis intervention	Disaster relief programs
	Victim assistance programs
Rural social work	Community service programs
	Hospitals and rehabilitation programs
Military social work	Military mental health and family service programs
	Deployment support programs
Community development	Nonprofit and public sector
Community organizing	Community-based programs
Advocacy	Community-based programs
Policy development and analysis	Nonprofit and public sector programs

TABLE 8.1

Fields of Practice and Practice Settings

narratives are their views based on their own experiences. Each practitioner has a social work degree and is working with a different population and in a different setting, thus highlighting the flexibility that social work degrees offer for working in a variety of settings with different populations throughout your career.

OLDER ADULTS

Practice with older adults, or **gerontological social work,** is a field of practice that is currently undergoing dramatic changes. With the anticipated increases in the older-adult population as the baby boomers reach their senior years and people live longer, the need for more health and social services is increasing. By 2030, nearly one-quarter of the U.S. population will have reached age 65, resulting in this population becoming larger than younger cohorts (NASW, 2004d; Scharlach, Damron-Rodriguez, Robinson, & Feldman, 2000). More social workers will be needed to provide services to this population and their family members and caregivers, particularly to older women, older persons of color, and the fastest growing segment of the population, the "old-old" (those over age 85) (Mizrahi & Baskind, 2003).

Currently, less than 10 percent of social workers identify practice with older adults as their primary field of practice. In addition, fewer than 10 percent of social workers report that they completed a social work course specifically targeted at working with older adults (Clark, 2003; Damron-Rodriguez, Villa, Tseng, & Lubben, 1997). However, as the over-65 population reaches nearly one-quarter of the U.S. population, between 60,000 and 70,000 social workers will be needed in a wide range of fields, which is approximately double the number of social workers currently working in gerontological practice (CSWE, 2001b). Therefore, all social workers need increased awareness and skills for working with issues related to aging.

Practice Considerations with Older Adults

Through recent initiatives, social work educators have become aware of the need for increased emphasis on preparing students to work competently with older adults regardless of the setting in which they work. One such initiative, "Strengthening Aging and Gerontology Education for Social Work" (CSWE/SAGE-SW), has developed the following 10 competencies as being crucial for all social workers:

- Assess one's own values and biases regarding aging, death, and dying.
- Educate self to dispel the major myths about aging.

- Accept, respect, and recognize the right and need of older adults to make their own choices and decisions about their lives within the context of the law and safety concerns.
- Understand normal physical, psychological, and social changes in later life.
- Respect and address cultural, spiritual, and ethnic needs and beliefs of older adults and family members.
- Examine the diversity of attitudes toward aging, mental illness, and family roles.
- Understand the influence of aging on family dynamics.
- Use social work case management skills (such as brokering, advocacy, monitoring, and discharge planning) to link elders and their families to resources and services.
- Gather information regarding social history such as: social functioning, primary and secondary social supports, social activity level, social skills, financial status, cultural background, and social involvement.
- Identify ethical and professional boundary issues that commonly arise in work with older adults and their caregivers, such as client self-determination, end-of-life decisions, family conflicts, and guardianship.

Gerontological social workers practice with older adults in a variety of settings. Because much of the aging-related service delivery is provided by multiple disciplines, social workers often work directly with older adults and their families in host settings. A host setting is an organization whose primary mission is the provision of services other than social services (for example, health care or education). Such settings include hospitals; rehabilitation programs; residential care facilities (for example, nursing homes, assisted living facilities, and senior independent living communities); adult day service programs; senior centers with congregate meal programs; home health agencies; and hospice programs. Gerontological social workers may work in agencies that provide case management services for older adults; they may investigate elder abuse, neglect, and exploitation; or provide supportive services for family members and caregivers.

Another important area of practice for gerontological social workers is policy practice. Influencing the development of legislation, policy, and programming for older adults is critical to the enhanced longevity and quality of life for the burgeoning older-adult population.

The Social Work Library

The article by Kahana, Kahana, and Kerder in the Social Work Library provides more information on the older adult population.

Carroll Rodriguez, BSW, Alzheimer's Association Chapter

I am the public policy director for a state coalition of Alzheimer's Association chapters (see Exhibit 8.1). I am charged with mobilizing others in an effort to

EXHIBIT 8.1

Alzheimer's Association

Alzheimer's Association St. Louis Chapter
9374 Olive Boulevard
St. Louis, Missouri 63132
www.alzstl.org
The mission of the Alzheimer's Association is to eliminate Alzheimer's disease through the advancement of research and to enhance care and support for individuals, their families, and caregivers. The association provides the following services: Family Assistance Programs—Helpline, Care Consultation, Family Care Planning, Early Diagnosed Programs, Support Groups, Respite Care Assistance, and Family & Community Education.

bring about governmental and legislative changes that will benefit persons with Alzheimer's disease, their families, and their care partners. I work with the four state chapters, coordinating the state and national public policy activities for my state.

The route to becoming a state public policy director was not a straight one for me. Upon graduating with my BSW, I worked as a social worker in a skilled care nursing home and an adult day program. In these positions, I was responsible for facilitating support groups, working with older adults and their families, and coordinating admissions and care planning. Following a relocation with my family, I continued my gerontological social work career in community-based services, working as a program supervisor with an area agency on aging.

In this position, I supervised senior center programs in rural communities and had the opportunity to open up several new senior centers in small communities that had not previously had services. From there, it was a natural progression for me to work for the Alzheimer's Association, where I started out working in the respite program in which I coordinated access to these much-needed services that provided a break for caregivers. These varied experiences gave me both valuable skills in working with families and insight into many different facets of care needed to maintain a quality of life for our older-adult population.

In my current position, I work to improve the laws and policies that govern the services provided to persons with Alzheimer's disease. Alzheimer's disease is one form of dementia (the terms are often used interchangeably), a progressive, degenerative disease of the brain for which there is no cure. As the most common form of dementia, it affects a person's memory, judgment, and ability to reason. More than four million Americans are living with Alzheimer's disease and millions more are impacted—the families and friends that serve as their caregivers. A person with dementia will live an average of 8 years and as many as 20 years after the symptoms appear. As they advance through the disease process, long-term care and support are critical.

My experience as a social worker working with older adults prepared me well for working at the policy level. Having direct practice experience with this population in a variety of settings enables me to understand the needs of older adults and their caregivers, the gaps in the service delivery system, and the importance of ensuring that policy-decision makers are well informed as they enact legislation and make policy.

The Alzheimer's Association chapters are part of the nation's largest voluntary health organization devoted to conquering Alzheimer's disease. Through a network of more than 81 chapters across the country, individuals with the disease and their care partners have access to a broad range of programs and services, and can participate in support for research and advocacy. Because the association is such a large organization that speaks on behalf of persons with Alzheimer's disease, we have the opportunity to influence state and federal policies for this population.

State public policy activities and platform development begin with issue identification. As I determine the areas for advocacy, I routinely ask the following questions: What are the greatest unmet needs? Where are the gaps in services? How can we build an enhanced long-term care delivery system to meet the growing demands of an aging population? Answers to these questions can be found by listening to the voices of persons with the disease and their care partners.

Through focus groups, surveys, support group visits, and other means of communication, the coalition that I direct has identified three current areas of greatest need: (1) enhanced access to a continuum of long-term care services;

(2) improved quality of care throughout the long-term care continuum; and (3) a cure for Alzheimer's disease. Identifying the conditions and needs is an essential first step in establishing the framework for development of a public policy platform.

Once a policy agenda is established, the next critical task is to develop potential solutions. This process involves coalition building and networking both internally, within the chapter network, and externally, with partners that have an interest in the issue. Health care providers, leadership within state agencies, researchers in the field of aging, and families with a vested interest in the issue are examples of partners that can aid in developing viable solutions and achievable goals.

Building on this process, I work with the coalition to outline a public policy platform that includes goals and objectives addressing the areas of focus. Some of the components that are necessary to advance a public policy initiative include drafting the language for proposed legislative bills; gaining sponsorship from legislators that are sensitive to and supportive of the issue; testifying at public hearings in front of legislators and voters; and building a broad base of supporters among voters, professionals, and legislators. Grassroots advocacy is at the core of this process. By mobilizing people that are passionate about an issue, a great deal can be accomplished, as shown by the following examples.

Every year, I travel with other advocates to my state capital and Washington, D.C., to talk with Congress about appropriations for funding research to find a cure for Alzheimer's disease, study the effects of this disease on individuals and their families, and to develop interventions to enhance their lives. Along with thousands of supporters, I write letters and e-mail and meet with legislators in the capitols and their home districts. As a result of these ongoing grassroots advocacy efforts, Congress has increased Alzheimer's research funding by more than $500 million over the last 13 years.

A current challenge for the families that I represent in my advocacy efforts is that both Medicare and private health insurance fail to address the chronic health care needs of persons with Alzheimer's disease. Medicaid serves as the safety net for long-term care services. The program supports community-based programs as well as nursing home care. Access to Medicaid services has become a primary area of focus for Alzheimer's advocates. Through grassroots efforts, we have worked to expand options, support, and access to home and community services.

A second area of challenge in my current advocacy work is promoting the quality of the care that is provided within those long-term care settings. More than half of all nursing home residents have some form of dementia, and the same holds true for assisted living facilities. My fellow advocates and I drafted and passed legislation in my state that requires all employees caring for persons with dementia to be trained in dementia care.

Working with a coalition of chapters to shape a public policy platform and mobilizing advocates to move that platform forward has required me to call upon a skill set acquired from both experience and education. With a BSW and 20 years of professional experience in the field of aging, I have learned the value of listening to others, the importance of negotiation and compromise, and the merits of networking and coalition building. However, of most importance is the realization that many voices can make change happen.

In terms of the future of my area of practice, it is projected that 14 million of today's baby boomers will develop Alzheimer's disease by midcentury. The annual cost of care is projected to be at least $375 billion, a cost that will overwhelm our health care system and bankrupt both Medicare and Medicaid. Succinctly stated by the Alzheimer's Association, "We are facing a race against time." Now more than ever, there is a need for social workers to engage in public policy advocacy in support of persons with Alzheimer's disease and their care partners.

CHILDREN AND FAMILIES

Working with children and families is the second largest area of practice for social workers and is particularly popular with those with BSWs (Gibelman & Schervish, 1997). Approximately one-quarter of social workers report that they work with children and families, and this number is expected to increase in the next decade, particularly in the area of school-based services (Gibelman & Schervish, 1997; O'Neill, 2002). Approximately 16 percent of social workers work primarily in children's services, while 12 percent provide services to families (NASW, 2004d).

Social work practice with children and families takes place in a wide variety of settings, including public child welfare agencies, residential care facilities, family service agencies, schools, mental health centers, chemical dependency and addiction treatment programs, agencies that serve persons with disabilities, and health care settings. Services to children and families can be provided in settings that are publicly funded, nonprofit, and in the emerging for-profit area.

Practice Considerations with Children and Families

Social workers' responsibilities are equally as broad as the settings. They work in residential group homes as case managers, child care workers, and therapists. In public child welfare agencies, social workers investigate referrals about child abuse and neglect; and they work with children and families in the areas of alternative out-of-home care, prevention and adoption services, and family preservation programs. In private family service agencies, social workers also work with children and families in the areas of adoption, family preservation, alternative care, and in-home therapy programs. In agencies that provide services to persons with physical or mental illness, addictions, or disabilities, social workers complete intake assessments, develop and implement treatment plans and follow-up, provide individual and group therapy, and work with the children and/or their parents.

Greater emphasis has been given in recent years to the prevention of out-of-home placement for children and to strengthening the family's ability to function. As a result of this effort, specialized programs have been developed that focus on family preservation. The goal of family preservation programs is to enhance the family's ability to cope and manage. As social work education emphasizes a strengths-based, systems approach, social workers are well trained to serve as family preservation professionals. Social workers provide therapeutic case management, parenting education, and life skills services to families in both the family's home and agency settings.

School social work is another area of growth and opportunity for social workers. Approximately 5 percent of social workers, primarily MSWs, are employed in elementary and secondary school systems (NASW, 2004d). In schools, social workers conduct assessments, serve as liaisons between the school and the family, facilitate groups, and participate in multidisciplinary teams to develop individual educational plans for students. Through the provision of one-on-one and family services as well as educational and prevention programs, school social workers also provide support for those students at risk for poor academic and social outcomes.

One of the most serious issues confronting social workers who intervene with children and families is child abuse and neglect. **Child abuse** occurs when a child is subjected to physical and/or emotional injury and includes sexual abuse. **Child neglect** is considered to exist when the child's caregiver does not ensure that the child's emotional, physical, nutritional, educational, or shelter needs are being met. Societal attention to child abuse and neglect has increased in recent decades, resulting in an increase in the number of cases reported (Ginsberg, 1995). Reports are made most frequently by school personnel. Other primary reporters include professionals from social service agencies, law enforcement, and health care organizations. Many professionals that work in these settings are legally mandated to report suspected cases of child abuse, neglect, or exploitation. Nonmandated reporters (for example, family, friends, neighbors, or observers) can make anonymous reports and are protected from prosecution as long as the report is not made with malicious intent. As a result of mandated reporting and increasing rates of reporting, the number of children entering the foster care system is increasing, with the number of children entering out-of-home placements each year exceeding the number that are returned to their homes.

Angela Chierek, BSW, Department of Social Services, Children's Division

I received my bachelor's degree in social work and am currently pursuing a master's degree in social work. I am employed by the state Children's Division as a Social Service Worker II in a Child Abuse and Neglect unit. My primary responsibility consists of responding to mandated reports of suspected child abuse and neglect, and preventive reports made through the agency's hotline. Mandated reports are made by professionals that work with children, including social workers, doctors, and day care workers, that are mandated by law to report suspected child abuse and neglect. A preventive report may be made by any concerned person and often relates to a family's need for services such as counseling or utility assistance referrals. Preventive reports do not usually contain any concerns of abuse or neglect by the child's parent or caretaker.

My position is unique in the respect that it is based in a public school, not in an office with other public child welfare services. My co-workers and I respond to concerns from the school in which our office is located and the surrounding area schools as well as the general community. Since a major focus of our work is to reduce the educational neglect of children, some of my co-workers collaborate with individual public schools to prevent school absences. Home visits are made when a child has missed a few days of school. If needed, intensive services can be provided and referrals made to Family Court for educational neglect or truancy.

In general, child welfare workers are very focused on their role in the child protection system. It is essential to have people working for as well as with the children, since the children cannot protect themselves. Using a strengths-based approach, social workers working in child welfare agencies emphasize the strengths of the families with whom they are working, as this is important in achieving positive outcomes for families. An emphasis on teamwork is also a strength within the Child Abuse and Neglect unit and the community as a whole. Social workers assist each other with resources to assist families and in the process of placing children in foster care. In addition, I see an increased emphasis on the use of community support for children and families. This emphasis is based on the idea that connecting children and families within their communities will serve as a safety net for them in the event of another period of crisis.

My work is challenging and demanding since different families come to the situation with varied issues concerning safety and risk to their children. The reasons for my involvement with a family can range from substance abuse to a need for parenting, conflict management, or help with appropriate discipline. One of the first challenges for any worker is to engage the families in their involvement with the Children's Division. A family may have anger regarding the report, which could be an obstacle to their active involvement in the case.

While sometimes challenging, my goal is to link families to the appropriate services to ensure the safety of the children in their home, so that the children do not have to be placed into out-of-home care (foster care). Knowing the available resources to which I can link families is essential for addressing the needs of a family.

Another challenge I face is the fact that there are some issues that cannot be addressed by providing services to families in the home. Situations such as severe physical and sexual abuse place the child's safety at immediate risk of suffering more abuse or neglect. In these cases, the child or children must either be temporarily placed with a relative with a safety plan to protect them, or the child must be taken into protective custody by the court and placed in foster care. If a child is temporarily placed with a relative, I investigate the allegations and make a decision based on evidence that is discovered during the investigation. If the child is placed into protective custody, there will be an initial protective custody hearing to determine whether the child will remain in foster care. The foster care worker and the parents will develop a service plan to work toward reunification of the parents and child.

It is challenging to properly support and provide services to families despite the typical large caseloads. This challenge requires a great focus on prioritizing the needs of some families over the needs of other families whose children are considered safe. Another challenge is attracting and keeping workers with an educational background of social work who want to work in the field of child welfare. Not all child welfare agencies require service workers to have a social work degree, but our social work training makes us well suited for working in child welfare because we are trained to fully focus on the needs of the family. I would like to see more degreed social workers working in positions like the one I have.

The future of the Children's Division rests in services that prevent children from being placed in foster care and in services that more quickly employ *wraparound* (comprehensive, coordinated service delivery system) services for families so that children in foster care can more quickly return home. Intensive In-Home Services is an innovative six-week program in which an in-home worker spends 20 hours per week with the family, with the aim of reducing the risk factors that place the child(ren) at risk for foster care placement. At the end of the six-week period, the team of workers determines whether the child(ren) can safely remain in the home. Intensive involvement services are also being used for speedier reunification of foster children and their families. Through these services, professionals work with the families to provide individualized services that fit their needs instead of typical court-ordered service plans that might include education on parenting and anger management. Social workers working in intensive involvement programs have small caseloads (for example, two families) so the families get more intensive involvement and more regular contact to ensure that they receive the needed services.

Being a social worker in children's services can be challenging and demanding, but also can be rewarding to any social worker. For me as a beginning social worker, working in children's services has been a great opportunity to hone my organizational skills and learn a variety of different intervention strategies.

IMMIGRANTS AND REFUGEES

The number of current U.S. residents born in other countries exceeded 32 million in 2002, representing a 64 percent increase since 1990 (Schmidley & Robinson, 2003). Persons born outside the United States who are living here may be in the country as a refugee or asylum seeker or here on an immigrant, student, business, or extended visa, or without documentation. In recent years, the number of immigrants from Mexico and other Central and Latin American countries is increasing, while immigration of persons born in Europe has decreased (Mizrahi & Baskind, 2003; Schmidley & Robinson, 2003).

The Social Work Library

Read De La Rosa's article to better understand poverty within the Latino community.

Practice Considerations with Immigrants and Refugees

Social workers in the United States have always worked with an array of international issues, including providing services to people who immigrate to this country from their homelands. In the area of international adoptions, social workers assist families in applying, conduct home studies, act as liaison to the international adoption organization, and provide postadoption support services. Social workers also provide services in international emergency and disaster situations and in administering U.S.-based programs that provide services in the international community.

In addition to working with international issues, social workers play a prominent role in working with immigrants and refugees living in the United States. The settlement house movement focused originally on the provision of services to recent immigrants to the United States. Training social workers who are culturally competent and sensitive to the needs of the many and varied populations of persons that are new to this country is a priority for the profession.

Working with persons born in other countries will span the spectrum of the social work population, thus requiring U.S.-based social workers in virtually every field of practice to have the knowledge and skills for practicing with diverse populations. Social workers may work in direct practice with individuals and families that have immigrated to this country, or they may work in the policy and advocacy arena on behalf of entire communities of persons who have relocated to the United States. Policies toward newer residents are often conflicted, thus creating a need for social workers to become the voice for this population (Mizrahi & Baskind, 2003).

Suzanne LeLaurin, MSW, LCSW, International Institute

I am a social worker who works with persons who have immigrated to the United States from other countries (see Exhibit 8.2). I am the senior vice-president for individuals and families at a refugee resettlement agency. I oversee several departments that provide a variety of services to immigrants and their families. In the social service department, we provide case management services for newly arrived refugees. The education department is responsible for teaching English to speakers of other languages. In addition, the education staff prepare clients for taking tests that are needed for working and going to school in the United States. The General Equivalency Diploma (GED) certifies that the person has knowledge comparable to a U.S. high school graduate. The Test of English as a Foreign Language (TOEFL) is an examination required for college admission to nonnative English speaker. This test provides verification of the person's ability to read, write, and understand English.

Social work is a second career for me. After spending over 20 years in the for-profit sector working for a large insurance company, I decided I wanted to work in the nonprofit sector, and chose to get my MSW because I want to help others gain access to needed services and enhance their quality of life. Since completing my MSW, I have obtained my license to practice clinical social work in my state.

To reflect on my social work practice working with persons living in the United States who were born in another country, I must include an emphasis

---

EXHIBIT 8.2

International Institute of St. Louis

International Institute of St. Louis
3654 S. Grand
St. Louis, Missouri 63118
www.intlinst.org
Since 1919, the International Institute has worked to strengthen the St. Louis community by helping immigrants and their families become secure and successful Americans and by promoting the value of ethnic diversity in the social, cultural, and economic life of the region. Its vision is a thriving community with an ethnically diverse and engaged citizenry. The institute serves as the community's central clearinghouse for information about St. Louis's diverse ethnic communities, and provides integrated and cost-effective adjustment services to almost 9,000 newcomers each year. Located on the Southside in the heart of the city's new American communities, it has been Missouri's largest refugee resettlement agency since 1980.

on politics and advocacy. The United States is a country of immigrants, but as a society, we have conflicting views about the importance of immigrants to our country. In the mid-1990s, Congress passed legislation that restricted access by noncitizens who entered the United States legally to benefits available to U.S. citizens. There have been initiatives to ease those restrictions, especially since they were harming some of the most vulnerable persons in our society—seniors that had been unable to learn English sufficiently to obtain citizenship and were increasingly at risk of homelessness as well as despair (which pushed some of them to suicide). In early 2001, the presidents of the United States and Mexico were discussing programs to ease migration into the United States.

Then came September 11, 2001, and the world changed. With the horrifying terrorist attacks on the United States, many of the moves to welcome the immigrant to our shores shifted once again. Security tightened for all immigrants attempting to enter the United States. The effects were most pronounced with refugee migration—the largest population with which I work—as the number of refugees admitted dropped from almost 70,000 in fiscal year 2001 to less than 30,000 in 2002.

Advocacy became paramount in social work with immigrants, as the rise in anti-immigrant fever increased. My own agency worked with an advocacy group to accompany our clients to their preferred farmer's market and doctors' appointments, just to protect them from shouts of "go home, terrorist" and worse. One of my own staff, a former refugee herself, slept with her clothes on and a stick and her cell phone with her, for fear of intruders. Thankfully, the panic from 9/11 has died down, but the events of that horrible day gave new impetus to the strong anti-immigration sentiment of those fighting political gains for immigrants.

Counterbalancing the political forces to keep immigrants out of our country are the needs of employers. With the baby boom generation aging and birth rates decreasing in the United States, employers and policy experts are beginning to recognize that future growth in employment forces will depend on migration into our country.

For the near future, it is likely that we will continue to see fewer refugees and other immigrants into the United States. In spite of the lower numbers, however, we will still see those born in other countries in our midst, both to fuel our economy through a skilled workforce and because, unfortunately, we still experience war and civil unrest around the world, leading to refugees needing safe haven.

For those social workers interested in working with persons with diverse national origins, there will be many opportunities to provide a variety of social work services for refugees, those who are forced to flee their homelands due to civil unrest, persecution, and violence. These persons are considered "reluctant immigrants," as they did not choose to leave their homelands, but were forced to do so by circumstances beyond their control. Typically, they arrive here with little more than the clothes on their backs. This population needs and will continue to need our support in basic necessities (food, clothing, and shelter), learning the English language, employment, adapting to U.S. culture (while hopefully holding on to the richness of their own culture), and mental health services for coming to terms with the horrors of trauma and torture. These needs will also exist for migrant workers that come into the United States intent on making enough money to support their families, with risk of exploitation by unscrupulous employers taking advantage of their undocumented status.

There is a growing need for cultural diversity training for those born in the United States that expands the definition of diversity beyond the traditional black-white-indigenous population categories into cultural diversity based on ethnicity. Our religious communities, while already pluralistic, will also shift beyond the dominant Judeo-Christian faiths, which will lead us to a need for diversity training for a variety of groups—other social service providers, employers, educators, medical professionals, and many more. We also need to adapt our social work services to accommodate the needs of those whose cultural norms are different from those of the United States. Social workers must ask themselves questions such as ones I ask myself. How do I, as a feminist, react to and serve a conservative Muslim woman who considers it immodest to show any parts of her body other than her hands and face; yet her clothing limits her ability to work in the only job I can find for her, such as a manufacturing job that requires clothing not get in the way of machines? How do I work with teenagers and parents experiencing family conflicts in which the teens are "Americanized" into thinking that adolescence is a time to "move away" from parents and become independent, while the parents come from a culture in which youth independence brings great shame on the family in their cultural community? How do I counsel an adult woman with an aging mother in need of long-term care, but who considers the idea of putting her mother in a skilled nursing facility a shameful rejection of her responsibilities as a dutiful and respectful daughter? As social workers, we will all be challenged to serve those with different values and beliefs from our own, and these differences will be much more pronounced with those who were born in other cultures.

The great joy—and challenge—of working with the persons from diverse national origins is that they help me see the world through a different cultural and political lens, influenced by their own life experiences, cultural norms, and beliefs that are so different from my own. I am in awe of the resilience and spirit of the refugees that come to my country, prepared to start building a whole new life after the one they knew was shattered and stolen from them. I am challenged to see my world through another person's eyes, and find myself questioning some of my own deeply held assumptions about my country and culture. The world has gotten so much smaller for me after working with an international population for so many years.

CHEMICAL DEPENDENCY AND ADDICTION

An area of practice in which social workers have long been involved, chemical dependency and addiction treatment has undergone dramatic changes in recent years. Early substance abuse treatment efforts focused primarily on the rehabilitation of the persons addicted to alcohol, and the treatment was in the form of Alcoholics Anonymous, a model focused on mutual peer support. Inpatient treatment programs emerged during the 1970s for the treatment of alcoholism and other drug addictions. Restrictions imposed on treatment programs by the health insurance industry regarding the amount of reimbursement for treatment resulted in the elimination of many in-patient programs because clients were no longer able to afford the cost. As a result, chemical dependency and addiction treatment is now typically provided through a combination of short-term in-patient treatment followed by a period of out-patient treatment known as aftercare.

The Social Work Library

Learn about the treatment of chemical dependency from historical and contemporary perspectives in DiNitto's article.

Practice Considerations in Chemical Dependency and Addiction

Despite the changes in the societal response to chemical dependency and addiction, the prevalence of chemical dependency has not dissipated. Of persons referred to employee assistance programs at their workplaces, nearly half are reported to have problems with alcohol or other substances that negatively impact their ability to perform their jobs (Ginsberg, 1995).

As a result of the shift away from large in-patient programs, a relatively small number of social workers identify substance abuse as their primary area of practice. Fewer than 10 percent of NASW members surveyed indicated alcohol and drugs as their primary or secondary focus, with less than 5 percent reporting substance abuse treatment as their primary practice area (Gibelman & Schervish, 1997). Social workers who work in chemical dependency and addiction treatment programs are typically employed by private for-profit and private nonprofit organizations. Interestingly, of the social workers that work in the field of chemical dependency and addiction treatment, men outnumber women.

Although a small percentage of social workers practice exclusively in the field of chemical dependency and addiction treatment, knowledge of substance abuse prevention and intervention is critical for social workers in virtually every field of practice. Substance use and abuse issues frequently overlap in such areas as mental illness, domestic violence, and corrections; therefore, social workers in these areas must be able to identify signs of chemical dependency and addiction. The number of social workers practicing in mental health–substance abuse treatment is expected to grow by nearly 40 percent in the next several years (O'Neill, 2002).

As you will read in the following narrative, the issue of dual diagnosis is prevalent in this area of his practice. **Dual diagnosis** occurs when the person is thought to be experiencing two diseases or conditions simultaneously, and the interaction of the two diseases can impede diagnosis and treatment. Within chemical dependency and addiction treatment, dual diagnosis is typically the presence of mental illness and chemical dependence.

Jon Hudson, BSW, Chestnut Health Systems, Inc.

I am a BSW student completing my practicum at a large agency that provides treatment for adolescents with chemical dependency. I want to practice clinical social work, and because clinical work often involves chemical dependency issues, I need to have experience in this area. I find it an honor to work with these young people as they struggle with issues of chemical dependence. Although this is my first formal social work practice experience, I gained experience through volunteering and working part-time in several social service settings before beginning my practicum. My volunteer and employment experiences helped me to determine the areas of social work in which I would like to practice and the populations on which I want to focus my practice.

The residential program at my practicum site is separated by gender. I work in the capacity of a chemical dependence counselor on the male unit. In this setting, a substance abuse counselor provides treatment to individual clients and their families, facilitates group therapy, and works in teams with other counselors to maintain the daily routine of the treatment unit. The unit where I work houses 20 boys ranging in age from 13 to 17 years. Nearly all of the residents are court mandated to chemical dependency treatment, but the reasons for their sentences are not always related directly to use or abuse of substances. More often, they are arrested for other crimes and discovered to be under the influence of substances during the arrest process. Most of the boys are from modest socioeconomic backgrounds, and their formal education has been interrupted as a result of their criminal activities and lack of family support.

Some of the boys are dually diagnosed with a mental illness and chemical dependence. Working with persons who are dually diagnosed presents a special challenge in treatment, as both conditions must be addressed simultaneously. Treatment of a person with a dual diagnosis usually results in a boy working with his counselor and a staff psychiatrist who provides medication and treatment for the mental illness. The counselor must be knowledgeable about the diagnosis and treatment of both conditions and balance the mental illness, chemical dependence, and oftentimes, legal issues all at the same time.

Persons who are dually diagnosed may not be aware of the existence of a mental illness and be shocked to learn of it. The client may have been abusing drugs as a way to deal with the symptoms of mental illness and have difficulty accepting that he now has to grapple with two crises. Typically, the boy unwillingly enters the treatment program without knowing what to expect. As a result, he has no idea how to cope, and the news of a dual diagnosis puts extra stress on him. As a result, he may appear to be getting worse after the first few weeks in residence. I think the thing that touched me most was that learning that he has a dual diagnosis often makes the young man or boy feel more broken than he already feels.

A program such as the one in which I am completing my practicum provides judges with the option of sentencing alternatives that are more appropriate for developing young men and women. The fact that the boy or girl may have committed a crime, possibly several crimes, is secondary to the consideration that jail is not appropriate for everyone who commits a crime, especially children and adolescents. The program introduces the young people to treatment and healthy recovery before they have become entrenched in a maladaptive pattern of misuse of chemical substances. The longer a person is chemically dependent and actively using substances, the more difficult it is for her or him to break the cycle of dependence.

In my practicum, I am learning that there are special considerations when a client and a clinician are dealing with issues of chemical dependence. Many substances require a long time to clear the body. This can result in the person being in the treatment and recovery process longer, which increases the chances for long-term abstinence and recovery. In many parts of the world, the length of time a person is in treatment has become the leading issue in the search for new models of addiction treatment.

Traditional models of substance abuse treatment are based on the 12 steps of Alcoholics Anonymous and have complete abstinence as the primary goal. Since its beginnings in the 1930s, this model has been effective for millions of men and women suffering from chemical dependence. The model dictates that sufferers must first stop using chemicals and then admit they are chemically dependent and powerless over their substance of choice. One of the challenges that I have identified in this field of practice is that, although the 12-step model has a long-standing history, the addict must cease all drug use before she or he can move through recovery. I have observed that this approach works well for some in a self-help environment. In the framework of a treatment model, however, if the goal is to stop using and remain abstinent, cessation should not be a requirement to begin treatment.

In my practicum, I have been exposed to a new model of substance abuse treatment. The Harm Reduction model is finding success in many parts of the world, but is still controversial in the United States. Harm Reduction is based on the idea that the longer a person is engaged in the treatment and recovery process, the better her or his chances are for long-term recovery. Harm Reduction encourages the client to prioritize goals and does not require her or him to become and remain abstinent at any point. The user may see her or his problem as cocaine and not alcohol, for example, even though both are being used in a maladaptive pattern. The social worker using a Harm Reduction framework recognizes value in the client's theory and builds on that strength. Why does the social worker, who can clearly see that the person has a problem with cocaine and alcohol, concur with the client's theory of the problem? The social worker knows she or he can keep the client engaged in the recovery process longer by working on what the person sees as the problem, and the longer the person is engaged, the more likelihood of long-term change.

An example of a Harm Reduction program may be a needle exchange program in a city where the incidence of intravenous drug use is high. Opponents of the Harm Reduction approach claim that needle exchange does not work because it does not reduce the number of intravenous (IV) drug users. However, the incidence of new HIV infection is reduced, and this creates a safer, less harmful environment for everyone by reducing or eliminating the incidence of needle sharing. Needle exchange ensures that IV drug users are introduced to the treatment and recovery process; thus the seed is planted and the process begins.

I decided on social work as a profession because I believe in values of social justice, the dignity and worth of the person, a person's right to self-determination, and the importance of human relationships as outlined in the National Association of Social Workers *Code of Ethics* (1999). Through my coursework and practicum, I have learned to engage, assess, and intervene with client systems. Also of importance are the skills of critical thinking and evaluation. Because I have learned the value of thinking critically about my practice, I have come to understand that treatment models for chemical dependence work can vary and are more effective with multidisciplinary professional teams that include social workers as integral, working parts of the models.

As a social worker I have been educated and trained in an approach that involves not only the person and her or his disorder. The social work perspective takes into consideration the person in her or his environment over time. This multidisciplinary approach transcends and includes approaches from the fields of psychology, sociology, anthropology, biology, and history. Social work theory helps me to understand that I need to integrate the biological, psychological, and social aspects of a person to understand her or his disease. In order to help a person in a competent and respectful manner, I need to know where the person lives, the education, family history, ethnic and cultural background, spiritual beliefs, and most importantly, the way in which the person perceives the condition or situation that prompted her or him to ask for help and the path to change.

CRIMINAL JUSTICE

One area of **forensic social work**, social work practice in criminal justice, is a growing area for social work employment. Forensic social work is the practice of social work in areas relating to the law and legal systems, including the criminal and civil legal systems. Examples include child, elder, and spouse abuse; child custody; juvenile and adult criminal issues; and corrections. Prompted by media attention, society has experienced an increased focus on crime and criminals (Ginsberg, 1995). An increasing number of persons are being jailed, most in state and county facilities. Half of the residents of correctional facilities are awaiting trial, and many are persons of color and of low socioeconomic status. More than half of persons who encounter the criminal justice system are under the influence of alcohol or other substances during the time in which the crime for which they are accused was committed. Although the majority of persons in correctional facilities are men, the number of female offenders is growing (Ginsberg, 1995).

Practice Considerations in Criminal Justice

Social work practice in criminal justice encompasses a wide range of settings and issues. Social workers in this field of practice may work in adult or juvenile correctional facilities, community-based probation and parole agencies, legal services organizations that represent the accused and the victims, juvenile or family court agencies, law enforcement agencies, or programs that respond to issues of domestic and family violence (Clark, 2003). Despite the fact that social workers have been involved in social work practice in criminal justice since the 1800s, the number of social workers that identify criminal justice as a primary area of practice is small (Clark, 2003). However, because of the array of settings, some social workers may identify their primary practice of focus in a related area (for example, mental health or chemical dependency and addiction treatment). Practice in criminal justice is an employment option for BSW social workers. A relatively new area of focus for social workers interested in the legal system is to complete both a graduate social work and law degree.

The Social Work Library

The article by Brownell and Roberts provides an overview of the first 100 years of social work in criminal justice.

Herbert Bernsen, MSW, County Department of Justice Services

I am the assistant director for a county Department of Justice Services (see Exhibit 8.3). I have a master's degree in social work. Through my involvement in the field of corrections, I have been designated a Certified Jail Manager by the American Jail Association. Because I have learned the importance of collaborating with others in the community whose services overlap with the criminal justice system, I am actively involved with several community organizations. I serve as the president of a drug and alcohol recovery and treatment organization, and am a board member for an organization that provides services to persons with developmental disabilities who encounter the criminal justice system. I began my career in criminal justice social work while I was a student in the MSW program. I worked as a probation and parole officer and have continued

EXHIBIT 8.3

St. Louis County Department of Justice Services

St. Louis County Department of Justice Services
100 South Central Avenue
St. Louis, Missouri 63105

The St. Louis County Department of Justice Services is responsible for the operation of the St. Louis county jail and the Division of Community Corrections. The county jail provides 1,232 beds for the county's minimum, medium, and maximum security inmates. The Division of Community Corrections is located in a nearby building and is responsible for the operation of the Work Release Center and the Alternative Community Services Program, including the Mental Health Court.

Photographs provided by Hellmuth, Obata, and Kassabaum, Inc.

in this field for the past 31 years. I have also served as a superintendent of the maximum and medium security correctional institutions.

My department is responsible for the operation of the county jail and the Community Corrections Division. The populations that we encounter are adult men and women, 17 years of age and older, charged with crimes ranging from felonies and misdemeanors to county ordinance violations. The capacity of the jail at which I work is 1,232 inmates. In 2002, 33,083 persons were booked at the jail, and the average daily population was 1,179 inmates. The population consists primarily of those inmates awaiting trial, but inmates are sentenced to the jail for periods up to one year. For sentences exceeding one year, inmates are normally sent to the state prison system operated by the Department of Corrections.

The management philosophy used in our general population housing area is considered direct supervision. Correctional officers are stationed inside the housing area pods enabling officers to take a proactive role in controlling inmate behavior and minimizing tension. We find that assaults against staff and other inmates are significantly reduced in our current direct supervision facility compared to our previous linear design facility. In the more traditional linear facility, officers only intermittently observe inmates when they conduct patrols in front of their cells. In direct supervision facilities, the officer is inside the living area and she or he can often stop problems early before they escalate.

Communication is the key skill for officers in dealing with inmates. Most inmates follow the rules because they want to live in a safe and secure environment. We set high expectations for inmate behavior, and this becomes a self-fulfilling prophecy. Inmates prefer to live in an environment in which the officer is the leader, not the toughest inmate. If an inmate consistently violates the rules, she or he is moved to an indirect housing unit with reduced privileges and restricted movement.

The most important part of the corrections department mission is to ensure inmate safety and security. As an administrator, I read daily reports and review incident reports. If there are numerous inmate assaults against other inmates or staff, we are not doing our job. Supervisors must make frequent inspections. Cells and inmate living areas must be routinely searched. If homemade weapons are being made, inmates cannot feel safe. Inmates are taught the rules and the possible sanctions for violating the rules. They also know that their right to a due process hearing to determine their guilt or innocence is affirmed.

The social worker in the corrections area works as a member of a multidisciplinary team. The social worker/case worker is responsible for conducting the initial assessment when the inmate is booked and processed into the jail setting. Often, this assessment involves crisis intervention, as the social worker must evaluate the inmate's current emotional state to identify issues such as suicidal ideation and mental illness. This assessment provides the basis for determining the part of the jail system in which the inmate will be housed. Secondly, social workers are responsible for coordinating and participating in the educational and treatment programs provided for the inmates. Casework also involves prioritizing the needs of the inmates through regular contact during their incarceration to assess how the inmate is functioning within the jail population and any issues that she or he is faced with from external sources (for example, family or financial). The social worker serves as a liaison with the legal system to monitor the inmate's case progress and with employers when inmates are participating in the work release program. Lastly, the social worker is often responsible for working with those inmates that need assistance upon release from jail to ensure that they are integrated effectively back into their communities.

One of the challenges of working in criminal justice is the high incidence of mental illness and drug abuse. In the early 1960s, there was an effort to deinstitutionalize vast numbers of persons with mental illness and provide the consequent community support and housing that would be needed. The community support for this effort fell woefully short. As a result, jails often became the place of last resort for those persons suffering from mental illness, not all of whom had committed crimes. We have certainly needed to hire psychiatrists, psychologists, and social workers to work with persons diagnosed with mental illness inside our jails. Many of those experiencing mental illness do not, however, belong in jail in the first place.

Because I was aware of the inappropriate placement of many persons that suffered from mental illness, I was instrumental in forming a mental health court task force consisting of community mental health providers and criminal justice agencies. The goal of this task force was to establish a mental health court to divert persons with serious mental health disorders from the criminal justice system to appropriate mental health treatment and services in order to improve their mental health functioning and deter future criminal behavior. To ensure the provision of comprehensive services, we worked closely with the police department to implement their Crisis Intervention Team (CIT) program. In this program, police officers are trained to intervene in situations involving persons with mental illness. Our other partners included an advocacy group, the state mental health agency, a nonprofit mental health agency, and a university social work program along with judges, prosecutors, public defenders, probation officers, and our corrections department at the county jail.

Another challenge faced by social workers in criminal justice is the issue of substance abuse. Along with mental illness, the inmate population contains many persons that use and abuse alcohol and other drugs. My department has made a significant commitment to the treatment of substance abuse within the jail through the Choices Substance Abuse Recovery Program. Using a 12-step model, the program provides 120 days of treatment for male and female inmates with the goal of empowering participants to choose a lifestyle free of alcohol and other drug addictions and criminal behavior. During the past five years, the Choices program served 1,275 inmates. Judges have embraced the program, and there has been a waiting list since the program's inception. Each year, faculty and students at a local university evaluate the program, and each year the program consistently shows positive results. For example, during the second and third years of operation, 67 percent of those inmates who completed the program resided in the community without being arrested for a new crime or having their probation revoked or suspended. By the fourth year of the program, 92 percent of the participants successfully completed the program.

I have learned that providing educational opportunities is also important for helping inmates to initiate changes in their life. Local school districts provide instructors to prepare inmates to take the high school equivalency exam. Inmates have the opportunity to be tested. In 2002, 83 inmates took the GED test, and 60 received their diploma.

The successful operation of our jail and the programs that I have described here also depends on volunteers. There are currently over 300 active volunteers at the jail. Programs conducted by volunteers include creative writing, individual counseling, religious services, literacy assistance, leadership classes, substance abuse education, and support groups for substance abusers. The volunteers have a positive influence on the well-being of the inmates both inside and outside of confinement.

The field of social work in criminal justice has many challenges. Jails and prisons are being inundated with inmates with mental health and substance abuse problems. Jails and prisons have the highest rates of suicide in our society. In these times of scarce resources and reduced budgets, it is important to form partnerships with community leaders and organizations to provide services for inmate populations.

The future for social workers working in criminal justice is promising. There are a myriad of opportunities for correctional officers, social service staff, medical and mental health staff, and administrators in this field of practice. Innovations in inmate supervision and treatment, public health, technology, and community aftercare are examples of areas for growth and development. The vast majority of jail and prison inmates will be returning to their communities. The resources directed toward inmate populations during and after incarceration will pay significant dividends to the individuals, their families, and the community.

HEALTH SETTINGS

One of many areas of growth for social work employment, medical and public health social work jobs are expected to increase by 31 percent in the coming years (O'Neill, 2002; U.S. Bureau of Labor Statistics, 2002b). Following mental health and social work with children and families, social work in the medical and health setting is currently reported as the third most frequently practiced area of social work (Gibelman & Schervish, 1997). Nearly one-third of social workers are employed in health-related settings—20 percent in hospitals and 12 percent in out-patient settings (NASW, 2004d).

Practice Considerations in Health Settings

Social workers who practice in health settings have the opportunity to work in a variety of organizations with a wide array of client systems and with a range of other disciplines. Social workers work in interdisciplinary teams in in-patient hospitals, out-patient medical clinics, health-specific educational and advocacy organizations, residential care facilities, and home health and hospice organizations.

Social work in the health field, however, requires the social worker to have knowledge of the biological, psychological, and social aspects of human functioning along with the skills to work with other professionals that provide health care services. Understanding the distinct and overlapping roles of all

The Social Work Library

Read Gorin's article to find out what social workers can do about inequality in the health care system.

the disciplines that work with the patient population is key to being an effective medical social worker. Medical social work involves an integration of direct practice with individuals and families as well as an awareness of the impact of policies and the willingness to serve as an advocate for patients' needs.

Jane Sprankel, MSW, LCSW, Neighborhood Health Center

I have a master's degree in social work and am a social worker in the health field (see Exhibit 8.4). I began my career as an educator, but chose social work because when I had the opportunity to hear several social workers discuss their work, a light bulb went on for me. I knew this was the work that I wanted to do. After I completed my MSW, a friend encouraged me to consider social work in the health field because this area is interesting, fast paced, challenging, and requires the use of all social work skills, from policy to therapy. I took my friend's

EXHIBIT 8.4

St. John's Mercy Neighborhood Health Center

St. John's Mercy Neighborhood Health Center
3846 Ohio
St. Louis, Missouri 63118
The Neighborhood Health Center, a collaboration of Mercy Medical Group and Mercy Neighborhood Ministry, provides adult primary care and social services in an effort to increase health care access for underserved communities. The program primarily serves persons who are refugees and immigrants and have limited English speaking skills.

suggestion and entered the world of medical social work. I discovered that her assessment of the work has been true throughout my career.

Medical social workers practice in a variety of settings—hospitals, clinics, physician offices, ambulatory care centers, public health facilities, home health and hospice programs, and residential care facilities, to name a few. I have practiced in three health care settings—a hospital, an in-patient rehabilitation program, and a community-based health care center. Each of these settings has afforded me opportunities for practicing social work and learning new skills. As an MSW social worker in the health field, I felt it was important to obtain the credentials that certify my competence as a social work professional. Therefore, I obtained my ACSW, a national credential that certifies me as a member of the NASW Academy of Certified Social Workers (ACSW), and a license to practice clinical social work in my state.

As a new hospital social worker, I began my work at a community-based hospital assigned to the rehabilitation/skilled nursing unit. The population I served was primarily older adults that have experienced a health event and are in need of physical rehabilitation or skilled nursing care because they are no longer able to care for their own basic, daily needs. I was a member of an interdisciplinary team comprising professionals in nursing; physical, occupational, and speech therapy; dietetics; and utilization review (staff that oversee the process of managing the financial resources for health care services). My responsibilities were to assist with discharge planning, coping with illness and injury, patient and family education, and community resource referrals. During my time in this position, I developed a patient education program and support group for caregivers, became a part of a team that provided diabetic education for patients and families, and facilitated a support group for patients with chronic pulmonary disease.

Along with the direct practice opportunities, I saw the impact of state and federal policy on our patients' ability to access services. Through professional organizations I participated in working on changing Medicare and Medicaid policies. Through these experiences, the issues affecting older adults and their families became an area of increased interest for me. When I first began to work with older adults, I realize I saw them through my eyes and my age; but with more experience, I now see them through their eyes and their years of wisdom and living.

After four years in my first social work position, I found myself wanting to specialize in the area of rehabilitation and obtained a position as rehabilitation social worker at an in-patient rehabilitation hospital. My work focused on young adults with spinal cord and brain injuries. Not unlike my previous responsibilities at the community hospital, I worked with patients and families in the areas of discharge planning, coping, patient/family education, and community resource referrals. As a member of the rehabilitation team, I participated in developing and maintaining program evaluation goals, team building, and staff education. I became active with the disability community, working on issues of access and services at the state and federal level.

In the nine years I worked as a rehabilitation social worker, I saw a trend in the aging of the population we were serving. People were living longer and were more susceptible to acquiring a spinal cord or brain injury. Because I had previously worked with older adults, I understood the dynamics of the developmental issues of this population and their families. These older adults and their families often faced different types of caregiving situations, discharge planning, and coping issues than the younger adults on the unit.

In 1999, I had the opportunity to be involved in a new project that was being developed to provide primary care and social services to new refugees and immigrants. I was intrigued with the idea of applying my medical social work skills in another area of the health care delivery system, the physician's office. I was also intrigued with working with non-English-speaking, new refugees and immigrants. My clients were primarily new refugees to the United States who may have arrived a few days or weeks prior to their visit to the community health care center where I worked. In most cases, the patients were coming from resettlement camps in their own or other countries willing to house them until they received approval to come to the United States. The health care they had received prior to coming here was often intermittent or minimal. These men, women, and children were entering a country they may have only known through the movies, a complex health care delivery system, and a culture different from their own.

My world as a social worker shifted dramatically with this new experience. I learned new skills, not the least of which was how to interview and provide counseling services through an interpreter. Because I was dealing with individuals and families from multiple countries, cultural competence took on a whole new meaning for me. I became acutely aware that, although I was a good medical social worker, I was going to have to reframe my practice to better meet the needs of this new clientele.

As I had the opportunity to get to know our clients and their health and social service needs, the nurse practitioner, physician, and I began to realize that many of our clients were suffering from post-traumatic stress disorder (PTSD). Hearing the stories of the war, their transitions during and after it, led us to understand that many of these people had suffered great physical harm, torture, and abuse at the hands of their captors. As the social worker on our team, I assisted these persons and their families in locating mental health professionals specially trained in war trauma and torture. Issues of access of care, policy implementation, and policy formulation became central to my practice with this population. Working as a part of a coalition of agencies serving refugees and immigrants, I was able to advocate for interpreter services provided by Medicaid that increased access to quality medical care.

In my current social work position at a university, I have the opportunity to work with new MSW students as a practicum advisor in a refugee health center and an adjunct professor for a health policy course. I currently serve as a member of a board of an agency that provides mental health services to refugees and immigrants suffering from war trauma and torture. My practice as a medical social worker is a source of personal and professional satisfaction and has provided me with the expertise to serve as a mentor and teacher.

The future of social work in the health field is intimately tied to the aging population. The traditional settings of hospitals and clinics remain an arena in which social workers can work, but nontraditional settings, such as physicians' offices and ambulatory care centers, are increasingly becoming options for employment. Such health concerns as Alzheimer's disease, multiple sclerosis, brain and spinal cord injury, pediatric medicine, and cancer care have recognized the contributions of social workers and seek them to serve on their interdisciplinary teams. Rural health is another arena of practice for social workers. Local community hospitals are in need of general practitioners to serve as part of the health care delivery team. Social work students wishing to practice medical social work will likely find themselves practicing generalist social work and then specializing in one of many areas.

MENTAL HEALTH SETTINGS

The social work profession is the largest provider of mental health services in the United States today, accounting for almost two-thirds of services. The remaining one-third are provided by psychiatrists, psychologists, and psychiatric nurses, as shown in Exhibit 8.5. As you might expect, mental health practice is also the largest area of practice for social workers, with over one-third of social workers reporting this category as their primary field of practice (Gibelman & Schervish, 1997).

After five years of practice as a social worker, the number of social workers that identify mental health as the setting in which they work begins to increase, supporting the idea that immediately following graduation, social workers gravitate to employment in the areas of aging, family and children services, and health settings and then shift their focus to the provision of more traditional clinical services after gaining experience. Mental health services are most often provided by social workers with an MSW or PhD. These social workers tend to be older, more experienced practitioners. Fewer social workers who are persons of color and of diverse ethnic groups identify themselves as mental health practitioners, creating a need for greater diversity among mental health providers (Gibelman & Schervish, 1997).

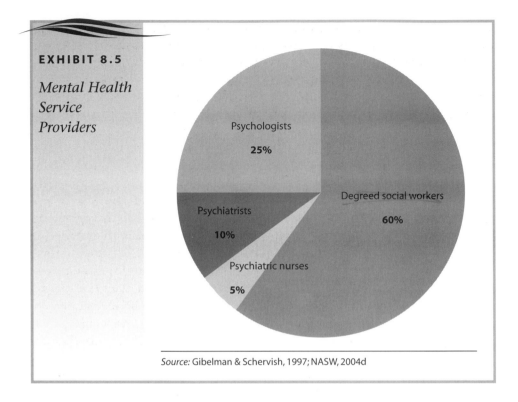

EXHIBIT 8.5

Mental Health Service Providers

Psychologists 25%

Degreed social workers 60%

Psychiatrists 10%

Psychiatric nurses 5%

Source: Gibelman & Schervish, 1997; NASW, 2004d

Practice Considerations in Mental Health Settings

Mental health services are provided in a variety of settings with diverse client populations. Social workers provide mental health services to children, adolescents, adults of all ages, families, groups, persons with physical and/or developmental disabilities; in correctional facilities, family service or mental health organizations, employee assistance programs, disaster relief programs, crisis intervention programs, victim assistance programs; and to persons from all races, ethnicities, and cultures. In sum, we are all potential consumers of mental health services provided by social workers.

Mental health services can be provided in the form of clinical therapy with individuals, families, and groups. Social workers facilitate support groups related to mental health issues, provide mental health education, and serve as advocates for those persons suffering from mental illness. More social workers providing mental health services are employed in out-patient mental health settings than in in-patient (hospital) settings (Gibelman & Schervish, 1997). Out-patient settings include public and nonprofit mental health centers and group and solo private practices.

A growing area of mental health practice for social workers is private practice. Over one-fifth of NASW members surveyed in the mid-1990s reported they were engaged in private or group clinical practice, making this the second ranked setting in which social workers practice (Gibelman & Schervish, 1997).

Nearly every major health insurance provider recognizes the graduate social work degree as a provider of mental health services, thus making clinical practice (private or agency based) a viable employment option for social workers with MSWs. Social workers in private clinical practice tend to garner the highest salaries within the social work practice community (Clark, 2003).

Barbara Flory, MSW, LCSW, Heritage House

I am a licensed clinical social worker employed in a program for families that have experienced domestic violence. My education includes an undergraduate degree in human services and a graduate degree in social work from a private university. My postgraduate training includes a certificate in family conflict management from a state university, and family therapy training from a program accredited by the American Association of Marriage and Family Therapy. My combined experience of family therapy and mediation has prepared me for the unusual position that I hold in today's social services environment.

Like me, many social workers are employed in intense, highly conflictual, often violent, settings. Nothing in our training prepares us for the assaultive nature of the work, which often leads to vicarious traumatization of the professional. Therefore, education in self-care is essential to support professionals who have chosen to work in this field. Having awareness of the need to care for oneself is one of the real issues facing the profession that require attention by social workers of tomorrow.

For the past seven years, I have been employed in a nonprofit mental health agency in a large metropolitan area. In my capacity as a program manager, I am responsible for all phases of program development, implementation, supervision of staff, and evaluation of program outcomes. Implemented in 1997, the program is a supervised visitation and custody exchange center implemented to meet the needs of family court and a special needs population of separated, divorced, and never-married families. The families are court mandated to participate in the programming out of three family court divisions: domestic relations (divorce and post-divorce child custody modifications), civil adult and child protection (time-limited protection orders sought by an adult), and juvenile dependency (child abuse and neglect cases resulting from a hotline call to child protection services).

As a public-private partnership between the local family court and the agency in which I work, this formal collaboration requires me to work at the interface between social services and the law, a unique position that requires knowledge beyond that which is traditionally a part of social work education.

Historically, supervised visitation between noncustodial parent and child is judicially ordered when the court determines that a child's safety is threatened by parental behavior. Supervised visitation is third-party guided contact between noncustodial parent and child for the purpose of maintaining or forming a relationship. Service delivery occurs on three levels to (1) ensure the safety of children when abuse is alleged, (2) reintroduce parent and child after a prolonged separation, and (3) introduce parent and child when no prior relationship exists. *Custody exchange transfer* is defined as the transfer of children from custodial to noncustodial parent for the purpose of temporary custody. In the context of child abuse and neglect, supervised visitation services have a well-established history as a means to facilitate family reunification. Supervised visitation is a relatively new service within the domestic relations arena that is gaining credibility as an effective intervention when domestic violence is an issue. Over time, the judiciary has slowly embraced the practice of ordering supervised visitation on domestic relations cases to ensure the protection of mothers and the children for whom they are responsible.

The population served is largely a violent group that engages in psychological and/or physical aggression as a way to resolve interpersonal conflict. Approximately 70 percent of the client population has a history of abusive behavior, most often male-on-female intimate partner abuse (generally referred to as domestic violence). In some instances, parental behavior excludes physical or sexual child abuse, and in other instances the children are abuse victims as well. Whichever the case, a violent home environment almost ensures diminished overall child well-being. Therefore, the program is structured to meet the unique physical and emotional safety needs of this abusive population.

In order to meet the needs of families, the program operates during nontraditional business hours, meaning evenings, weekends, and holidays, including Christmas day. Weekdays and Sunday begin at 4:00 p.m. when parents begin arriving to visit with their children under the supervision of a social worker. The social worker's responsibilities include ensuring children's safety during noncustodial parent visitation, teaching parenting skills and age-appropriate communication skills, and facilitating attachment and bonding as needed. Other noncustodial parents arrive at the center to pick up their children to spend time with them in an unprotected setting (for example, at home). The center is open on Saturday from 10:00 a.m. to 4:00 p.m., thus enabling parents to have flexible hours in which to spend time with their children.

Many of these parents have untreated, often undiagnosed, mental health disorders that contribute to their violent tendencies. Consequently, safety is paramount at the center, and off-duty police officers oversee the operation. A no-contact policy is necessary; that is, participating parents do not come face-to-face while at the center, or communicate with each other outside the center. It is encouraging to see that most parents can be good parents when offered the right circumstance. Unfortunately, sometimes circumstances dictate third-party intervention and court-restricted parental contact to ensure the cessation of violent behavior. I often find myself called upon to negotiate situations that are a crisis for the stressed parent, whereas they are situations of little consequence for most parents. The level of anger and distress of the stressed parent is often disproportionate to the event and can lead to violent outbursts with little provocation. Consequently, staff members are hypervigilant about safety and take all necessary precautions to ensure their personal safety as well as client system safety.

Supervised visitation is an emerging field of practice in social services that enjoys both praise and criticism from mental health and legal professionals. There is limited research about the effectiveness of services, with my team and myself being among a handful of social workers that have conducted research in this field. As practitioners, we conducted an exploratory study that showed that the service can be very efficacious in promoting noncustodial parent/child safe contact, reducing interparental violence and promoting child well-being (Dunn, Flory, Berg-Weger, & Milstead, 2004; Flory & Berg-Weger, 2003; Flory, Dunn, Berg-Weger, & Milstead, 2001). Since few social workers conduct research in their settings, my research experience and professional publications have resulted in consulting roles, such as judicial training for a national organization and participation in a federal task force charged with developing standards and guidelines for the profession.

The program that I manage is only one small piece on a continuum of care needed to sustain families in the modern-day world. The agency in which I work offers a broad scope of intervention services to include individual and family counseling, addictions treatment, workforce development, employee assistance services, suicide prevention, youth mentoring services, teen pregnancy prevention, and in-home geriatrics support services. I am fortunate that my employer values and supports innovative programming. Supervised visitation and safe custody exchange services emerged out of grassroots organizing that will support future programming, albeit at a limited level. Future expansion of services is largely in the hands of family courts faced with budgetary cuts due to shrinking state and federal budgets. There are, however, promising legislative efforts at the federal level to support noncustodial parental access to children. The national task force of which I am a member demonstrates a commitment to shape an emerging field that meets public policy expectations, thus legitimizing services and helping to ensure the future evolution of the field.

The Social Work Library

Danis' article sheds light on the issues facing social workers in the field of domestic violence.

RURAL SETTINGS

Rural communities are typically described as being more than 50 miles from a metropolitan area and having fewer than 50,000 residents (Ginsberg, 1998). Social work practice in rural communities is an important area of practice, but one that can go unnoticed. Oftentimes, social workers may, in fact, be the

The Social Work Library

Check out the article by Davenport and Davenport for a broad overview of social work in rural settings.

only providers of mental health services in rural, nonmetropolitan areas (Clark, 2003). Social workers with BSWs tend to be more commonplace in rural communities than MSWs and doctoral-level social workers. They are thus required to function at multiple levels, for which they are prepared as generalists, and to be knowledgeable about a wider array of issues and resources than may be needed in an urban area.

Early pioneers in rural social work focused on political and policy changes that were needed to increase the availability of social work services in rural communities (Brown, 1933; Ginsberg, 1998; Martinez-Brawley, 1983). However, despite the small numbers of citizens and lack of services, rural communities are diverse populations. The Rural Social Work Caucus notes that social work employment opportunities in rural communities are on the rise. However, rural social workers often come from urban environments and "must adapt their practice model significantly to do a credible job in rural areas" (CSWE, 2003).

Practice Considerations in Rural Settings

As generalist social work practice is the method best suited to practice in rural areas, social work educators are being called upon to include rural social work practice within social work curricula (DeWeaver, Smith, & Hosang, 1989; York, Denton, & Moran, 1989). Such a focus can help rural social workers to conceptualize the possible differences between urban and rural practice and incorporate these differences into the training of other social workers. A set of 19 assumptions has been developed by the Southern Regional Education Board Manpower Education and Training Project's Rural Task Force that includes guidelines for social workers in rural settings (Southern Regional Education Board, 1998). For example, rural communities may be diverse, but the people who live in them, as well as their needs, are more similar to people who live in urban areas than they are different. Although rural communities may lack basic services, greater priority is placed on services to sustain life than on those to enhance the quality of life. Rural communities have unique characteristics that can include geographically scattered poverty; existence of generational poverty; resistance to formal services and professionals, particularly those who are not members of the community; and more informal service networks.

Practice in small communities can provide social workers with a uniquely rewarding and challenging opportunity. In addition to being trained in generalist practice, social workers who practice in rural communities are required to develop knowledge, skills, and values appropriate for that community. These may include an understanding of the unique aspects of that community and the ability to use the community's customs and traditions as a basis for interventions; the willingness to respect the culture and values of the community; the ability to work within the informal network of services and resources; and the skills to develop new resources as needed (Southern Regional Education Board, 1998).

The social worker often plays overlapping roles in a small community. Whereas an urban setting typically offers a social worker anonymity, in smaller communities, social workers often have not only a history with, but also multiple ties to, persons to whom they will provide services. Such complex roles are not impossible in a larger community, but the potential is greater in a rural area due to the smaller population. Multiple roles can serve as both a strength and a liability in the social work relationship. Knowing a person's background, support system, and resources can be an asset in engaging her or him, assessing the situation, and developing and implementing an intervention. On the other hand, having extensive prior knowledge can compromise the social worker's professional objectivity.

Ellen Burkemper, PhD, MSW, LCSW, LMFT, RN, School of Social Service

For the last 25 years, I have provided a number of social work professional services in my small, rural community. I have found that social work practice in the small community is varied and requires that I be flexible and able to engage in services at the individual, family, group, and community levels. Through funding from the Department of Health, I participated in a program in which social workers obtain MSWs to provide mental health services through and in rural physicians' offices. Already a registered nurse, I was particularly well suited to this program, as I was familiar with the medical setting and terminology and lived in a rural community.

Upon completing my MSW, I had the opportunity to work in my community's mental health center as the center's coordinator and social work clinician. This practice opportunity brought forth all of my MSW generalist and clinical education and training. I was already knowledgeable about the services in my community and knew the local physicians and clergy that serve as the primary gatekeepers for referrals for mental health services. I felt this was a proactive way to bring the practice of social work to my community.

My responsibilities in the rural community mental health center included working with individuals, families, groups, organizations, and the community. Some of my practice activities included

- Providing clinical services (therapy) for individuals and families.
- Working with other agencies to identify and develop community services.
- Representing the center at community meetings and events.
- Organizing fund-raising events.

- Collaborating with other programs involved in the provision of services to persons living with chronic and persistent mental illness.

- Making presentations to community groups on the services provided by the center.

- Serving as a member of the agency's advisory board.

- Writing newspaper articles regarding mental health concerns.

Due to a lack of funding and a need to consolidate services, the center closed after I had worked there for 10 years. Having the center close might have been a crisis, but I realized that I had gained considerable expertise in clinical and administrative practice. Because of the confidence that I had gained as a social worker, I decided to establish a private clinical practice as a solo practitioner. Concurrent with the opening of my private practice, I continued my education, ending with a doctoral degree in marriage and family therapy. I also began to work as a trainer and consultant for therapeutic foster parents for child protective services in my county.

The opportunities I have had to provide services in my small community have been rewarding. In small communities, there is a need for mental health services, and social workers are ideally suited to provide these services. As generalists, social workers are trained to engage in all levels of practice, and that versatility enables us to exercise our talents and education.

Working in a small community can present challenges. I had to be familiar with the NASW *Code of Ethics* (1999). In particular, rural social workers are knowledgeable about the special implications of the possible dual relationships that can occur in a small community. My family and I are active in my community, and living and working in a small community means that I am likely to run into clients while grocery shopping, attending weddings, church, professional gatherings, or school events. I learned to be careful to keep office work at the office. Of considerable importance is ensuring that client systems have knowingly provided informed consent for the social worker to discuss their cases with other professionals and that the social worker will not discuss them with friends, family members, or acquaintances. Clients must fully understand the social worker's role and functions, and the special implications of confidentiality in a small community. I talk with the client about the likelihood that we will encounter one another outside the professional social work setting. I inform clients that should that occur, I will not acknowledge them until they acknowledge me. By placing the decision to communicate in a public setting with clients, I am providing them with the right to self-determination.

Social workers are needed in small communities. Social workers that live and work in the small community have a view that is fuller than those who drive to the job and return home to other communities. Having been a member of a family in this farming community, my knowledge of the community helps me understand the culture in which the client system lives. This insight has provided me with a more efficient understanding of my clients' backgrounds, social environments, and rural ethic.

I see small-community social work as a viable field of practice. It offers the opportunity to engage in all levels of practice. In some cases, a benefit of rural practice is the ease of getting tasks accomplished due to the fewer numbers of individuals who need to be consulted. Social workers living and working in small communities are a minority, but rural areas can be an opportunity for employment, and for the expression of professional talents and education.

CONCLUSION

Although vastly different in terms of the settings in which they practice, populations with whom they work, and challenges they face, these "voices from the field" share a number of similarities and themes. Each social worker possesses a social work degree, not a degree in gerontology, substance abuse treatment, or counseling. Upon completion of the requirements for the social work degree, the social worker is, thus, equipped with a set of knowledge, skills, and values that enable her or him to practice at multiple levels with diverse populations in different settings. Specific knowledge of a population and setting is required, but the engagement, assessment, intervention, and evaluation process is common regardless of the targeted client system or setting.

Other similarities can be identified across the fields of practice. Having knowledge of aging issues is obviously important for working with older adults, but can be critical for working in every other field of practice described in this chapter. Because a significant amount of health care resources are devoted to older adults, knowledge of aging is essential for social workers in the health care setting (Clark, 2003). With increasing frequency, grandparents are rearing grandchildren or are living in three-generational households, thus requiring the social worker to have knowledge of those issues faced by the older adults in their clients' lives. Older adults can develop addictions or mental illness or become part of the criminal justice system as a perpetrator or victim. Older immigrants and refugees can present unique challenges as they strive to create a life in a new culture.

Advocacy and policy practice are two additional areas about which the social workers are united in their perceptions. In each of the narratives, the social worker states implicitly or explicitly that working on behalf of the client population is part of being an effective social worker. Advocacy is a vital skill, especially when resources are a critical factor and policies are limiting. The social workers who shared their stories highlight the need to advocate for improved services, more liberal policies, increased funding, and more effective treatment modalities. To achieve better access to services, social workers must be on the forefront of the legislative advocacy efforts for such issues as universal health insurance coverage, equity in mental health benefits, economic reform, and better access to services for those groups whose voices are not being heard by policy makers (for example, older adults, children, persons with disabilities, refugees and immigrants, battered women, and persons in the criminal justice system) (Clark, 2003). To be effective advocates, social workers must be knowledgeable about the functioning of organizations and communities, the workings of the political system, and the role of social and economic development (Mizrahi & Baskind, 2003).

Several of the narratives provide insights into the opportunities to build on the practice skills used with individuals and families in order to move into administrative and management roles. Herb, Suzanne, and Barbara all write of their administrative functions, but each is grounded in her or his knowledge of the issues that social workers that work with individuals, families, and groups face in working in their respective fields of practice.

Each of the social workers emphasizes a strengths-based perspective in terms of their fields of practice. Being able to identify the assets and resources that a client system or population possesses contributes to being an effective advocate, an ethical practitioner, and a partner with the client system in the change process. The narratives provide evidence of the importance of critical thinking as a valuable social work skill. In Jon's narrative on working in chemical dependency and addiction treatment, he describes a traditional treatment modality for substance abuse. Moreover, he voices skepticism regarding the effectiveness of that particular approach for all substance abusers and offers his insights into an alternative framework. Jon's social work training instilled in him the value of questioning and examining his social work practice so that all possibilities can be explored.

I want to point out that shortages do exist in several of the fields of practice described here. More social workers are needed to work with older adults, in chemical dependency and addiction treatment, and in the child welfare arena (Gibelman & Schervish, 1997). Although a variety of initiatives have been launched to increase the number of degreed social workers in aging and child welfare, for instance, still more initiatives are necessary to meet the needs of these and other areas. To gain the experience to respond to these emerging needs, social work students can seek out elective courses in working with specific populations and settings, gain field experiences in the areas in which a need exists, and participate in research to develop enhanced treatment approaches and policy recommendations (Mizrahi & Baskind, 2003).

You may not know the area of social work practice that is right for you. I encourage you to work in a variety of areas so that you can find the area or areas that are the best professional fit for you. You can begin by working with a population or in a setting that is familiar to you, but I also encourage you to explore an area or setting with which you are completely unfamiliar. Using a strengths-based approach, you can assess your strengths and explore areas in which those strengths can be assets.

MAIN POINTS

- Social workers' range of knowledge and skills should include knowledge of human behavior and biology; the philosophy of other disciplines; awareness of cultures, laws, policies, and social systems; and the ability to work with a diverse population of clients and other professionals.

- With a social work degree, you can practice in a variety of different fields within the same career, including mental health, chemical dependency, and criminal justice. Within the field, you work with a variety of client systems at various levels.

- Eight social workers present their experiences in eight different fields, from working with older adults to working in a rural community, with the goal of sharing the diversity, challenges, and rewards of the social work profession.

- The diverse fields are held together by the commonality of social work practice. For example, working with older adults requires knowledge of medical and health issues. Further, working in mental health involves interactions with the legal and health systems.

- Although opportunities in the fields of practice presented here are increasing, other growth areas for employment exist in employee assistance programs, forensic social work, and school social work.

EXERCISES: PRACTICING SOCIAL WORK

Roberto Salazar

Using the Sanchez family interactive case study, review the information regarding Junior Sanchez and answer Roberto's Critical Thinking Questions.

Emilia Sanchez

Using the Sanchez family interactive case study, review the information regarding Junior Sanchez and answer Emilia's Critical Thinking Questions.

Gloria Sanchez Quintanilla

Using the Sanchez family interactive case study, review the information regarding Junior Sanchez and answer Gloria's Critical Thinking Questions.

EXERCISES: THE SOCIAL WORK LIBRARY

Exploring Fields of Practice: Part I

Select one of the fields of practice described in this chapter. After reading the article(s) in the Social Work Library that correspond to this area of practice, respond to the following:

1. Describe the field of social work (i.e., setting, client populations, major issues, etc.).

2. Describe the roles/opportunities for social work in this field.

3. Discuss your potential personal interests and skills in this area.

OTHER EXERCISES

Exploring Fields of Practice: Part II

Go to the www.naswdc.org, click on Issue Fact Sheets, and read about the various fields of practice that are included in this chapter.

Exploring Fields of Practice: Part III

With assistance from your instructor, identify a social work student with whom you can conduct an interview regarding her/his primary field of practice interests. Your assignment is to dialogue with your fellow student to gain insight into the reasons she/he has chosen social work for a career, the pros and cons of majoring in social work, and the life and academic experiences that she/he perceives to be helpful in pursuing a social work career.

Forward Vision

You have been given the opportunity to read about various fields of action in social work practice. Imagine that you are working in one of these fields of practice. Given your previous experience, respond to the following questions:

1. How might you see political, economic, and social issues impact your work?

2. What are the potential "isms" that you might encounter in this field of practice?

3. How might you adjust to the issues that you identified in the previous two questions?

CHAPTER 9

Social Work Practice with Individuals and Families

Emily's career has taken her down many paths, but the knowledge and skills she developed for working with individuals and families have proved invaluable in all her practice experiences. She has learned to develop rapport, establish trust, build relationships, conduct interviews, and employ skills of engagement, assessment, intervention, and evaluation, and this has formed the foundation of Emily's social work career. Emily has applied these skills when working with children, families, young adults, and older adult clients.

In this chapter, we explore the area of social work with individuals and families. Providing services to individuals, couples, and families is the cornerstone of social work practice. Also known as **micro practice**, working one-on-one with individuals and families is the primary focus of most practicing social workers. In fact, an NASW study conducted in the 1990s indicated that 65 percent of social workers with BSWs, 71 percent of those with MSWs, and 40 percent of doctoral-level social workers were engaged in direct practice (Gibelman & Schervish, 1997). Moreover, social work practice with individuals, couples, and families is an area that continues to grow. Not surprisingly, a larger proportion of younger and more recently graduated social workers are employed in direct practice areas, while many older, more experienced social workers often move into supervisory, administrative, management, teaching, and research positions. Practitioners who work with individuals and families continue to work primarily in traditional settings such as health and mental health and family service settings, but they are also found in educational, religious, and correctional settings. This chapter focuses on the history and meaning of this level of practice. It also identifies practice skills that are essential for direct practice with individuals and families.

HISTORICAL PERSPECTIVE ON SOCIAL WORK PRACTICE WITH INDIVIDUALS AND FAMILIES

As you learned in Chapter 2, the history of social work is, in many ways, the history of social work practice with individuals and families. The friendly visitors, outdoor relief, and eventually, the Charity Organization Society movement of the 19th century all served as the forerunners of modern-day social work practice with individuals and families. Focused on providing aid to the individual or family unit, the work of these early practitioners evolved into a methodology referred to as social casework. Recall from Chapter 1 that this is a method of social work practice in which social workers, through direct contact with the client system, help individuals and families to resolve personal challenges.

Using the medical profession as a model, Mary Richmond, in her 1917 book, *Social Diagnosis,* introduced the concept of social diagnosis as a method for the friendly visitors to objectively gather information and make assessments. This concept became the model for the social casework that social workers practice today. Moving beyond the concept of social diagnosis, Richmond's 1922 book, *What Is Social Case Work?* provided the basis for the teaching and practice of social casework for many decades to come. Richmond proposed social casework as a method for helping individuals adjust to their situations by identifying needs, goals, and resources (Brieland, 1995). Early caseworkers were trained in the idea that one approach—social casework—could be used to help individuals and families resolve problems caused by "deviations from accepted standards of normal social life" (Brieland, 1995, p. 2251). For example, social workers who engaged in casework during this period may have worked with an immigrant family to obtain housing and jobs, helped a widow to obtain financial assistance, or facilitated the adoption of an orphaned child.

The Social Work Library

Is casework dead? Read what Perlman has to say on this issue.

Introduced later, group work and community organization concepts encouraged the profession to accept the person-in-environment, ecological, and systems constructs. However, social casework continued to be the prevailing model for social work practice well into the 20th century. This exclusive focus on the individual changed when the social upheaval of the 1960s brought the issues of race, ethnicity, poverty, and human rights to the forefront of societal attention (Pinderhughes, 1995). This attention prompted social workers to incorporate a broader, more holistic perspective when intervening with client systems.

Contemporary concepts for practice with individuals and families emerged as a result of the changes of the 1960s and 1970s. Practice with individuals and families then shifted to include the emergence of the ecological model that encompassed the environmental perspective, the need for research to support and guide practice, and the birth of the generalist model (Pinderhughes, 1995). The generalist model emphasized an ecological, systemic, and strengths-based approach to working with individuals, groups, and communities. From that basis, social workers can develop a broad-based set of skills for working with any population.

THE CHANGE PROCESS IN SOCIAL WORK PRACTICE WITH INDIVIDUALS AND FAMILIES

Change is the goal of the social worker's involvement with client systems at all levels of practice. Change for the client system involves embracing new attitudes or behaviors. Within the context of the social work relationship, establishing goals for change is a key component of the plan developed to achieve the goals set by the client system. Change is a part of the intervention and is agreed upon by the social worker and the client system.

Social workers become involved in a wide variety of change efforts in working with individuals and families. For example, social workers help client systems in such situations as:

- Beginning or ending a phase of life, for example, marriage, divorce, parenting, career change, caring for a family member, retirement, or grief.

- Relationship difficulties, for example, friendship, family, marital, parent/child, or employment.

- Life crises, for example, physical or mental health problems, violence, natural or economic disasters, or legal problems.

- Chemical dependency and addictions, for example, alcohol, drugs, food, gambling, sexual, or spending.

All interventions revolve around **planned change**, a process in which the social worker and client collaborate to plan and then execute a series of actions designed to enhance the client's functioning and well-being. Planned change for interventions with individuals, families, groups, organizations, and communities consists of four phases: engagement, assessment, intervention, and evaluation. See Exhibit 9.1 for a depiction of the planned change model.

Change is a fluid process that involves unexpected starts and stops. The client system may be able to establish goals for change, but the process may be interrupted when real-life factors intervene; for example, the client may be seeking employment, but her or his car breaks down or child care arrangements fall through. The social worker's responsibility is to monitor and support the change process by helping the individual anticipate and respond to challenges and crises that affect the change process.

EXHIBIT 9.1

The Four Phases of the Planned Change Model

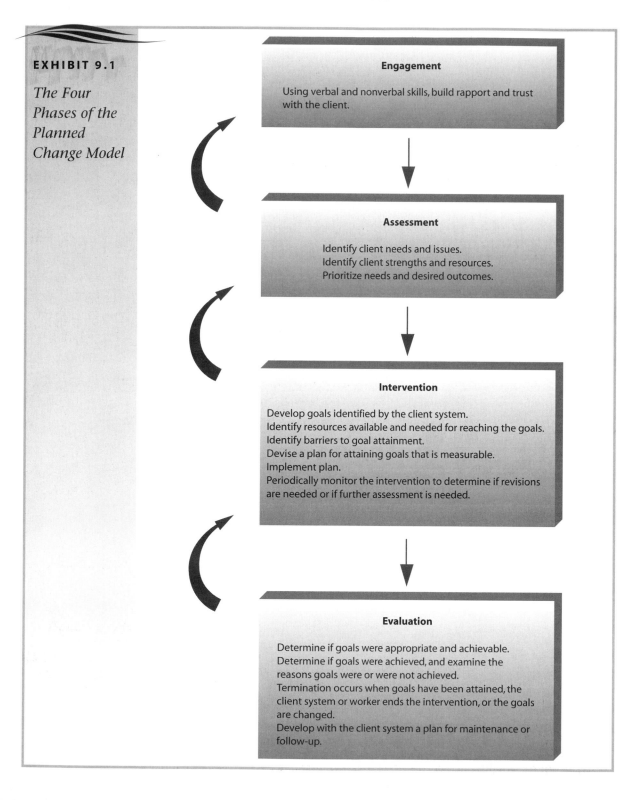

Engagement

Using verbal and nonverbal skills, build rapport and trust with the client.

Assessment

Identify client needs and issues.
Identify client strengths and resources.
Prioritize needs and desired outcomes.

Intervention

Develop goals identified by the client system.
Identify resources available and needed for reaching the goals.
Identify barriers to goal attainment.
Devise a plan for attaining goals that is measurable.
Implement plan.
Periodically monitor the intervention to determine if revisions are needed or if further assessment is needed.

Evaluation

Determine if goals were appropriate and achievable.
Determine if goals were achieved, and examine the reasons goals were or were not achieved.
Termination occurs when goals have been attained, the client system or worker ends the intervention, or the goals are changed.
Develop with the client system a plan for maintenance or follow-up.

BOX 9.1

Checklist of Personal Communication Styles

You may use the following checklist of personal communication styles to assess your own communication style. After answering the questions, identify those areas that may warrant attention in order to enhance your communication as a social worker.

- Are you more comfortable listening or talking?
- Do you view your role as being to give advice or explore options?
- When listening to someone describe a difficulty or challenge, do you feel compelled to immediately offer solutions?
- Do you find it difficult to pay attention when others are talking?
- Do you find that when others are talking, you are thinking of what you are going to say next?
- Do you find that you notice nonverbal communication as well as the verbal message?
- Do you become so consumed with the details of a story that you miss the essence of the story?
- Do you have a difficult time listening to a story without interjecting your own personal experiences or biases?
- How do you determine if you got the essence of the story?
- Do you find that you are easily distracted when conversing with another person (for example, watching other activities, thinking of things you have to do later)?
- How do you react to people who have difficulty communicating in a straightforward manner (for example, nonfocused, tangential), are uncommunicative, or hostile?
- Does your speech include "ums," "ers," "you knows"?
- Do you feel that you communicate in a straightforward manner?
- What is your nonverbal communication style—use of hands and gestures, volume and tempo of your voice, posture, and so on?

Source: Adapted from Corey & Corey, 1998, p. 69

To facilitate planned change, the social worker understands the situation from the perspective of the client system. Some clients want to change something in their lives and feel capable of doing so, whereas others who desire change feel incapable of doing so. Still other clients perceive no need for change. The saying "starting where the client is" guides social workers in gaining insight into the client's perception of the problem and the desired goal. This approach helps the social worker understand the client system's motivation and capacity for change and will prevent the social worker from making assumptions regarding the client's thoughts, feelings, and values. Understanding the client's stance

The Social Work Library

To learn more about "starting where the client is," read Goldstein's article.

on change can serve to deter the social worker from imposing her or his desired goals on the client.

The social worker is a collaborator in the planned change process. Recall from Chapter 7 that according to the strengths-based perspective, the client is the expert on her or his life, and the social worker's role is to support and empower the client to enhance her or his function and well-being. Staying true to this social work approach often requires social workers to take stock of their thoughts and feelings about the client's situation, choices, and goals. As one example of this process, Box 9.1 provides a checklist of questions that you can use to inventory your personal communication style.

To use the strengths-based perspective properly, social workers must consistently compare the client's goals with their own to ensure that the goals being worked toward are the client's and not the social worker's. As we all know from our personal experiences, our motivation is likely to be much higher when the goal we are working toward is one in which we are invested and one that we think has the most possibility for success. Because social workers sometimes work with clients who did not voluntarily seek assistance, goals can be quite different. The goals of the client who is not voluntarily seeking services may be to end the professional relationship as soon as possible. Even with that apparent disparity of goals, the social worker's responsibility is to "start where the client is" and identify the common ground on which to build a working relationship. In this case, the common ground may be the mutual desire to terminate the relationship.

SKILLS FOR SOCIAL WORK PRACTICE WITH INDIVIDUALS AND FAMILIES

To practice social work with empathy and efficacy, the social worker must possess a repertoire of specialized skills. In this section, we explore beginning social work skills for each of the four phases of the planned change intervention—engagement, assessment, intervention, and evaluation. These basic skills are essential for practice at all levels, and they serve as the foundation for the more advanced skills that social workers develop to address specific situations.

While working at the domestic violence program, Emily responded to a call from a convenience store manager late one night. A woman had come to the store and asked to use the telephone. Her swollen face and bleeding lip suggested that she had been physically assaulted. Recognizing the customer from previous visits to the store, the manager asked if she could help. The woman, Victoria, burst into tears and told the manager she had been attacked by a man she did not know as she was entering her apartment. He dragged her into some bushes, beat and sexually assaulted her, and then left her in the bushes as he fled on foot. Victoria agreed to allow the manager to call Emily's agency, but not the police.

Emily first met Victoria in the manager's office. As Emily entered the room, she observed Victoria lying on a couch in a fetal position and crying. When Emily moved toward her and said her name, Victoria visibly flinched. Emily recognized that as a result of the trauma that Victoria had experienced, building trust with Victoria was critical to being able to help her.

Emily's first step was to sit down near Victoria, but not too close to threaten her. She told Victoria who she was and that she was there to help in any way that she could. She asked Victoria if she could get her a tissue. As she spoke to Victoria, Emily spoke slowly in a warm and soft tone. She leaned forward toward Victoria but made no attempt to touch her. She told Victoria that the manager had informed her that Victoria had been attacked. Emily then suggested that if Victoria was willing and when she was ready, they go to the hospital so that Victoria could be examined and could call the police to report the assault. Emily was careful not to use graphic, medical, or legal jargon at this point, focusing instead on helping Victoria to feel safe.

Emily sat with Victoria for an hour before Victoria said she was ready to go to the hospital. Emily assured Victoria that she would stay with her through the examination and the police interview. As Victoria rose from the couch, Emily asked for Victoria's permission to physically assist her in getting up and walking to the car. During the trip to the hospital, Emily explained to Victoria what she could expect when they reached the hospital. She continued to speak softly, calmly, and with empathy, assuring Victoria that she was now safe and in control of the procedure.

Engagement of Individuals and Families

In order to conduct a complete and accurate assessment of the client system, the social worker's first task is to establish a working relationship that encompasses rapport, trust, and respect—three distinct phenomena. Rapport is the client's perception that she or he and the social worker have established a congenial relationship that promotes a sense of trust in which the client can share personal information (Shulman, 1999). When the social worker respects the client, she or he will treat the client with esteem and dignity.

Engaging the client is the first step in building a successful relationship. **Engagement** is the process of eliciting information in an open and trusting manner using both verbal and nonverbal communication. To engage the client system and build rapport, the social worker should attend to the following aspects of verbal communication:

- Speak at a pace that the client can easily follow, particularly with clients whose first language is different from yours or clients that have a hearing impairment.

- Speak at a level that the client can easily hear, but not too loud.

- Speak with warmth and empathy.

- Use language appropriate to the client's culture, ethnicity, and social group, but do not attempt to use language that is unfamiliar to you.

- Use language appropriate to the client's educational level.

- Avoid professional jargon that may be unfamiliar to the client.

- Use respectful language to refer to individuals and groups, paying particular attention to avoiding language that promotes the isms.

- Patiently listen while the client tells her or his story without interrupting, prompting, or interjecting words.

- Avoid "ums," "you knows," and other unnecessary language.

Attention to nonverbal communication is as important as verbal communication characteristics. Important nonverbal issues to consider include

- Ensure that you and the client are both physically on the same level (for example, both sitting).

- Maintain direct eye contact when culturally appropriate. When working with a family or small group, maintain equal eye contact with all members of the group. To look at one or more persons more than others can imply a preference or bias and can hamper your ability to establish trust with all members.

- Look at the client while speaking instead of looking out the window, at forms, or the client's chart, for example.

- Maintain physical and emotional focus on the client when the client speaks, as opposed to thinking ahead to the next question or comment.

- Avoid distractive behaviors (for example, playing with pencil/hair, swinging leg, tapping on the desk).

- Directly face the client.

- Lean slightly forward to indicate attentiveness.

- Use nonverbal gestures that are typical and comfortable, but ensure that they are not excessive to the point of distraction.

- Demonstrate appropriate facial expressions such as interest, warmth, and varied responses that are appropriate to the client's remarks. Facial expressions should be consistent with the words.

Assessment of Individuals and Families

Emily stayed with Victoria through the physical examination, the collection of evidence for the rape kit, and the police interview. Because these events took several hours, Emily had an opportunity to become more familiar with Victoria's situation. She learned that Victoria had moved to the city to attend college. She now was a management trainee at a department store in the mall and lived alone in a ground-floor apartment. She was engaged, but her fiancé lived in another state and visited only once a month. Her family was in her hometown several hours away. By asking questions in a gentle, unobtrusive manner, Emily was able to begin the assessment process. Emily was careful not to ask questions that were not relevant to gathering information for responding to Victoria's immediate need of safety. Emily learned that Victoria's attacker likely knew where she lived and possibly that she lived alone. She learned that Victoria had friends from school and work, but did not know anyone at her apartment complex, as she had just recently moved there. Victoria admitted that she was terrified to return to her apartment, but she did not want to leave town because she had work and school commitments.

Assessment is the professional activity conducted with the client that provides the basis for understanding the client system's situation and planning the intervention. In conducting an assessment at the individual, family, group, or community level, the social worker gathers relevant information and then uses theoretical frameworks to evaluate the information and determine its meaning for the client system. At the same time, the worker must evaluate the level of functioning for the system—with a focus on strengths—as well as the resources available to the system. When the social worker has completed this process, she or he works with the client to define and prioritize the issues to be addressed within the intervention. They then begin to develop the intervention, paying specific attention to the time frame, the necessary resources, appropriate strategies and activities, and desired outcomes (Meyer, 1995).

The next step in the assessment process is for the social worker to consider the types and quality of questions to ask the client. Questions should be focused on gathering only that information relevant to the situation at hand (and not just interesting). They should be grounded in the strengths-based perspective, and they should convey a sense of genuine support and empathy to the client. To elicit as much relevant information as possible and to optimize client comfort, assessments should also emphasize the following (Collins & Coleman, 2000):

- *A balance of open-ended questions and responses and closed-ended questions and responses:* **Open-ended questions** and responses (questions that ask what, how, and feelings questions) are helpful for gathering information and affirming the client's control of the situation. **Closed-ended questions** and responses (questions that can be answered by yes, no, or short answers) are more directive and allow the social worker to control the interview.

- *Avoidance of excessive questioning:* A good rule to follow is to ask no more than two questions in succession without pausing for reflection.

- *Periodic reflection:* Recapping or paraphrasing the client's response, known as **reflection**, enables the social worker to clarify her or his understanding of the client's words. Recapping not only makes the client feel validated and understood, but also enables her or him to clarify any misunderstandings by the social worker. At the same time, it enables the social worker to consider the information that has been shared and to plan for future comments and directions for the interview.

- *Silence:* Not speaking is an important social work skill. Pausing after asking a question enables the client to consider her or his response in a thoughtful manner.

The Social Work Library

Hartman's 1981 article on working with families continues to be an important reading for social workers today.

In addition to these guidelines, there are numerous behaviors that social workers should either embrace or avoid in developing an assessment. Table 9.1 gives additional examples of assessment don'ts and dos.

When conducting an assessment with a family, the social worker employs the same skill set that is appropriate for use with individuals, but with several additional considerations for the challenges inherent in assessing family issues. The family is a system, and working with a family essentially means working with a group and can be overwhelming at first. The family assessment provides the social worker and the family with insights regarding patterns of individual

ASSESSMENT DON'TS	EXAMPLE	ASSESSMENT DOS
Excessive utterances, excessive head nodding.	Frequent use of "That's good." "Really?"	Occasional use of these comments can serve as prompters or encouragers.
"Why" questions.	"Why did you hit your son?"	"What were you feeling when you struck your son?"
Use of poor grammar (for example, "that," "it").	"What did it feel like when it happened?"	"How did you feel when your daughter told you about the abuse?"
Closed questions.	"Do you want to tell me what brought you here today?"	"What brought you here today?"
Talking more than clients talk.	Social worker does the majority of the talking.	Client does the majority of the talking.
Machine gun questioning—series of "grilling" questions.	"Where were you when that happened? How did it feel? What did she say?"	The client's response should guide the next question.
Leading questions.	"I'm sure you told him that you would leave him if he didn't stop drinking, didn't you?"	"What did you say to your husband about his drinking?"
Placating.	"Now, Mrs. Smith, there is nothing to worry about."	"Mrs. Smith, I will be here to support you through this experience."
Minimizing.	"I'm sure you're keeping so busy that you don't really miss him that much."	"Missing a loved one who dies is a normal reaction."
Rescuing.	"I'll make sure that you don't get evicted."	"How can I help you with your housing situation?"
Fidgeting.	Twirling hair, playing with a pen/pencil, or moving about in the chair.	Movement is normal, just not to the point of distraction.
Poor attending skills.	Looking out the window, through papers, or responding to a beeper.	Focusing on the client during the encounter is essential to the social work relationship.
Giggling at inappropriate times or during silences.	Giggling, in general, conveys an unprofessional air and is offensive.	Laughing with the client at appropriate times is supportive.

TABLE 9.1

Assessment Don'ts and Dos

TABLE 9.1
continued

ASSESSMENT DON'TS	EXAMPLE	ASSESSMENT DOS
Use of repetitive words (for example, "you know," "like," "OK," "uh-huh").	"I'm like, you know, happy to set another appointment with you, OK?"	"I will be happy to schedule another appointment with you."
Giving advice.	"I definitely think you should have the procedure."	"Let's explore the pros and cons of having the procedure."
Multiple, double-barreled questions.	"When did you separate? Have you filed for divorce?" (Client may not know which to answer, or answer one and leave worker with the wrong impression.)	Ask a question, wait for a response, and continue.
Slouching.	Slouching implies a posture that suggests this is a casual relationship and the worker may not be taking the situation seriously.	Sitting upright and leaning slightly forward suggests a professional, interested posture.
Letting the client ramble.	Allowing the client to wander off the topic to the point that assessment cannot be completed.	Clients can often provide useful information while talking, but the social worker should monitor.
Mimicking cultural traits or language or client's behaviors.	Using language or gestures that are not typical, but done only for the benefit of the client.	Use appropriate language, but do not "experiment" on the client.
Taking sides with the client.	"I know you meant well."	"My role is to be objective and neutral."
Giving false reassurances or agreeing when that is inappropriate or unknown.	"I'm sure the doctor will be able to give you good news on your tests."	"If you would like, I can be with you when you get your test results."
Ignoring cues about the client's subjective experiences and only focusing on the objective issues (for example, getting the form completed).	"Now, what was your annual income last year?" (asked while client is sobbing).	"You seem very upset. Would you like to talk about it?"

ASSESSMENT DON'TS	EXAMPLE	ASSESSMENT DOS	
Judgmental responses.	"I am sure you want to take care of your mother at home instead of putting her in a nursing home."	"Have you thought about your mother's care? Let's discuss the options."	**TABLE 9.1** *continued*
Inappropriate use of humor.	"You know how they (*fill in the group*) can be."	If initiated by the client, the social worker should confront the inappropriate humor.	
Premature problem solving.	"I've heard enough. Let me tell you what I think."	"I need more information before we can discuss options."	
Criticizing or belittling clients or behaving in a condescending way.	"You're not being fair." "You shouldn't worry about that."	"You seemed concerned about that."	
Overreliance on chitchat.	Anything beyond the usual greeting and pleasantries is too much casual conversation.	Greeting the client, asking about her or his well-being and responding briefly to any inquiries is appropriate.	
Overprotecting clients by avoiding clear cues to implicit information.	"I think there may be some concern about your son's academic performance" (when, in fact, the son is failing).	"I am concerned that your son's grades are below the level needed for him to pass."	
Inappropriate response to information shared by client.	With wide eyes, "Wow, you have got to be kidding!"	Empathetically stated, "You must have been surprised."	

Source: Adapted from Collins & Coleman, 2000

behaviors, family functioning, relationships, communication patterns, and dynamics among family members.

The first step in conducting a family assessment is to determine the composition of the family. This process requires the social worker to have a broad concept of family, given that the definition of family has changed considerably in recent years. The accepted social work definition of **family** is a group of persons, usually residing together, who acknowledge a sense of responsibility for one another and function as a unit. As defined by the U.S. Census Bureau (2001), the number of "family" households (co-residents related by birth, marriage, or adoption) rose 11 percent between 1990 and 2000. During the same period, however, nonfamily households (persons living alone or persons living with nonrelatives) grew by 23 percent, suggesting that social workers need to rethink traditional definitions of family.

Adopting a broad definition of family helps the social worker to conduct a thorough family assessment. Social workers routinely intervene with family units that do not conform to the traditional definition of family. Examples are gay, lesbian, bisexual, and transgendered couples; people who share a residence but are not biologically or legally related; blended families that include the children of multiple marriages or relationships; single parents; grandparents serving as parents; and foster and other kinship relationships.

When conducting a family assessment, the social worker must determine which family members are to be included in the change effort. Several factors may contribute to the composition, including the goal(s) of the persons seeking services, the willingness and availability of family members to participate, and the relationships of the family members with one another. For example, in an adoption process, all members of the family should be involved, as the addition of a new member will affect everyone. Engaging with each family member can be particularly difficult if one or more members has not voluntarily sought the services of a social worker or has different needs and agendas for the intervention. Involuntary participants may feel anger, resentment, or hostility. The skills of engagement described in this section become critical as the social worker strives to establish rapport with each family member and the family unit as a whole, while observing the interactions among family members and between the family and their external environment.

Intervention with Individuals and Families

Using the information that she had gathered from Victoria during the assessment process, Emily developed an immediate and short-term plan for intervention with the agreement that Victoria would allow Emily to follow up the next day. With Emily's help, Victoria was able to state that her immediate need was a safe place to stay. In response, Emily arranged for Victoria to stay with a friend from work. Being sensitive to the trauma that Victoria had experienced, Emily did not want to overwhelm her with a request to establish long-range goals.

Over the next several weeks, Emily had regular contact with Victoria. Emily told Victoria that she was there to support her through this period, but their goal will include phasing Emily out of Victoria's life as Victoria recovers and regains emotional strength. Together, they established a list of objectives as prioritized by Victoria. Victoria wanted to return to living independently, feel safe, and be able to talk with her family and fiancé about her experience. Emily identified several types of services that would be most helpful to Victoria. Working together toward the goals identified by Victoria, Emily helped Victoria to return to her apartment complex, although she relocated to a third-floor apartment in another building. Emily referred Victoria to several services that helped her to meet her goals: the community police program for an in-home safety assessment, a support group for sexual assault survivors, and a clinical social worker to help her address her feelings of guilt and violation and to work with Victoria's family and fiancé.

Once the social worker has engaged with the client and gathered relevant information to assess the client's situation, the worker and the client can jointly begin the process of planning and carrying out the intervention. **Intervention** is the phase of the social work relationship in which the actual work is completed. During the assessment phase, the social worker and the client engage in the process of identifying needs, issues, strengths, and resources. Using that information, they next focus on prioritizing the client's needs and mobilizing the client's strengths and resources to facilitate the desired change.

The social work intervention involves two steps: planning and implementation. In planning an intervention, the social worker and the client identify the areas of change on which the client system wants to focus the intervention. Initially, the goals may be broad or overwhelming. Through discussion, the social worker and the client will prioritize the goals and define each goal in specific behavioral and achievable terms. This is the point in the intervention in which the social worker and the client negotiate and document a contract that is mutually agreed upon, clear, measurable, and specific.

Once the intervention is planned, the next step is implementation. Reviewing the contract on a regular basis enables the client and the social worker to monitor progress and determine whether the goals and strategies are realistic or if they should be changed or eliminated. Applying the concepts of the strengths-based approach to planning and implementation, the social worker recognizes the client as the expert on her or his life and respects the client's right to self-determination in facilitating the change process.

The intervention phase can be a time of gratification and fulfillment, but it can also be a time of frustration and struggle. Changing lifelong behaviors and patterns of interaction is sometimes difficult and even painful for clients. Social workers, too, can be challenged when clients are unable or unready to change their lifestyles. Nevertheless, when social workers and clients commit to mutually agreed-upon goals and agree to make adjustments as needed, the intervention can produce a positive outcome. A written contract, mutually agreed upon by both the social worker and the client, is a valuable tool in the development and implementation of an intervention. Box 9.2 provides an example of a contract format that can be used to develop goals and strategies for the planned change effort.

Although the intervention phase may seem to be the culmination of the client–social worker relationship, evaluation and termination of the intervention are equally important.

Evaluation and Termination of Individuals and Families

After Emily worked with Victoria for three months, she reminded Victoria that their goal was to terminate the relationship when Victoria felt she no longer needed Emily's support. The two of them took this opportunity to evaluate their work together. Using the contract they had negotiated as a basis for their evaluation, they reviewed each of the objectives. By that time, Victoria had settled into her new apartment. With the community police officer's help, she had taken a number of personal and environmental safety measures. She was regularly attending the sexual assault survivor support group and had seen the clinical social worker three times. She wanted to continue with the support group because she felt they understood her fears, setbacks, and uneasiness in talking about the event with others. Because the goals that they established were specific and measurable, Emily and Victoria were able to determine that their work together was a success and Victoria was ready to terminate her relationship with Emily.

Evaluation is the process by which the social worker and client system assess the progress and success of the planned change effort and determine whether it is time to terminate the relationship. In order for the social worker and the client to conduct a meaningful evaluation, the assessment and intervention phases must have been conducted in a comprehensive, well-conceived, and collaborative manner. In turn, these phases can be completed successfully only if the goals and objectives were developed with specificity and clear-cut strategies for measurement.

Evaluations can focus on assessing both the social work intervention itself (for example, the dynamics of the social worker–client system relationship) and the success of the intervention in attaining the defined goals (Shulman, 1999). The social worker may want to conduct periodic evaluations throughout the

Client Name(s):

Victoria H.

Client System's Description of Issues to Be Addressed:

Feel safe

Remain independent

Goals and Tasks:

Goal	Client Tasks/Date	Social Worker Tasks/Date
1. Arrange for safe, alternative housing	Inquire about apartment above ground floor.	Provide referral to community police program.
2. Talk with my family and fiancé about the rape.	Attend survivor support group and meet with therapist.	Provide referral to survivor support group and therapist specializing in rape trauma.
3. Assume control of my life.	Journal daily and share journal with social worker.	Provide support as needed.

Date Contract Will Be Reviewed:

3 months from date of contract

I agree with the above stated goals, to complete the contracted tasks, and participate in a review and evaluation of the contract on the specified date.

Victoria   Emily

Client   Social Worker

Date   Date

BOX 9.2

Sample Contract for Client System and Social Worker Intervention Planning

course of the intervention to monitor its progress. If progress is not being made, the social worker and client can refocus the intervention strategy in a direction that is more likely to promote a successful outcome.

Although periodic evaluations are helpful, evaluating the intervention at the time agreed upon in the contract is critical. This allows the social worker and client to address some fundamental questions: Can the relationship be terminated because the goals have been successfully achieved? Were the goals not achieved and should they be renegotiated? Should the relationship be terminated because there is no longer a need? Determining whether the intervention facilitated the change that the client desired also serves as a way of evaluating the social worker's practice (for example, is the social worker offering appropriate and helpful input?). Using the contract as a basis for evaluation, the social worker and client can scrutinize each aspect of the intervention to determine whether the social worker upheld her or his commitment to the client and the change effort, adhered to professional ethical standards, and met the obligations to which she or he contracted.

As in so many areas of social work practice, a variety and combination of methods and skills are available for conducting evaluations. Some specific strategies for measuring the success of practice approaches include evaluating programs and change. Measuring clients' attitudes and behaviors before, during, and following an intervention provides evidence of change. Obtaining the client's feedback regarding services and benefits is a common strategy for evaluation. Client satisfaction measures should be interpreted with caution, however, as satisfaction, or lack thereof, does not necessarily determine success or effectiveness. Another effective strategy is to monitor change through the life of a contract. Developing the contract to identify mutual goals, strengths, and resources; strategies for achieving the goals; and barriers to goal achievement will give the social worker and client a working document for evaluating change throughout the intervention.

Agencies that fund social work programs and services have placed increasing importance on evaluating social workers' services as a way to determine funding levels. In other words, social workers can no longer just try to "help people." Rather, they now must verify that people were helped, and they must identify change that occurred as a result of the intervention. Within the profession itself, evaluating social work methods and practices enables social work educators to develop curricula that will train new social workers to be effective and efficient.

After completing their evaluation of their work together, Emily and Victoria planned for termination. They agreed they would meet one more time. At that meeting, they again reviewed the goals they had established and the progress that Victoria had made in meeting her goals. They discussed plans for handling situations in which Victoria felt her safety was being threatened, and they antici-pated such events as the anniversary of the rape and her upcoming marriage. Emily offered Victoria the option to contact her in the future if she felt a need to talk or just to let Emily know how she was doing. Emily commended Victoria on her strength in handling this situation, and she told Victoria she appreciated Victoria's willingness to work with her. Victoria told Emily that she had been a "lifesaver" and she would forever be grateful to her. She admitted that she would miss Emily, and she was grateful to know that she could call Emily if she felt a need to talk with her.

Termination, defined as the official breaking off of the social worker–client relationship, is the goal from the first encounter. Failure to establish termination as the ultimate objective can lead to situations in which the client becomes de-pendent on the social worker. Individuals and families can come to feel comfort-able in their relationships with the social worker and be reluctant to lose the sup-port and caring that the worker provides. Because the mission of social work is to empower clients to enhance their functioning and well-being, social workers are obligated to engage the client, assess the situation, plan and carry out an inter-vention, evaluate the intervention, and then terminate the planned change relationship. The social worker who empowers the client to make changes in her or his life and devises a plan for maintaining that change provides a greater ser-vice than a worker who creates a relationship in which the client continues to look to the worker for help with each life crisis. Of course, if future events create a real need for assistance, services can be resumed.

Terminations occur for a variety of reasons and in a variety of ways. The so-cial work relationship can be terminated in the following situations:

- The goals have successfully been achieved.

- The client withdraws from the relationship because she or he no longer agrees with the plan established within the contract.

- The client is no longer eligible to receive services.

- The social worker feels that the goals cannot be achieved or the client is unwilling to comply with the contract.

- The social worker or agency is no longer the most appropriate service provider for the client.

Ideally, the concept of termination is introduced at the first social worker–client encounter. It is then built into the intervention, routinely discussed, and carried out in a planned manner. Planned terminations enable the client to enter into the contract and work through the intervention with a clear focus on the desired outcome, knowing that when the specified goals are reached, the planned change relationship will be terminated. Determining the point at which termination can occur often influences the planning and implementation of the intervention. For example, when working with a person who identifies self-sufficiency as a priority, the social worker can design an intervention aimed toward independent living and economic stability. When the person has secured housing and a regular income, the planned change relationship can then be successfully terminated.

Successful termination of the social work relationship includes the following processes:

- Reviewing the goals and objectives included in the contract to determine whether these goals have been met, to identify barriers to meeting the goals, and consider future goals.

- Developing a plan for maintaining change after the relationship has been terminated. This plan must anticipate issues such as the client's response should the crisis occur again, as well as the skills, resources, and strengths developed and needed for the client's response.

- Discussing continued professional contact between the social worker and the client, anticipating such questions as when and under what conditions future contact would be acceptable and the appropriate parameters for that contact.

- Expressing feelings about ending the relationship. The nature of the social work relationship can be intense and personal, and both the client and social worker can feel anxious or sad about ending that part of their lives. Therefore, discussing feelings is an important ingredient in a successful termination.

A skillfully facilitated termination can be gratifying for both the client system and the social worker. Client systems can achieve a sense of closure and, if permitted by agency policy, can be reassured that they can contact the social worker in the future if the need arises. Also feeling a sense of closure, the social worker can end the planned change relationship with the client, having addressed the progress, developed a maintenance plan, and discussed their feelings about the work they have completed together.

CONCLUSION

Social work practice with individuals and families can be approached systematically using the steps of engagement, assessment, intervention, and evaluation. Although such an approach provides a structure for working with individuals and families, facilitating a planned change is not always straightforward, simple, or without complications. During the intervention phase, the social worker should routinely revisit the original assessment to determine whether it is accurate. Working with client systems whose lives can be steeped in crises, unexpected twists and turns, and external pressures requires social workers to be flexible and patient. Social workers must be willing to renegotiate or delay plans for interventions in order to respond to unplanned changes in the planned change effort.

In the next two chapters, we explore the process of engagement, assessment, intervention, and evaluation in the context of social work practice with groups, organizations, and communities. Although the client systems at the group and community levels are larger, the same basic premise provides the foundation for the social work intervention. Having the knowledge and skills to build rapport and trust, gather information, develop a planned change effort, and evaluate and terminate the intervention is the same regardless of the size or makeup of the client system.

This chapter has provided you with the framework from which you can expand your social work knowledge and skills. The agency in which you work will determine the specific assessment tools, intervention protocols, and evaluation methods that you will use, but having a well-grounded knowledge of the change process will enable you to transfer the knowledge and skills to the setting.

MAIN POINTS

- Direct social work practice with individuals and families is the process of working one-on-one with the client system to identify and assess a need and develop a plan for facilitating a change.

- The client system's investment in the change process is key to the success of the social work intervention. The social worker is a collaborator in the planned change process.

- Developing a social work intervention using the strengths perspective is essential for identifying the assets and resources possessed by the client system and for planning a successful intervention.

- Social workers practicing with individuals and families use a variety of skills within the context of engagement, assessment, intervention, and evaluation.

- Engagement is the building of rapport and trust with the client system.

- Assessment includes gathering information about the client system and the client's perception of her or his strengths, resources, and needs.

- With the client, the social worker plans an intervention that includes determining desired goals, priorities, barriers to change, and strategies for making change.

- Evaluation consists of assessing the progress and/or success of change and the change process, the effectiveness of the social work intervention, and readiness to terminate the client-worker relationship.

EXERCISES: PRACTICING SOCIAL WORK

A Case from Start to Finish

It is now your turn to apply the knowledge of individual and family social work practice that you have acquired by reading this chapter. Using the Sanchez family interactive case study, you will have the opportunity to experience a social work relationship from engagement through evaluation.

Assessment through the Ecolens

Click on Assess and Ecolens. Review each of the four lenses. Click to open the panel for the Sanchez family. Review each of the four eco-perspectives. Select one of the eco-perspectives, click on a topic in the center circle to select it, and answer each of the questions that appear.

   After you have completed these questions, complete Tasks 1–3 for this section.

Intervention

Click on Intervene. Continuing with the client that you selected in the Assessment segment, develop an intervention plan. Following the prompts, define goals and needs, identify tasks for the client and social worker, and complete the timeline. Complete Tasks 1–3 for this section.

   Click on the Interaction matrix. Match the client with whom you were working previously with the members of her/his family by clicking on Plot the Interaction. Identify the issues or barriers that exist between your client and her/his family members.

Termination and Evaluation

Click on Evaluate. Continuing with the client that you have been focused on, complete Tasks 1–3 for that specific client.

EXERCISES: THE SOCIAL WORK LIBRARY

Is Casework Dead?

After reading "Casework is Dead" (Perlman, 1995), write a brief paper reflecting on your reactions as you read the article. Specifically:

1. What thoughts did you have as your read the letter from Mrs. Jones?

2. Identify the needs of the Jones family.

3. Comment on your position regarding the author's original premise that casework is dead.

Starting Where the Client Is

After reading "Starting Where the Client Is" (Goldstein, 1983), respond to the following:

1. Describe your understanding of Goldstein's premise that competent social work practice is grounded in "starting where the client is."

2. Reflect on the possible strengths and challenges related to starting where the client is.

3. Consider the following scenario and describe the way in which you would start where the client is:

Mr. J. is a 61-year-old male. He was diagnosed with probable dementia of the Alzheimer's type. Mr. J. is experiencing increasing memory problems; he has been unable to find his car in the mall parking lot on three occasions, and has begun to lose his possessions (e.g., glasses, keys, etc.) on a regular basis. He works as a shipping and receiving foreman for a discount chain store. Given that the typical course of Alzheimer's disease is eight to ten years from time of diagnosis to death, the physician has recommended that Mr. J. consider early retirement within the next year and that he be evaluated by the Department of Motor Vehicles to determine if he is safe to drive. The physician has asked you to followup with Mr. J. and his family to implement these recommendations. Mr. J. and his family—which includes his wife and adult son—are adamantly opposed to both recommendations, stating that his forgetfulness is just normal aging and that everyone misplaces small items and gets lost in large parking lots. Where do you begin?

What Knowledge Do Social Workers Need?

After reading "Knowledge for Direct Social Work Practice: An Analysis of Trends" (Reid, 1997), respond to the following:

1. Summarize the major shifts that occurred in the social work profession in the last quarter of the 20th century.

2. As you think about our contemporary world, what are the primary issues and challenges that face social workers today?

OTHER EXERCISES

Social Work Scripted

Write a script as though it were a play. The script will focus on a social worker interviewing an individual or family client system. Include in the script the questions that the social worker would ask in her/his assessment of the individual or family. Also include the facial and body language of the social worker and the client system. Include the client system's responses to the social worker. At the close of the script, draw an ecomap of the individual or family system and identify the individual and family strengths and areas for growth and change.

Journal Entry #4—Changes

Describe a change you have made in your life, how you were able to do so, why you made the change, and the long term effects of the change on you and those in your environment. Discuss how this experience might impact your work and professional development.

CHAPTER 10

Social Work Practice with Groups

Over a period of time, Emily began to notice that the clients staying at the shelter for battered women and their children shared a common concern regarding parenting. In working with the women with children, Emily heard many women voice apprehension about the effects of domestic violence on their children. Emily was uncertain as to the most effective method for addressing this issue. Emily determined three possible strategies for responding to the need for parenting information: (1) the Community-wide Domestic Violence Coalition could develop a program; (2) Emily could approach a local clinical social worker about forming a therapy group for women who had been victims of domestic violence, and parenting could be incorporated as a therapeutic goal; or (3) Emily's agency could form a support group for current and former residents of the shelter.

In this chapter, we will learn more about each of the options Emily proposed and the one that best met the needs of Emily's clients.

Working with groups has long been a part of social work practice. Also referred to as **mezzo (meso)** practice, **group work** is a practice method in which the social worker works with a multiperson client system to develop a planned change effort that meets the needs of the group. The goals of group work focus on addressing individual issues, a need for information and education, support, or social problems. The social worker's role in a group can be as a facilitator, therapist, resource person, or consultant.

Social work practice with groups emphasizes group interdependence, interaction, and support as the vehicle for change. Group practice is built on the concept that change occurs as a result of the ongoing and changing group dynamics and group members' interactions with one another. Thus, group social work practice has a dual role—the group and the individual change as a result of the group intervention (Schopler & Galinsky, 1995). Essentially, the strength of group work is that a group can accomplish more as a group than a person can alone, whether the desired change is on the individual or community level. Moreover, the concept of "people helping people" can be empowering, de-pathologize problems and stigmas, and reduce social and emotional isolation (Gitterman & Knight, 2000, p. 15).

Group work is increasingly a part of most social workers' career experiences. Most social workers engage in some form of group social work practice as a part of their social work positions, but may view group work as just one of many activities in which they engage. The NASW *Code of Ethics* (1999) includes working with groups as one of the ethical principles for social work practice. The *Code* charges social workers to strengthen relationships and the well-being of people at all levels of social work practice, including social groups. The *Code* also mandates that social workers practice with competence, thus providing the basis for all social workers to have knowledge and skills for working with groups.

This chapter highlights the historical development of group work as a method of social work intervention and the role of group work within generalist social work practice. We will explore the types of group work methods along with an introduction to skills needed to effectively deliver group services.

HISTORICAL PERSPECTIVE ON SOCIAL WORK PRACTICE WITH GROUPS

First used in the settlement house movement of the late 1890s, a group approach was most effective for the reform of such social problems as inadequate housing and working conditions, a concept still present in contemporary community-based organizations (Schopler & Galinsky, 1995). Group work for the promotion of recreational and educational activities then emerged after World War I. Mary Richmond, known primarily for her contributions to the development of practice with individuals and families, began to draw attention to the practice of group work during the 1920s, but it was not until the 1930s that group work was recognized within the profession as a method for intervention (Brieland, 1995). Before the introduction of training specific to group social work practice, group work was considered primarily a recreational or nonprofessional activity.

The term group work was first used in 1927 and provided the basis for introducing curricula to train social workers in professional group facilitation (Brieland, 1995). By the 1930s and 1940s, group work had become an intervention method for professional social workers working with hospitalized patients, persons with developmental disabilities and mental illness, and returning World War II veterans. The depression of the 1930s contributed to the growth of social work practice with groups as social workers mobilized groups for the purpose of social change and coping with the devastation of the depression (Garvin, 1997). However, controversy regarding group work's place within social work practice continued as professionals debated whether group work was a recreational activity, a social work method, or a separate profession.

Interest in incorporating group methods into social work practice continued to grow and expand into more settings over the next several decades. During the 1960s, the profession began to view group work as a part of social work practice and began to promote a similar skill set for casework and group work (Garvin, 1997). By the 1970s, social workers were participating in a variety of experimental groups focused on self-improvement. Over the next 20 years, group work became an integrated part of social work practice for social workers addressing clients' challenges and issues at the individual and family, organizational, and community levels.

BOX 10.1

Standards for Social Work Practice with Groups

- Familial, social, political, cultural context of member identity, interactional style, and problem—members are viewed as citizens capable of change and helping one another.

- Attention to the whole person using such concepts as systems theory, person and environment and biopsychosocial perspectives, member-in-group, and group-in-community.

- Competency-based assessment with an emphasis on member strengths as well as concerns.

- Mutual aid function—the group consists of multiple helping relationships and the worker's role is one of helping members help one another.

- The democratic process characterizes groups—members are helped to own the group, members and social workers have equal worth, egalitarianism, and reciprocity.

- Group emphasizes empowerment—group goals focus on individual growth and social change and the social worker promotes individual and group autonomy.

- Assessment and intervention are flexible and eclectic.

- Group behavior is characterized by the group being viewed as an entity separate and distinct from individual members, the phases of group development foster change over the life of the group, and recognition that group process shapes and influences individual members' behavior.

- Groups are formed for different purposes and goals—the type of group influences the social worker's role and methods of goal attainment.

- Monitoring and evaluation are conducted through observation and measurement of outcomes and processes.

Source: AASWG, 2004

Group social work practice is now recognized as part of the profession's mission to empower and promote well-being through the social worker's serving in the roles of broker, teacher/educator, enabler, advocate, mobilizer, mediator, and case manager. The profession recognizes the value of educating all social workers in group knowledge and skills. As a result, all social work students are exposed to group work theory and practice through coursework and field experiences. In 2000, the Association for the Advancement of Social Work with Groups (AASWG) developed its Standards for Social Work Practice with Groups. Listed in Box 10.1, the standards specify the core knowledge and values needed for social work practice with groups.

MODELS OF CHANGE IN SOCIAL WORK PRACTICE WITH GROUPS

Building on the knowledge and skill base established for working with individuals and families, group work practice has evolved into distinct change approaches with similar theoretical underpinnings. Three models for group work were introduced at a 1966 meeting of the Council on Social Work Education that continue to influence contemporary social work practice with groups (Garvin, 1997). The three models include goals related to social issues, remediation, and reciprocity. Influenced by the collective works of a variety of scholars, all three models are grounded in systems theory and emphasize a goal-oriented outcome. As this century unfolds, group social work practice has become integrated into social work practice that draws on an eclectic variety of theoretical frameworks.

Each of the models described in this section has multiple uses and similarities. As you will learn from Emily's situation, one issue can be addressed by more than one intervention. While distinct in nature, each group shares the similarity that change can occur as a result of the group effort and could not be reached as effectively with only individual efforts.

Social Action Groups

Aimed at facilitating social change on the organizational or community level, social action, or social goals, groups originated from the early work of reformers, but continue to be a primary approach used by social workers striving to achieve social change today. Groups with a social change focus are built on a democratic philosophy that individual growth occurs through changes being made within the environment (Schopler & Galinsky, 1995). A key component of social work practice with organizations and communities, social goals groups may be established for the purposes of accomplishing specific tasks, carrying out the goals of an organization, changing a law or policy, or developing a new program. The social worker may serve as initiator, participant, or consultant of a social change group. Professionals or nonprofessional persons may lead social action groups. Typically, the group's goals determine the leadership.

Groups whose aim is goal specific can be short term if there is no need for the group to continue once the goal is achieved or the time limit has expired for the goal to be achieved. For goal-specific groups that have an ongoing mission, longevity may be indefinite.

The following are examples of task-oriented social action groups.

- *Neighborhood groups that promote a safe environment:* Such a group may hold regular meetings to strategize ways to improve and monitor neighborhood safety. The group may be composed of neighborhood residents, social service professionals that work in the neighborhood, and law enforcement personnel. Such a group is likely to be long term, but the focus may shift from establishing a plan for safety to one of maintaining the plan. Due to their involvement in the community, social workers are often in a position to identify the need for a neighborhood group; so they may serve to mobilize the group, but not to lead the group. Neighborhood residents with an investment in their community are usually most effective as group leaders.

- *Members of the Alzheimer's Association:* Such a group may be formed to lobby legislators to introduce and pass legislation requiring mandatory dementia education for long-term residential care workers caring for patients with Alzheimer's disease. This group may be composed of family members of persons suffering from dementia, representatives from the residential long-term care industry, and health and social service professionals. This group may exist over multiple legislative sessions, but the lifetime of the group will be determined by the success or failure of proposed legislation. Should the legislation be enacted, the group may refocus its efforts on implementing and monitoring the mandatory educational requirements, or they may redirect their efforts to other legislation to protect persons living with dementia. The social worker's employment position or personal interest in the issue will determine her or his role.

- *Child welfare workers from various public and private agencies that monitor the foster care system:* To ensure that children in the foster care system have timely and permanent plans developed, such a group might meet regularly to provide oversight of all foster care cases in a city, county, or region. Group members can include professionals from multiple disciplines, such as social work, education, health, and law. This group essentially provides a quality assurance function and could exist indefinitely. The social worker's role may be as a leader, participant, or both.

Faced with the dilemma regarding the best approach for strengthening the parenting needs of women receiving services from the domestic violence program, Emily asked to have the issue placed on the agenda for the monthly meeting of the Community-wide Domestic Violence Coalition. This group of social, medical, and legal service professionals had organized for the purpose of enhancing communication among the community's domestic violence services, influencing legislation, and training members of the community to respond effectively to victims of domestic violence. Because they developed programs to address specific domestic violence–related needs, Emily thought the group might be appropriate for creating a program for parenting. After hearing Emily's proposal that such a program be developed, Coalition members determined that the provision of direct client services was outside the purview of their mission. Coalition members felt that such a service should be provided by individual agencies to simplify such issues as leadership, funding, and comfort level of potential participants.

Remedial Groups

With an exclusive emphasis on problem-focused individual growth and change, remedial, or therapeutic, goals groups are professionally facilitated groups aimed at helping group members enhance their social functioning. Also known as treatment groups, group therapy, group psychotherapy, and clinical group work, the goal for the person in a remedial goals group is to eliminate or cope with a specific social, emotional, or behavioral issue (Barker, 2003). Clinically oriented group work was first incorporated into social work practice in rehabilitation settings (Garvin, 1997). As discussed in the next section, on reciprocal groups, not all group work focused on individual growth and change is in therapeutic or treatment groups. The distinguishing factor for therapeutic groups is the presence of a professional group leader and the development of treatment goals specific to individual change.

Group dynamics—interacting with other group members, hearing their experiences, and strategizing personal attitudinal and behavioral change—is influential in promoting change within the group members, but group goals are secondary to the goals of each group member. The role for the social worker is typically as a leader or facilitator. Social workers may also serve as co-leaders of certain types of therapy groups, particularly in cases of single gendered groups, groups that are conflictual in nature, or groups that encompass emotionally sensitive issues.

Therapeutic groups often arise when a professional identifies several individuals within the agency's client population that share a common presenting issue. In the case of the mothers at Emily's shelter, Emily determined that the agency was serving a number of clients who shared a common concern. Therapeutic groups may meet for a specified number of sessions or weeks or have an open-ended time limit or number of sessions. They may also be closed or open: Closed groups have a designated group membership that does not change during the lifetime of the group, whereas group members can move in and out of open groups as needs arise.

The following are examples of groups that might be formed for the purpose of therapeutically focused group work.

- *Persons hospitalized for mental illness:* Social workers working in psychiatric facilities often conduct group therapy on a daily or weekly basis with patients hospitalized for newly diagnosed or chronic mental illness. These social worker–led groups usually supplement individual therapy, but the interactions among group members serve to support and enhance individual treatment. The group itself is typically open and ongoing, the membership changing with admissions to and discharges from the facility. Group membership may be determined by diagnosis, time and duration of admission, or gender.

- *Survivors of childhood incest:* A group composed of persons who are victims of incest is likely to be single gendered due to the emotional intensity of the issue and the fact that incest raises considerable trust problems for the survivors. A survivor group may be formed within an agency by the administrative or clinical staff and can either be time limited or ongoing and open or closed. In determining the type and timing of a survivor group, the social worker is sensitive to the nature of the trauma and the situations of the individual members of the group.

- *Male batterers:* A group of men identified by the social service or legal system as batterers can be composed of involuntary or voluntary members. Involuntary groups, particularly ones with members that have a history of violence, can be challenging groups to facilitate due to members' hostility and resentment regarding their participation in the group. A group for batterers is typically a highly structured group with a focus on behavioral change. Such groups are often led by co-facilitators to enable a balanced response to disputes and angry outbursts.

Behaviorally focused groups are typically time limited and closed in order to enhance the therapist's ability to provide information and promote individual change and group cohesion.

Emily considered forming a therapy group to respond to the need for parenting information for the shelter's residents. With a BSW, Emily was not trained to conduct a therapy group, so she explored the possibility of co-leading a treatment group with a local clinical social worker in private practice. Emily developed a concept that the therapist would offer a weekly therapy group for women who had been battered by their partners. The voluntary, open-ended group would be accessible to women in the community, and the therapist could incorporate parenting issues for children who have also been victimized by domestic violence. After discussing her proposal with the clinical social worker, Emily and the clinical social worker jointly agreed that a therapy group was one effective approach for addressing the women's feelings regarding their life experience, and parenting issues would naturally become a part of the discussion. The two social workers agreed that they would not include a formal parenting education curriculum in this group.

Reciprocal Groups

Also referred to as the mutual aid, self-help, and support group model, reciprocal goals groups emphasize the concept of common interest and exchange as the basis for change. Group members come together out of a shared interest or experience. Personal growth and change occur as a result of group members sharing those commonalities, exchanging support with one another, and receiving information about their shared issue. Receiving support from others who have similar experiences can be validating and empowering for the membership. Based on a member's needs and personality, support groups can be used to augment individual treatment or can be beneficial as a stand-alone resource. Mutual aid groups differ from therapy groups in several areas: (1) leaders can be professional or nonprofessional, (2) individual members do not typically have specified treatment goals, and (3) the intervention occurs as a result of the members' interpersonal relationships.

The group and the reasons for its origins often determine the social worker's role. Being on the forefront of service delivery, the social worker may identify a common need among her or his clients and be instrumental in creating the opportunity for a support group to meet at the agency. The social worker may serve initially as the group's facilitator and turn that role over to the group itself. The leader's role is often to facilitate exchanges and supportive relationships aimed at individuals meeting their similar goals (Schopler & Galinsky, 1995). Support groups are typically less formal than therapy groups and are open so that members can move in and out of the group as they feel a need.

The following are examples of self-help, support-focused groups.

- *Addictions groups:* The 12-step model that originated with Alcoholics Anonymous is an example of a self-help group with members providing the leadership. Addictions self-help groups have expanded beyond alcohol to include other drugs, food, gambling, and sexual behavior. Social workers can play a leadership role in addictions groups, but in a traditional 12-step model, there is no formal or professional leadership. Most addictions-focused groups are open ended, with members using the group to sustain their recovery process. Members may stop participating as they feel confident in their behavioral change.

- *Adoption or sibling groups:* Groups for families that are acquiring new members through adoption, remarriage, or birth may focus on providing education about such issues as the adoption or birth, but they also provide an opportunity for the members to identify and share their feelings about the change.

- *Disease/health condition groups:* Groups for persons suffering from a particular health condition are often facilitated by hospital social workers or social workers in organizations that advocate for and educate the public on specific health concerns. Groups are formed for persons with a variety of conditions, such as cancer, multiple sclerosis, strokes, and pregnancy.

- *Significant-other groups:* Support groups for the families and friends of persons experiencing a particular life event or health condition have increased in recent years. For example, such groups provide considerable support for the family and friends of persons newly diagnosed with an illness or injury; gays, lesbians, bisexuals, and transgendered persons; persons that have been victimized by an assault or disaster; and persons experiencing an addiction.

Investigating the third option in her pursuit of a parenting program, Emily approached the administration of her own agency. Emily described the need that she and other workers had identified among the mothers being served by the agency.

She proposed that the agency offer a psychoeducational group (one that includes both education and emotional support) so that the clients could be exposed to parenting education, share their concerns, and strategize about ways to respond to their children's experience with domestic violence. Emily felt she could make a greater impact on this issue through a group, as she could provide information on parenting, a group experience could complement the individual work she and her co-workers were engaging in with each woman, and the women could support one another. The agency director agreed with Emily's assessment and gave approval for Emily to develop the group and advertise it to her co-workers and former and current residents. Although several potentially viable options for responding to a client need emerged from Emily's ideas, she was confident that the support group approach could provide the parenting support and information needed by the mothers.

SKILLS FOR SOCIAL WORK PRACTICE WITH GROUPS

Social work practice with groups builds on many of the skills that are used in working with individuals and families. Establishing a group for persons with a common cause, need, or agenda does not ensure that the group process will be mutually beneficial for all members (Shulman, 1999). Without understanding the concepts and power of group practice, the social worker becomes the sole "helper" in the group; whereas using group practice skills, the entire group serves as helpers (Gitterman & Knight, 2000). Group work also uses the skills of engagement, assessment, intervention, and evaluation that were introduced in Chapter 9. We will focus on these skills as they apply to the phases of group work. Despite the type, makeup, purpose, or structure of a group, all group experiences have three phases—beginning, middle, and end. The beginning phase encompasses engagement and assessment activities, the middle phase includes the intervention, and the ending phase involves evaluation and termination. As the group intervention moves through the planned change effort, social workers often notice that conflict becomes a normal part of the group process and can be a part of the intervention itself.

First, the group must be formed and membership determined. When social workers have the opportunity to determine group membership, they may be able to ease the process of engaging group members by attending to the factors that influence group dynamics. Forming a group that is optimally configured in terms of goals, member characteristics, and logistical issues contributes to group and worker cohesion, enabling the group to progress more quickly to the tasks at hand. However, social workers may not always have free rein in determining group members. The following factors that affect group membership may or may not be influenced by the social worker:

- Individual and group criteria and goals determine who may be eligible or interested in joining the group.

- The pool of group members from which the social worker can draw will vary.

- Logistical issues such as time, location, cost, duration, and accessibility (for example, open versus closed) should accommodate group members' needs.

- Size varies; for example, 6 to 8 members is optimal for a therapy group, while 15 to 20 is acceptable for support and educational groups.

- Some groups thrive on a mixture of personality types, ages, and gender, while other groups need homogeneity of personality types for a successful experience. For example, young children can be in mixed gender groups, but adolescents may find mixed gender groups uncomfortable, particularly if issues of sexuality are to be discussed.

Once Emily had permission to form a parenting support group for current and former shelter clients, she began by gathering information from her co-workers regarding their perceptions of client needs in the area of parenting. She also obtained input from clients at one of the weekly house meetings in which staff and current clients discuss house issues. Her idea was favorably received, and she went ahead with the planning. The group was scheduled for a time and location that Emily felt best served the clients. She arranged for the group members' children to be supervised by a volunteer. Emily created flyers to post around the house and to mail to those former clients that she knew it was safe to contact. (For their safety, women who return to live with batterers cannot always be contacted by the social worker.) Because this group has a psychoeducational focus, Emily felt that diversity in age, race, and ethnicity would be an asset.

During the first session, Emily began by explaining the origins and purpose of the group. She asked each member to introduce herself and say as much or as little about herself as she wished and to state one goal she had for herself in join-ing this group. Next, Emily and the group developed some general rules related to frequency of sessions, attendance, speaking out of turn, handling conflicts, and sharing information about group members outside the group meeting. Because Emily knew each of the group members from her stay at the shelter, the first ses-sion was comfortable, and the members began to bond with one another.

Engagement of Groups

The first step in engaging the group is to perceive the group as the client system. Although groups are made up of individual members and the social worker en-gages each of those individual members, she or he engages the entire group as well. Regardless of the type of group work being practiced, the beginning stage includes group formation and first meeting activities:

- *Introductions:* Group members have the opportunity to introduce them-selves by the name they wish to be called during group meetings and to share with the group any information they feel is relevant for the group experience.

- *Explaining the purpose of the group:* The person who convened the group (this may be the group leader) is responsible for explaining the reason the group has been formed and to share her or his role and expectations for participating in the group.

- *Establishing group rules, norms, and boundaries:* An important step in en-gaging group members is to provide the opportunity for each person to voice her or his feelings about individual and group goals and expecta-tions for the group experience. Enabling all the members of a group to contribute to a set of group rules, norms, and boundaries enhances their connection to the leader and to one another, thus motivating them to continue with the group's work. For example, group members may choose to establish rules regarding attendance, timeliness, conflict management, sharing information outside the group, and even respon-sibility for refreshments.

- *Attending to group members:* Just as attending skills are important for engaging individuals, a similar skill set is required for developing effec-tive group work skills. Focusing on verbal and nonverbal engaging skills to enhance communication, clarify exchanges, and create an en-vironment in which the person feels safe is somewhat more complex at the group level, as the social worker attends to all members of the group at the same time. Keeping the perspective that group work involves facilitating relationships with individual group members and the group itself helps to distinguish the group practitioner from a caseworker in a group setting (Shulman, 1999). During this early phase of group development, social workers also want to be aware of and sensitive to members' feelings about participating in a group (AASWG, 2004).

The engagement, or beginning, phase in group practice is essential for the process of building group cohesion and trust. Being part of a group process requires the individual to take risks in sharing thoughts, feelings, and ideas. Members of groups that are effectively engaged by the group leader are likely to feel a higher level of connection to each other and the leader and trust the safety of the group process.

Assessment of Groups

Despite the fact that Emily knew all of the group members before they joined the group, she needed to assess their current situations and, specifically, their concerns and strengths in the area of parenting children exposed to domestic violence. Emily began her assessment of the group members as they introduced themselves, shared their stories, and stated their expectations for the group. This process enabled Emily to learn about the level of violence to which the children had been exposed, the way in which the mothers had handled that exposure, whether the children had been physically abused as well, and behaviors exhibited by the children that concerned the mother.

In addition to assessing each individual, Emily was able to assess the group members in terms of their strengths as parents and the areas in which they could build on those strengths to enhance their parenting skills. Other factors she thought about were the members' investment in the group process, their ability to bond with and support one another, and how they might handle emotional and conflictual situations that could occur within the group.

Following engagement, the next phase of the group process is the assessment of individuals within the group as well as the group as a whole. In addition to identifying individual members' goals, the social worker's role is to help members determine a set of goals for the group. Focusing on the following issues will help to achieve this:

- *Group development:* The social worker's role is to determine whether the group's level of cohesion can support mutual goal setting and sharing that will result in a positive impact on group members (Schopler & Galinsky, 1995). Therefore, assessment of group bonding is critical. The social worker can help group members become aware of their commonalities and their ability to support the goals of the individual members as well as the group. Even the process of establishing group norms, rules, and goals can provide the social worker with information for assessing individual members' communication and interpersonal styles as well as the group's ability to function collectively.

- *Group diversity:* As part of the assessment of group development, the social worker is aware of the influence of member diversity on the group building and work processes (AASWG, 2004). Group member characteristics that can impact group dynamics include race, ethnicity, gender, cultural background, age, and values. The group process can be a useful strategy for increasing awareness of and educating individuals on stereotypes and diversity issues.

- *Group members' strengths and resources:* In conducting initial and ongoing group assessment, the social worker helps both individuals and the group as a whole to identify strengths, resources, and areas for growth and change. Different from individual assessment, group assessment shifts the emphasis to members of the group, who ask questions, share experiences and insights, and identify resources previously unknown to other members or the social worker.

- *Balance of personal and group goals:* Each group member shares her or his motivation for participating in the group experience and identifies her or his expectations for that participation. The social worker is aware that the change process is a *group* process and balances attention appropriately with each group member. The social worker helps link personal needs to group needs and goals (AASWG, 2004). Group members can be a resource for identifying the concerns and priorities of other members, thus involving all members of the group in the personal change process. Such a strategy fosters development of individual assessment as well as group cohesion. To achieve balance and involvement of all members, the worker uses a combination of open- and closed-ended questions and encourages other members to engage in questioning one another as well.

Ongoing assessment is particularly important in group practice. Because the group experience involves a variety of individual personalities and life experiences, the goals, concerns, and dynamics change constantly. The social worker's role in practice with groups is to be aware of the interactions among group members and to monitor individual and group process and progress. Individual and group goals and group structure (for example, rules, norms, or membership) may change as a result of ongoing assessment. Vigilance and flexibility regarding changing group dynamics allow group members and the social worker to develop plans and interventions to fit the changing needs of the group members as well as the group itself. Ongoing assessment is also a facet of the evaluation process that enables the client and social worker to monitor individual and group progress toward goals.

Intervention with Groups

Using the individual and group goals identified by the group members, Emily proposed that each session have two components: education and support. Each meeting would begin with a "checking in" period in which the members could share successes or ask for help with their parenting. The second half of the session would include a presentation by Emily or another professional on a topic specific to parenting children that have experienced trauma. Together, Emily and the group developed a list of possible topics to cover, being flexible in case additional topics arose. Throughout each session, Emily monitored the interactions of the group members with her and one another and noted individual growth and change. Emily routinely provided feedback to the group on her observations and asked the members to do the same with her and one another.

As with social work interventions at the individual and family practice level, group interventions occur in two phases: planning and implementation. Working with a group in the middle phases of its life, the social worker continues to help establish individual and group goals and begins to develop a plan for achieving those goals.

Keeping in mind the dual emphasis of individual and group goals is necessary for both planning and implementing. Even if the group is able to develop a mutually agreed-upon set of group goals, individual perceptions of the tasks and activities needed to achieve those goals may vary considerably. In addition, the group may reach consensus on group goals, but individual goals are bound to be distinct and unique, just as the group members are distinct and unique persons. Moreover, both individual and group goals may change over the lifetime of the group, requiring the group leader to be aware of and responsive to the need for periodical review of goals. The social worker is responsible for monitoring and overseeing the changing balance of issues.

Planning activities at the group level include establishing goals and documenting the agenda for the group experience.

- *Establishing goals:* The social worker helps the group create goals for the individual within the group and the group itself, using specific and measurable tasks and outcomes. Working with all group members, the social worker provides input into the development of the goals, weighs the advantages and disadvantages of proposed goals, identifies barriers and available and needed resources, and provides links between the individual and group proposals (AASWG, 2004).

- *Documenting the agenda for the group experience:* For remedial and reciprocal goals groups, developing individual and group working agreements helps the participant focus on her or his personal commitment as well as the commitment to the larger group. For social action groups, the agreement can be in the form of a working statement of the purpose, goals, and activities of the group while delineating the roles of the individual members. Box 10.2 shows an example of a working agreement, similar to the individual contract in Chapter 9, that can be used in remedial, reciprocal, and social action goals groups.

Implementation of individual and group goals begins by taking action. The social worker and group members put into action the individual and group goals that have been established. As they proceed, the social worker and the group engage in ongoing assessment of their individual and collective work toward individual and group goals to determine whether goals need to be revised. The implementation stage of group practice may provide the greatest challenges for the social worker and group members, as this stage involves the actual changing of attitudes, behaviors, and completion of tasks. The social worker watches for and addresses individual and group issues that can impede the work of the group. Let us look at some aspects of group dynamics and suggestions for addressing them:

- *Conflict:* Differences may arise as members work toward the contracted goals at varying paces, and conflict can occur concerning individual and group values or when needs change. The social worker may often be confronted with member-to-member conflict as well as member–to–social worker conflict. The social worker can model conflict

Group Members:

Olivia M.	Tammy R.
Shirley B.	Megan S.
Cynthia W.	Angela G.

Group Goals as Agreed on by All Group Members:

Identify our strengths as mothers.

Improve parenting skills.

Have a safe place to talk about our experiences.

Group Rules and Expectations:

Group will meet weekly; members attend as needed.

Members will respect one another's right to speak.

All information shared will be confidential.

Individual Group Member Goals and Tasks:

Group Member	Goal	Client Tasks/Date	Social Worker Tasks/Date
Olivia	1. Be able to share my situation with others.	I will share at least one personal item each meeting.	Each meeting, I will support Olivia by asking if she would like to share.
	2. Identify my strengths as a parent.	I will report at least one positive thing I did during the week as a mother.	I will provide information on "parenting without spanking."
	3.		

Date Contract Will Be Reviewed:

8 weeks from today

I agree with the above stated goals, to complete the contracted tasks, and participate in a review and evaluation of the contract on the specified date.

Olivia M.	Emily
Client	Social Worker
Date	Date

resolution by responding directly to the conflict and involving group members in facilitating a positive outcome.

- *Violation of group rules and norms:* Even if rules are clearly outlined during the group's early development, members may find themselves unable to comply or to fulfill expectations. Responsibility for confronting violations falls to the group leader. Asking the group to review the previously established rules and to address the infraction empowers the group to act as a unit in determining an appropriate response.

- *Disruptive members:* Group process can suffer from having members that create obstacles to achieving the desired goals. Behaviors that impede the group's progress include talking too much or too little, not fulfilling obligations (for example, attendance or tasks), and being overly critical. A group leader minimizes the disruption by monitoring for such behaviors and addressing the disruptive behaviors either within the group session itself or outside the group meeting. Offering alternative strategies for interacting with the group and modeling appropriate behaviors while in the group provide members with options for appropriate interaction.

The purpose and goals of the group influence the development and implementation of the intervention. For example, an intervention for an anger management group focused on teaching the members appropriate skills for handling their anger may be highly structured and formalized, whereas a group for persons recently widowed may be less structured to foster the sharing of feelings and supporting one another. Despite the type of intervention, relevant strategies are needed that build on individual and group strengths, meet individual and group needs, and focus on specific and measurable outcomes.

Evaluation and Termination of Groups

During the beginning phase of the group's work, Emily and the members agreed the group would meet weekly for eight weeks, and at that point they would evaluate the future of the group. The members also completed a standardized parenting questionnaire at the first and eighth sessions to determine a baseline and changes in parenting style and knowledge. At the eighth session, the group asked that Emily continue the group, but open it to other current and former shelter residents to join. Through these two evaluation strategies, Emily and the group members were able to assess both individual and group goals and make decisions for the future.

The final phase of group work includes evaluation and possible group termination. This segment of group work provides the opportunity to integrate the process of the group experience with the content addressed during the group interactions, thus enabling the social worker and the group members to review learning and changes that occurred (Shulman, 1999). Evaluation at the group level can be more complicated than when working with individuals. Individual and group goals are evaluated along with the group process. In general, strategies for evaluating a group experience evolve from the structure of the group, goals, and intervention tasks and activities. For example, structured groups benefit from more formalized evaluations, while less structured groups (for example, ongoing support groups) may be able to informally evaluate process and progress on a regular basis.

Evaluation is part of the group process from the time the group is formed, but building evaluation into the ending phase serves a variety of functions. Evaluating progress toward individual and group goals can be empowering. The social worker and group members identify personal and group changes that have occurred, assess the impact of the group experience on the members' lives, and determine whether future intervention is needed (AASWG, 2004). On the other hand, individual or group goals may not have been achieved, and an evaluation provides an examination of that outcome as well, to determine whether the goals or the intervention were not appropriate or resources were not available (Schopler & Galinsky, 1995).

To capture the complexities of the group experience, a multifaceted plan for conducting a group evaluation might include the following:

- Audio- or videotaping, with group members' informed consent, to enable the social worker to observe group dynamics and her or his skills.

- Obtaining information from group members in such areas as needs assessments, measures of attitudes or behaviors, or physical measures before and after the group experience.

- Obtaining group member feedback regarding satisfaction with the group experience and the leadership.

- Reviewing individual and group goals.

Groups that are time limited or based on a specific goal or activity may terminate as a group at this stage. In these situations, the termination process encompasses the entire group. On the other hand, open-ended groups may not terminate as a group, but individuals terminate as they leave the group. Therefore, evaluation may occur for the individual at the time of her or his departure from the group, but this can still involve those members that are not leaving the group.

In addition to assessing change in any type of group, the social worker facilitates group termination and follow-up using a common set of skills:

- The social worker and group members share feelings about ending the group experience and leaving the group.

- Plans for maintaining change are developed.

- Group members discuss their feelings about having contact after termination from the group (for example, returning to the group, having contact outside the group, or having group reunions).

Although social work practice with groups requires specialized skills for engagement, assessment, intervention, and evaluation, each phase uses those skills developed for working with individuals and families. At the group level, the processes of engagement, assessment, intervention, and evaluation can be fluid and dynamic, particularly in groups that are open ended or in groups in which the goal or purpose may change after the group is formed. Monitoring individual and group progress toward goal achievement requires the social worker to move back and forth comfortably between phases of work.

CONCLUSION

Groups can be a powerful experience for both the social worker and the members of the group. Groups often achieve far greater accomplishments than a person could alone, but a group intervention is not for every person or every issue. The effective social worker uses her or his engagement and assessment skills to determine whether a group intervention is the optimal approach to use in a given situation.

While emphasizing the group, the social worker uses the skills of engagement, assessment, intervention, and evaluation that were introduced in Chapter 9 for work with individuals. In group practice, the social worker must simultaneously build rapport with the individual group members and facilitate group cohesiveness, being careful not to focus too much attention on one group member or issue. Group members can come together to provide input into the development of the individual and group intervention plan and participate in a groupwide evaluation of the experience. Working with a group of people at one time may seem like a daunting task, but the social worker's skill in viewing strengths from a systemic perspective can be an asset.

MAIN POINTS

- Group work is a method of practice in which the social worker works with a group of persons to address individual issues; a need for information and education; support; or social conditions. Introduced in 1927, group work soon became an established part of the social work educational curriculum.

- The main group work models are in the areas of social action, individual growth (or remediation), and self-help and support (or reciprocity). The goal of a social action group is to initiate or change a policy, law, or program; individual growth groups emphasize clinically oriented treatment for a personal issue or concern; and support groups are mutual aid groups based on a common life experience.

- In the practice of social work with groups, the social worker forms the group, facilitates a group meeting or session, provides resources for the group, or works with the group to develop strategies to meet the desired goals.

- The outcomes for the group are based on the individual members' ability and willingness to be interdependent and interact with one another for the purpose of achieving the goals. Although change occurs for the individual members of the group, the focus of the intervention is on the group as a whole.

- As with social work practice with individuals and families, skills for group work focus on the areas of engagement, assessment, intervention, and evaluation.

EXERCISES: PRACTICING SOCIAL WORK

What Type of Group is It?

Below are descriptions of three groups in which the Sanchez family may be participants. Read the descriptions and, utilizing the group practice models highlighted in this chapter, complete the items that follow the descriptions.

Group #1—Grandparents Raising Grandchildren

Hector and Celia are members of a group for grandparents rearing grandchildren. The group, which meets for a monthly potluck meal, shares strategies and resources related to rearing grandchildren. The group was organized by a social worker who has custody of her granddaughter. Occasionally, the group meeting includes a presentation by a professional on a topic of interest to the group (e.g., legal and financial issues and childrearing strategies).

Group #2—Women's Group

Celia Sanchez is a member of a group for persons experiencing depression. The group meets weekly for 90 minutes at the mental health center. Facilitated by two clinical social workers, the group is comprised of eight women who were referred by other mental health professionals. Celia was referred by the social worker working with Hector and her to facilitate Joey's adoption. The adoption social worker noted that Celia had experienced episodic depression throughout her life and was currently reporting depressive symptoms. Each group member was interviewed by the group leaders to determine her appropriateness for the group. The group addresses such issues as identifying causes and symptoms of depression, treatment strategies, and strategies for coping with depression.

Group #3—Grandparents for Justice

Through their involvement with the grandparents group, Celia and Hector became members of a group in their state that is working for improving the state laws that determine the rights of grandparents. The group was formed by several grandparents who struggled with the state's child welfare system to gain custody of their grandchildren. The group's goal is to see legislation passed that will protect the rights of grandparents.

Complete the following:

Group #1—Grandparents Raising Grandchildren

Type of Group _____
Indicators that identify the type of group

1)

2)

3)

Group #2—Women's Group

Type of Group _____
Indicators that identify the type of group

1)

2)

3)

Group #3—Grandparents for Justice

Type of Group _____

Indicators that identify the type of group

1)

2)

3)

The Group Process

Select one of the group scenarios described in the previous exercise. Using that scenario, identify skills appropriate for each phase of the group process.

Engagement

1)

2)

3)

Assessment Skills

1)

2)

3)

Intervention Skills

1)

2)

3)

Evaluation and Termination Skills

1)

2)

3)

Launching a Group

As you read in the first exercise, Hector and Celia have become involved in a group working for improving the state laws that dictate the rights of grandparents. Using the knowledge that you have gained regarding the types of group process and the phases of the group process, develop a list of strategies that the group might use to develop a plan and focus local and state attention on their issue.

EXERCISES: THE SOCIAL WORK LIBRARY

Group Practice Overview

After reading "Group Practice Overview" (Schopler & Galinsky, 1995), develop a plan for conducting an online support group. Sketch out a general overview of strategies for recruiting members and conducting the group (i.e., rules for interaction, confidentiality, and handling conflicts). As you consider the development of an online group, reflect on the ethical and practical challenges.

The Social Worker in the Group

After reading "The Social Worker in the Group" (Schwartz, 1961), compare and contrast the descriptions of social work practice with groups offered by Schwartz with those presented thirty years later in "Group Practice Overview" (Scholpler & Galinsky, 1995). Recall that Schwartz wrote about the importance of the mediating function of social work. Using the conception of the mediating function, what is the social worker's role in group practice?

CHAPTER 11

Social Work Practice with Organizations and Communities

In Chapter 7, Emily worked with Marietta to arrange home-based services so that she could continue independent living. Home health care is one of the services that Emily arranged for Marietta to receive. As a result of policy changes in the reimbursement of home health agencies for services provided to recipients, a number of the older adults with whom Emily worked, including Marietta, had their home health services decreased or terminated altogether. Emily began to see negative consequences occurring for these older adults. Some of the older adults were no longer able to live independently and had to move in with family members or into a residential care facility, thus losing their independence.

Viewing her role as an advocate as well as a case manager, Emily compiled case examples detailing the negative effects of the policy changes. With her agency's support, Emily shared her data with a community coalition of agencies and organizations that engage in legislative advocacy on issues related to older adults. The advocacy group used Emily's data in their campaign to introduce legislation that would increase the reimbursement rates for older adults receiving home health services. Emily worked with the advocacy group to prepare testimony for a legislative committee. She arranged for family members of the home health care recipients to travel to the state capitol and testify before the committee on the negative impact of the cutbacks. As a result of this collaborative effort, legislation was passed to increase reimbursement for home health services for older adults.

In the previous chapters, we examined social work practice on the individual, family, and group levels. In this chapter, we explore social work practice that targets change efforts at the organizational, community, and societal levels. Also referred to as **macro practice**, **community-level practice** is a method of social work practice that promotes changes in practices, policies, and legislation that impact groups of people in an organization, community, state, country, or even the world. When policies are punitive or bureaucracies are large and impersonal, the social worker can serve as an advocate for the client system in facilitating change in the system that is intended to serve the client system.

Influencing social change encompasses a range of different practice approaches and interventions. Although many of the terms and concepts that describe social work practice with organizations and communities are used interchangeably, they are, in fact, distinct practice approaches and are not synonymous. The advocacy effort made by Emily on behalf of her client, Marietta, which brought about the policy change, is an example of one of the many roles that a social worker can play while practicing at the organizational and community level. Table 11.1 provides descriptions of various activities performed by social workers practicing with organizations and communities.

Social workers have worked for change at the organizational, community, and societal levels throughout the history of the profession. Organizational and community practice is often combined with direct practice; in fact, among secondary functions, management responsibilities are ranked number two by NASW members (Gibelman & Schervish, 1997). As you know, social workers commonly begin their careers by working with individuals and families and then move into areas that include administration, management, teaching, or research. This career path means that administrators, supervisors, and teachers have insight into the issues and challenges of social work practice with individuals and families.

Although organizational and community-level practice may not be their primary focus, all social workers are ethically and professionally obligated to advocate for social justice. The NASW *Code of Ethics* (1999) prominently addresses ethical obligations to practice at the organizational and community level. Four of the six ethical principles emphasize this responsibility. For social work practice at the community level, the *Code* charges social workers with the responsibility to (1) promote social change "with and on behalf of vulnerable and oppressed individuals and groups" in the areas of poverty, unemployment, discrimination, and other areas of social injustice; (2) serve both client systems and the larger society and address the needs of organizations and communities as well as individuals, families, and groups; and (3) practice with integrity within organizations (NASW, 1999).

Addressing social injustice is considered to be a social work responsibility because social injustice "harms people and limits their opportunities to live as fully human persons with inherent worth and dignity" (Horejsi, 2002, p. 12).

SOCIAL WORK APPROACH/INTERVENTION	DEFINITION
Advocacy (1) Advocacy with legislative decision makers (2) Advocacy with nonlegislative decision makers	Championing the rights of individuals, groups, and communities to change policies, laws, and practice. Legislative advocacy involves influencing elected officials at local, state, or national levels on behalf of a group of clients, organizations, coalitions, or communities. Nonlegislative advocacy efforts focus on agency and organizational institutions, such as streamlining the application process for services or helping clients to have input into the service delivery system.
Social and political action (1) Campaigning and electoral activities	Building political pressure to resolve a social problem or address a social need at the institutional or policy level. Electoral activities involve working to elect candidates who support issues important to a group, organization, or community, or working to pass legislation important to a group, organization, or community.
Community organization	Facilitating the creation or maintenance of a "collective body" that shares a common concern related to a social problem and to work toward resolution of the shared concern.
Public education	Providing information on a community-wide basis.
Administration/management	Providing leadership at the agency level to develop and attain goals, seek and allocate resources, supervise personnel, and oversee service delivery. Supervision enhances the professional socialization and development process and provides quality assurance for effective practice.
Research	Examining social issues and developing theory and knowledge through systematically collecting quantitative or qualitative data.

TABLE 11.1

Types of Social Work Practice with Organizations and Communities

TABLE 11.1
continued

SOCIAL WORK APPROACH/INTERVENTION	DEFINITION
Teaching/training	Contributing to the professional educational process.
Policy practice	Analyzing, evaluating, and implementing policies that inform practice.
Social planning and development	Achieving social change by calling on experts or professionals to identify a need and conduct an assessment, develop a plan for intervention, and carry out an evaluation.
Community development	Developing or improving infrastructures (for example, employment base, housing stock, and roads and sewer systems) within a geographic community.

Source: Barker, 2003; Gibelman & Schervish, 1997; Gummer, 1995

Moreover, Standard 6 of the *Code of Ethics* focuses on social work practice within the broader society in the areas of

- social welfare;
- public participation through influencing policies and institutions;
- public emergencies; and
- social and political action through working toward equity in access to resources, opportunities, and policies.

In this chapter, we explore the third level of generalist practice, beginning with a review of the historical development of social work practice with organizations and communities. To understand the underpinnings of the many and varied facets of working with organizations and communities, we will examine the models of change used in this level of practice and the skills that are essential for being an effective practitioner.

HISTORICAL PERSPECTIVE ON SOCIAL WORK PRACTICE WITH ORGANIZATIONS AND COMMUNITIES

The origins of social work practice with organizations and communities can be found in the early efforts of the Charity Organization Society and settlement house movements. Charity Organization Society workers advocated for change with organizations regarding the sharing of client information, while early settlement house activists fought for improved living conditions for the poor through legislative advocacy (Brieland, 1995). In fact, Jane Addams and her colleagues at Hull House were the first to engage in large-scale advocacy efforts to address sanitation problems in Chicago, resulting in Addams's appointment as sanitation inspector (NASW, 1998).

The role of community practice continued to grow throughout the first half of the 20th century. The depression of the 1930s, in particular, focused the country on the need for community-level interventions to address the issues of widespread poverty, unemployment, and hunger. Through the New Deal programs, the federal government assumed responsibility for the development and implementation of community-level interventions for the first time in U.S. history. The social upheaval of the 1960s galvanized the role of community organization and advocacy for the social work profession. Social workers were involved in advocacy efforts in the areas of civil rights, employment, the Vietnam War, and welfare rights. With an emphasis on social work practice with individuals and families, interest in organizational and community change waxed and waned through the 1970s and 1980s. By the 1990s, the efforts of several social work organizations had created a resurgence of interest in such arenas as political campaigns and advocacy.

Acknowledging the need for social workers to have competence at multiple levels of intervention contributed to the development of the generalist social work practice model in which social workers strive to address social problems with individuals, families, groups, *and* communities. Such recognition has enabled the social work profession to reach a point in the 21st century in which practice at the organizational and community level is an integral part of the profession.

Social work practice at the organizational and community level often faces funding challenges; however, the profession's commitment to community organization, advocacy, and other organizational and community-level service activities remains strong. The Council on Social Work Education has shown its commitment to ensuring that all social workers have knowledge and skills for organizational and community practice in the current curriculum guidelines, which state that social workers should be prepared to work with organizations and communities as well as individuals and families (2001a).

MODELS OF CHANGE IN SOCIAL WORK PRACTICE WITH ORGANIZATIONS AND COMMUNITIES

Aimed at facilitating change within systems of all types and sizes, social work practice with organizations and communities can be achieved using a variety of approaches. Achieving change within a system is a challenging endeavor due to the many and varied persons, policies, and needs involved. In order to facilitate systemwide change, social workers need to determine whether the system is ready for a change or alternatives can be explored. If a change is viable, the social worker's role may focus on identifying the key persons and resources that are needed to facilitate the change process.

In an effort to address social injustices at the organizational or community level, social workers are instrumental in working toward change within political, social, and economic systems. The concept of community is thus defined to include the physical or geographic environment or a social group or organization. Upon defining the community to be targeted and the goal of the change effort, the social worker selects the most appropriate approach to achieve the desired outcome. Three models of community organization have been developed that enable social workers to match the community, the goals, and the strategies for intervention: locality or community development, social planning, and social action (Rothman, 2001).

Locality or Community Development

Change efforts in the **locality or community development** approach focus on a specific geographic area. This approach assumes that members of the community are invested in enhancing the environment in which they live, and efforts are typically aimed at a specific problem or need that exists. By developing goals related to community competence and social integration, building a sense of community is the desired outcome of this approach (Rothman, 2001). Effectiveness of a locality development change intervention is increased as member participation increases. Change is based on the assumption that community members can engage in a cooperative, self-help process with one another and with outside individuals and groups because they desire change and can change. In essence, the client system and the change agent system are the same population.

The social worker's role in locality or community development varies from initiator to participant. As a professional working in the community and interacting with a range of people and groups, the social worker may be in a unique position to identify a community need that residents of the community do not view as a community-wide problem. Therefore, the social worker may initiate a social change effort by mobilizing key persons within the community, following the social goals model of group practice described in Chapter 10. The social worker may train a community member to assume leadership and then relinquish the leadership role to the community. In situations in which community members identify the condition needing change, the social worker helps to facilitate the change. Lastly, the social worker may also be a participant in the change effort based on her or his residence in the community, position within an organization, or as an outside consultant to the change effort due to a particular expertise or by virtue of membership in the community.

Let us look at some examples of locality or community development change efforts.

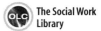

The Social Work Library

To learn more about the challenges of community development, read the article by Arches.

- *Neighborhood residents concerned about health care access:* The decreasing accessibility to health care of residents in a neighborhood largely composed of low-income, older adults comes to the attention of a social worker in a community center. With the help of the agency's neighborhood advisory committee, the social worker conducts a needs assessment to determine the extent of access problems and learns that many older adults have not seen a physician regularly since the nearby clinic closed several years earlier. The advisory committee approaches the local medical school to propose opening a small free clinic in the agency to serve outpatient needs. The medical school faculty seizes the opportunity to provide a training site for medical students, and a partnership is born.

- *Refugee-owned businesses:* Clients and former clients of a refugee resettlement agency approach social work staff about refugee-owned business owners being harassed. In recent months, a number of the refugee-owned businesses have been vandalized. With the support of the local business owners, the social worker convenes a task force comprising representatives from the refugee-owned businesses, Chamber of Commerce members, law enforcement personnel, and the community development agency. The task force conducts an assessment of the neighborhood and finds the problem to be widespread. They agree to address the issues of vandalism, increased security, and community relations. The social worker assists initially by chairing the task force, but later works to identify a leader from the refugee business community to assume that role.

- *Agency expansion:* Former recipients of services provided by an urban domestic violence program initiate an expansion into their rural community by contacting the agency and requesting that a satellite office be opened in their area. The domestic violence program conducts its own needs assessment to determine that the rural community lacks services for battered women, approaches key persons in the community for support, and establishes the program. A social worker working for the shelter may be called on to conduct the needs assessment, develop the program, or to manage the satellite program. A social worker may also be a key person in the rural community, whose support and involvement can help the program to gain acceptance.

In locality and community development activities, the experts are the members of the community. The social worker's role is to support and assist the community in developing and implementing a change to enhance the lives of those in the community.

Social Planning

Within a **social planning** approach, change efforts are aimed at policy-level or community-wide change, but do not necessarily involve members of the community themselves as the initiators of the change effort (Rothman, 2001). Orchestrated by professionals, outside consultants, and influential decision makers, social planning is implemented to address a special need within the community. Based on the belief that experts, who have access to empirical data and technical expertise, best orchestrate change, social planning involves social change at the institutional and bureaucratic levels (versus at the community level). The social worker's role may be as a member of a professional team involved in identifying issues, collecting data, analyzing policy, and planning a program to address needs.

The following are examples of social planning change efforts.

- *Neighborhood redevelopment:* Municipal officials, concerned about the deterioration of one of the city's historic neighborhoods, conducts a community assessment to determine the extent of decline. Upon determining that the number of businesses, owner-occupied households, and the tax base have drastically decreased, the city's Office of Community and Economic Development applies for federal funding to restore the neighborhood. The funding enables the city to offer tax breaks for new homeowners, low-interest loans for new business owners, funds for rehabilitation and beautification of buildings, and grants for development of social service programs. The social worker may be in a position to gather and analyze data, facilitate the interactions of local officials, publicize the redevelopment effort, review applications, and oversee program development.

- *International social work education:* Dramatic social, political, and economic changes in former communist countries have created a need to restructure the social service delivery system within the countries. Recognizing that the expertise to build a social service system based on democratic ideology did not exist within the professional community of these countries, social workers from the United States are called in to assist in the rebuilding effort. The social worker's role in this change effort is to serve as a trainer, facilitator, educator, and consultant, working with professionals to develop organizational practices, fund-raising mechanisms, and evaluation processes that are consistent with the new social structure.

- *Rural domestic violence services:* Consider the earlier example of the domestic violence agency establishing a satellite program in a rural community from a different perspective: Instead of the idea originating with the former recipients of services, an example of a social planning effort may be the result of hospital staff identifying a need. Noticing an increase in the number of battered women presenting to the emergency room, the hospital staff determine that local services are needed. The nearest domestic violence program is 30 miles away in the county seat. The hospital administrator contacts that program and asks for their help in establishing a satellite program at the hospital. The administrator and shelter director apply for a grant to provide start-up funding for a hospital-based social worker to provide services for battered women who are seen at the hospital. Once that program is in place, an advisory group is formed and plans are made to seek long-term funding to keep the program running on a permanent basis.

Social Action

Aimed at addressing a social injustice, **social action** change efforts increase political pressure on decision-making processes so that oppressed groups receive equitable services, resources, and power. Sometimes referred to as community organizing or grassroots organizing, social action often involves advocating for rights on behalf of or with a group that does not have a strong voice within the decision-making process. Advocacy can occur at the organizational, community, governmental, and legislative levels and may involve a range of activities, from public education campaigns to confrontational meetings and public protests. Working from a systems framework enables the social worker to grasp the meaning and inadequacies of the client-system interaction and to facilitate change that will enhance the functioning of both parts of the system (Shulman, 1999).

The Social Work Library

Schneider's article provides a rationale for social workers' involvement in advocacy efforts at the state level.

Social activists may also choose to direct their resources toward the election of political candidates who support political agendas favoring the agency or organizational mission. The social worker's role in social action change efforts is to identify and raise awareness regarding the need for social action, organize and lead an advocacy effort, work on a political candidate's campaign, or form a coalition that works collectively for change. Box 11.1 provides ideas for social action activities that social work students, faculty, and professionals can be involved in to make a difference.

The following are examples of social action change efforts.

The Social Work Library

The Lens & Gibelman article uses welfare reform to provide a basis for better understanding advocacy.

- *Welfare reform:* In the wake of budget cuts that reduced the state's public cash assistance programs, the director of a statewide welfare rights organization puts together a coalition of welfare recipients, social service professionals, and the ministerial alliance to engage in a high-profile advocacy effort. Pooling their resources, the coalition mounts a campaign that includes letters, e-mail, local visits, and telephone calls to

BOX 11.1

Making a Difference: Influencing State Policy

WHAT STUDENTS AND FACULTY CAN DO!

- Get out of your comfort zone.
- Ask your professors for advocacy and policy assignments.
- Identify an issue or problem that you want to change.
- Form a group at work or school to help you advocate.
- Contact your legislators and ask them to help you introduce a bill.
- Develop fact sheets and policy briefs.
- Identify and track a bill in the state legislature that affects your field agency.
- Enter the national contest, "State Policy Plus," for cash and commitment.
- Plan a social work "rally day" at the state legislature annually.
- Serve as an intern in the office of a state legislator.
- Visit state senators and representatives personally or as a class and inform them of your concerns on a particular bill.
- Organize a group to prepare testimony at a public hearing or subcommittee.
- Write letters to your state legislators.
- Track state legislation using the Internet. Visit www.statepolicy.org.
- Work with your state chapter of NASW in lobbying for its legislative agenda.
- Design a research project analyzing the current impact of state welfare reform.
- Join a coalition or advocacy group and assist them in setting their agenda.
- Organize a forum or luncheon for state legislators, lobbyists, service providers, and clients on a proposed bill or policy.
- Prepare and deliver testimony before a legislative committee.
- Analyze and compare a particular policy or bill among all 50 states or internally.
- Write position papers for candidates who are campaigning for legislative office.
- Volunteer to work in a political campaign to support a candidate.
- Conduct a survey of candidates or legislators on their views about proposed bills or significant issues.
- Persevere and be very determined.

Source: Influencing State Policy (http://www.statepolicy.org)

legislators; educational sessions to teach effective lobbying techniques to church groups; trips to the state capitol to lobby key legislators; and public service announcements to air on radio and television. The social worker may be involved in any of these activities directly or indirectly as a facilitator.

- *Political action:* The political action committee for NASW members (PACE—Political Action for Candidate Election) has chapters in every state. On behalf of NASW members, state chapter PACE committees endorse candidates at the local and state level, and the national PACE committee endorses candidates at the national level. Candidates are endorsed based on their platform on issues related to the social work profession. NASW members participate in campaigns, assist with voter registration, and contribute to campaigns.

- *Agency advocacy:* Residents of an apartment complex request help from a community-based social services agency in getting needed repairs made to their apartment buildings. The landlord has refused to replace inefficient, potentially dangerous heating and cooling equipment, maintain the exterior of the buildings, and replace hallway and outdoor lighting. With the assistance of the residents, the agency's social worker conducts an on-site assessment of their concerns and contacts a local attorney in the housing division of a legal services agency. Together, the legal services attorney and the social worker compile a report and form a team made up of the attorney, the social worker, and representatives from the residents' group. The team present the report to the landlord, and the landlord promises to make repairs. Repairs are not made within the six-month period promised. With the social worker's help, the residents organize a picket outside the landlord's office. The changes are then made promptly.

- *Community-building:* One definition of community-building is "an organized effort to make older and lower-income neighborhoods self-sustaining parts of a productive economy" (Naparstek & Dooley, 1997, pp. 78–79). Blending community development, social planning, and social action, residents join together with one another and with professionals to mobilize and build community resources to enhance the economic and social functioning of an area. Another example of community-building is a neighborhood that works with housing organizations to develop new, affordable housing for current and potential residents; yet another is the neighborhood that unites around the issue of having the public transportation system extend to their neighborhood so that access to and from the neighborhood is enhanced.

In terms of identifying and intervening with organizational and community issues, social workers have a unique vantage point because of the profession's commitment to social justice, enhancement of client and community well-being and functioning, and empowerment. Having a working knowledge of the three models of change described here enables the generalist social worker to effect change at the organizational and societal level. Knowledge of multiple approaches further provides the social work practitioner with the ability to move back and forth among the models and use the aspects of each model that will best meet the need.

SKILLS FOR SOCIAL WORK PRACTICE WITH ORGANIZATIONS AND COMMUNITIES

Organizations and communities are made up of persons and groups; therefore, effective practice with organizations and communities is built on the skills learned in working with individuals, families, and groups. Similar to social work practice with groups, the client in organizational and community practice is a group of individuals. For example, the client system may be residents in a neighborhood or community; social service agencies seeking adequate funding; or persons that share a common diagnosis, life event or style, or need.

As in social work practice with individuals, families, and groups, practice with organizations and communities encompasses multifaceted and varied roles. The role of the social worker in an organizational or community intervention is the same as it is at other levels of practice, but focuses on a larger client system. For example, the social worker may function in one or more of the following ways:

- *Broker:* In a brokering capacity, the social worker working with organizations and communities forms connections through the building of collaborations, coalitions, networks, and partnerships.

- *Enabler:* Community-level practitioners empower clients and others to participate in change by organizing and coordinating the efforts of individuals and groups committed to a common issue or concern. As many of the tasks and activities of organizational and community practice involve group meetings, social workers require skills to facilitate meetings, including planning, agenda development, and leading. Also included in the enabler role is evaluation. As funding sources increasingly require verification that funding is supporting programs that are making a positive impact, social workers are required to develop and carry out evaluations, analyze findings, and compile evaluation reports to staff, boards of directors, and funders.

- *Advocate:* Advocacy involves articulating the needs of a group to those in decision-making positions in the form that is most effective with the targeted decision makers (for example, press releases, letters, lobbying, public education campaigns, demonstrations, political lobbying, and petitions). Advocates must be willing to take risks and have realistic expectations regarding success.

- *Mobilizer:* Grant writing and organizing fund-raising campaigns (for example, events, mailings, and telethons) are examples of activities engaged in by social workers in the mobilizing role. This role also encompasses program development and planning. Organizational and community practice often involves establishing new programs, which means identifying the need for a program, conceptualizing and designing the program, securing funding or administrative support, overseeing program operations, and evaluating program outcomes.

- *Mediator or negotiator:* Through reflective listening, the social worker can aid opposing groups in establishing a common ground and a mutually agreed-upon resolution of the issues. In the role of mediator, the social worker serves as an unbiased party, while the role of negotiator typically involves the social worker having a preference for one side over the other.

- *Administrator:* Social work administration activities include overseeing program development and operations, budgets, fund-raising, and personnel.

Just as with individual, family, and group work, social work at the organizational and community level can be practiced using the concepts of engagement, assessment, intervention, and evaluation as a method for structuring social work practice processes and activities. The roles just described can be used within each phase of the social work intervention at the organizational or community level.

As a BSW student, Emily completed a practicum at a multiservice community center that provides social services to the residents of an urban neighborhood. Emily had the opportunity to gain generalist social work experiences working with children in the after-school program, taking applications for the utility assistance program, and co-facilitating a job skills group with mothers in the welfare-to-work program. To provide Emily with organizational and community experiences, the field instructor invited her to participate in the Neighborhood Advisory Council. This group provided input to the staff on the needs of the community.

During Emily's first meeting with the Neighborhood Advisory Council, one of the neighborhood resident council members suggested that neighborhood children and youth needed access to an after-school tutoring program. The council voted to create an ad hoc committee to explore the development of a tutoring program. Together with her field instructor, Caroline, Emily served as co-chair of the ad hoc committee. The committee began to investigate the possibility of adding tutoring to the services provided by the center.

The ad hoc committee chair's first task was to identify persons that would have an interest in this issue of tutoring and could provide support for launching the program. The first meeting was scheduled at the center (in the room that could house the tutoring program) with representatives from the center's Children and Youth Department, the school district's Office of Administration, the council, and neighborhood parents. Participants introduced themselves and described their personal or professional role. Caroline explained the reason for forming the ad hoc committee, the purpose of the gathering, and asked each member to share her or his thoughts (or the feelings of the constituency being represented by the member) regarding the need for a tutoring program. Although the group was generally in agreement on the concept of a tutoring program, questions were raised regarding neighborhood residents' support for a tutoring program, resources needed to mount a program, and staff or volunteers to operate the program. Emily volunteered to conduct a needs assessment and report back to the committee at next month's meeting.

Engagement of Organizations and Communities

Organizational and community-level concerns or needs are often addressed in a fragmented manner in which all relevant parties are not communicating with one another, and key participants may not be involved in the change process. In order to effectively work at this level, social workers use a systems approach and involve all those persons that can influence the change or can be affected by the change.

As with group work, the first step in engaging the client system is to identify the persons and groups that can contribute to the change effort. Several different groups may be involved, depending on the type and goal of the organizational or community change effort. For example, a welfare rights coalition (group one) may be representing welfare recipients (group two), and front-line workers in the welfare agency that have insight into the needs of the target group are in a third group. A group may come together naturally, as in the case of the earlier example of refugee business owners, or may have to be formed, as in the case of the neighborhood redevelopment example. Criteria for determining participants relate to those contributions that each person or group can make to the change effort. Contributions may come in the form of knowledge, resources, influence, funding, credibility, or access to other groups or resources.

During the engagement phase of an organizational and community change effort, all participants have the opportunity to articulate the needs, resources, contributions, and barriers to participation for themselves or the groups they represent. In addition, each participant contributes to the development of the purpose, goals, decision-making process, and allocation of resources and responsibilities. A key to sustaining participants' investment in the change process is to ensure that each participant has a clear understanding of the tasks and activities for which she or he is responsible. Each participant's contribution is affirmed and valued in the process.

The social work skills of reflective listening, interpreting both verbal and nonverbal communications, and negotiation can contribute to the group's ability to bond around a common concern. As with social work practice at the individual, family, and group levels, the social worker practicing at the community and organizational level will use empathy and rapport-building skills to engage with individuals and groups.

Assessment of Organizations and Communities

In formulating a strengths-based assessment approach, Emily and her field instructor developed the following plan:

- Clarification of purpose: *The council wanted to know if there was an interest in and need for a tutoring program as well as the viability of launching and sustaining such a program.*

- Data collection strategy: *In an effort to determine neighborhood interest and need for a tutoring program, Emily and Caroline developed a multimodal approach to collecting data. To ascertain community attitudes regarding a tutoring program, Emily and a representative from the residents' committee conducted a door-to-door survey of 50 neighborhood households using a survey developed by Emily and approved by the committee.*

> *Next, Emily contacted the board of education to gather information on existing tutoring resources in the area and the process for creating a tutoring program that would build on current resources. Emily then contacted other tutoring programs and gathered information regarding development, staffing, funding, and evaluation.*
>
> ● Compilation of data: *Emily compiled information from the various sources, contacted possible volunteer sources, and at the next committee meeting, presented a written and verbal report highlighting the interest, assets, and potential outcomes for a neighborhood-based tutoring program.*

An essential component of developing a plan of intervention for effecting change within an organization or community is the assessment process. The first assessment activity is to identify the organization or community targeted for change. Once identified, the organization is assessed to determine whether change is needed, desired, feasible, and sustainable. The assessment process may actually be a component of the intervention itself, particularly in the case of grassroots efforts (Tropman & Erlich, 2001). Gaining familiarity with the target group and identifying and organizing a core group of supporters can, in fact, contribute to the change process. Assessment of organization and community needs encompasses an array of activities, including determination of goals in order to identify the information to be gathered and the way in which the information will be used.

The next step is to develop and conduct an assessment. At the organizational and community level, having a plan for gathering information or data is critical for the future phase of organizing, analyzing, and interpreting the data. Data that is useful in the development of a plan includes in-person, telephone, or mail surveys; focus groups; official government data; agency records on services provided; and in-depth interviews with key stakeholders.

The assessment could then focus on the following:

● *Strengths and available resources:* Identify the availability of existing resources and assets possessed by the target group or community.

● *Organizational and community attitudes:* Having input from the key players and others involved in the change process contributes to the development of the plan and intervention and, ultimately, to the success or failure of a change effort.

● *Barriers to change:* An extension of identifying attitudes toward change, determining the existence of any obstacles to change is included as part of the planning process. Barriers may include such factors as attitudes, perceptions, funding, political support, space, and participation.

● *Viability of sustaining a change:* Determining the organization's or community's ability to maintain a change is critical information to have before implementing a change plan.

● *Assessment of similar change efforts:* Identifying organizations and communities that have developed similar programs, policies, or changes and evaluating the success or failure of those efforts are included within a needs assessment

Intervention with Organizations and Communities

Using the data from Emily's needs assessment, the ad hoc committee developed the following plan:

● *Goal: Develop a plan to establish a tutoring program building on the assets and capacities of the neighborhood residents, and implement it by the start of the next school year.*

● *Objectives:*
  ● *Using information gathered from the board of education and other tutoring programs, develop a schedule, curricular plan, budget, and staffing coverage.*
  ● *Present plan to the ad hoc committee and council for approval.*
  ● *Publicize the program to neighborhood parents and youth and school personnel*

After receiving approval of the plan from both the ad hoc committee and the council, Emily and Caroline implemented the intervention by developing a curricular plan for tutoring and a training program for the tutors; obtained funding from the agency for supplies and refreshments; recruited volunteers to serve as tutors; advertised the program to parents, youth, and teachers; and prepared the room designated for the program. Once the program was under way, Emily served as on-site supervisor, and she and Caroline met weekly with the volunteer tutors. With permission from students' parents, Emily contacted teachers on a monthly basis to monitor student performance.

Organizational and community interventions comprise planning and implementing activities that involve balancing multiple sets of needs, agendas, and resources. The social worker's role may be to negotiate a plan and intervention between groups whose goals and perceived obligations conflict. Having a realistic understanding of the organizations, policies, and limitations involved in accomplishing the goals can help the social worker create viable alternatives for addressing the need(s) identified during the needs assessment. With the skills that a generalist social worker possesses, helping the opposing parties to establish a common goal and to compromise regarding the intervention plan may fall within the purview of the social worker's responsibilities to the group.

Goal development means prioritizing the needs identified during the needs assessment process and articulating overall goals while attending to the individual needs of constituent groups. In organizational and community interventions, practitioners ensure that the goals address the needs of all involved participants and that responsibility for meeting the objectives is equitably shared by all groups. Although participants may contribute different skills, resources, or influence, all participants have a clear role that contributes to the achievement of the established goal. Moreover, each goal should be specific and measurable so that the change effort can be evaluated.

A priority in establishing goals is achievability. The strategies for action contain specific objectives toward achieving the desired change. The goals, action strategies, and evaluation methods are mutually agreed upon, documented, and shared with all relevant constituencies. As members of the change effort carry out the tasks and activities designed to meet the goals, regular communication and ongoing evaluation are used to monitor progress.

Evaluation and Termination of Organizations and Communities

Evaluation of the tutoring program began with the development of the program plans. The needs assessment yielded information to suggest that a program was needed; therefore, creating the program fulfilled that need. However, simply creating a service to meet a need does not equate to success. Maintaining regular contact with the volunteers, students' parents, and teachers provided ongoing input into such issues as student participation, parent and student satisfaction with the program, and student performance at school. Documenting the input from the involved groups enabled Emily and Caroline to report to the council that the tutoring program was meeting a neighborhood need and to recommend continuation.

Evaluation of organizational and community interventions is an ongoing and complex process. Because many interventions are long-term change efforts that are implemented over months or years with a large and varied number of persons and groups involved, evaluation may be compartmentalized and conducted on an ongoing basis. Evaluation strategies that are applicable for organizational and community interventions include

- Review of the needs assessment and goals to determine whether identified needs and goals have been met.

- Pre- and postintervention measures to determine whether change occurred and the extent of change.

Program outcomes and continuous quality assurance can be evaluated by assessing such change-related efforts as quantity and quality of services provided, revenue generated, decreased spending, or behavior change.

Termination of organizational and community-level change may indicate success or failure of the change effort. As in the case of program development, the intervention can be terminated when the program is operational, but with a stabilization effort incorporated to enable the program to be sustained. In an advocacy effort, termination may occur when a policy is or is not changed or law is or is not enacted. In these situations, the change effort may shift to focus on the implementation of the change. In other situations, termination is moot because the purpose of the intervention is to facilitate an ongoing change.

CONCLUSION

Social workers have skills that can influence large-scale changes in organizations, communities, and the society as a whole. To facilitate change at these levels, social workers use the knowledge and skills learned for working with individuals, families, and groups but apply them on a larger scale. Working at the organizational and community level, social workers have to advocate on behalf of a client, develop a new program, obtain funding, interpret data for program evaluation, or analyze the impact of a new policy on their clients. Therefore, social workers must keep abreast of the policy issues that are being proposed that could affect the lives of the persons they serve. Working at the organizational and community level often requires the social worker to have vision and patience—vision to see the possibility of large-scale change and patience to traverse the multiple and complex steps to achieve the change.

For additional information on social work practice with organizations and communities, check out the following groups:

- Influencing State Policy (www.statepolicy.org) is an organization for social work students, faculty, and professionals that provides information on advocacy and current legislation.

- NASW (www.naswdc.org) provides the latest information on the association's advocacy efforts, issues, updates, and political action. See information on the NASW publication *Social Work Speaks: NASW Policy Statements, 2003–2006*, a comprehensive guide to social and political issues that affect the social work profession.

- Association for Community Organization and Social Administration (www.acosa.org) is an organization for community organizers, planning activists, administrators, policy practice specialists, students, and faculty.

- International Federation of Social Workers (www.ifsw.org) is a global organization striving for social justice, human rights, and social development.

- Alliance for Justice (www.allianceforjustice.org) is an association of organizations focused on civil rights in the areas of mental health, women, children, consumers, and the environment. This group sponsors the First Monday Campaign, an effort to raise awareness about public policy and advocacy.

- NetAction Internet Resources (www.netaction.org) is a resource for community activists.

MAIN POINTS

- Social work practice with organizations and communities is defined as working toward large-scale change in a practice, policy, program, or law that affects people's lives.

- The roots of the social work profession are well grounded in practice at the organizational and community level as evidenced by the work of the settlement house workers whose goal it was to improve the living conditions for persons in the neighborhoods in which they worked.

- Models for facilitating change within organizations and communities include community or locality development, social planning, and social action. Community or locality development emphasizes bringing about change in a specific geographic area; social planning focuses on organizing a group of people to facilitate change that may span different geographic locales, but affect people experiencing similar life situations; the goal of a social action intervention is to organize people around a particular issue in an effort to influence decision making related to that issue.

- As at the other two levels of social work practice, skills for working with organizations and communities use the approaches of engagement, assessment, intervention, and evaluation.

- Specific social work skills needed for organizational and community practice include negotiation, fund-raising, collaboration, organization, advocacy, analysis, administration, program planning, evaluation, and supervision.

EXERCISES: PRACTICING SOCIAL WORK

Community Resources

Click on the Sanchez Family Town Map. What are the assets of the community for meeting the needs that you have identified for the family.

Community Resources Needed

Click on the Engage button for the Sanchez family. Complete Task #3 for this section.

Community Activism

Using the Sanchez Family interactive case study, you have learned that Hector and Celia have two children with disabilities. As you know from Chapter 10, they have become involved in a community group that advocates for additional funding for children with disabilities. Based on the knowledge you have gained from the current chapter, strategize about ways in which this group can be successful in launching a fundraising campaign.

EXERCISES: THE SOCIAL WORK LIBRARY

Challenges and Dilemmas in Community Development

After reading "Challenges and Dilemmas in Community Development" (Arches, 1999), select one of the five dilemmas for analysis. Specifically:

1. Describe the dilemma.

2. Identify the social work roles and skills that would be appropriate for responding to the dilemma.

3. Develop a list of strategies for responding to the dilemma.

OTHER EXERCISES

Influencing State Policy

Because laws impact the lives of everyone in our society, but particularly those persons served by social workers, having an awareness of legislative activity in your state is essential for effective social work practice. After reading "Influencing 'State' Policy: Social Work Arena for the 21st Century" (Schneider, 2002), go to the Internet site for Influencing State Policy at http://www.statepolicy.org and follow the instructions on the first page. Click on the flag and follow the directions to link up with Stateline.org. At Stateline.org, select "Welfare and Social Policy" under the heading, "Issues." Review the current policy issues for that day in selected states, or click on any state on the map and investigate the social welfare policy currently in the news. Prepare a two-minute presentation on an example of that state's policy and deliver it orally in class. Bring a one-page written version of the two-minute presentation to class with enough copies for your fellow students and the instructor.

Source: R. Schneider, Virginia Commonwealth University, 2002

Speaking Out

Advocacy is an important social work skill and one that requires the social worker to be able to articulate her/his points on behalf of the client or issue being advocated. In this exercise, you will have the opportunity to advocate for an issue that has been written about in a newspaper or other publication. Using the Internet or a hard copy of a newspaper or publication, identify an article that describes an issue, event, or pending legislation about which you have an opposing view. Write a letter to the editor of that publication articulating your point of view. The following guidelines may help you in making your points and being published.

Tips for Getting Your Letter to the Editor Published

- **Timeliness is key.** A letter to the editor is usually only as hot as the news of the day.

- **In the body of the letter, distinguish fact from opinion and support your opinions with adequate factual evidence.** Facts and figures are important to support your point, but do not rely solely on them. Take a position. Offer your opinion.

- **Write informally** (i.e., as if you are writing a letter to a relative).

- **Clarity is crucial.** Keep sentences short, simple, and to the point. Use language the average person can understand. Avoid jargon suited only to your expertise, age group, or cultural group.

- **The first sentence is the most important.** Summarize your thesis and tell the readers why they should care.

- **Do not forget the last sentence.** Give your ending as much thought as your start. A concise summary is vital.

- **Offer solutions.** Do not just address the problem, but discuss ways it can be fixed.

- **Keep it short.** Most letters to the editor should not exceed two to three short paragraphs.

- **Revise and rewrite.** Eliminate unnecessary words and sentences. The more you edit your piece, the less likely the editor will.

- **Add personal anecdotes** only if they help make your point.

Sources: Saint Louis University Marketing and Communications and Michael Johnson

CHAPTER 12

The Social Work Profession

*Emily has been fortunate to provide a range of services to a diverse group of peo-
ple in a variety of agency settings. Her social work degrees have enabled her to
easily secure employment with each of her transitions. She values being part of a
profession that not only embraces people with empathy and compassion but also
provides her with the knowledge, skills, and values to empower others to enhance
their lives. As Emily's story ends, yours begins.*

As you have learned in this introductory course, social work as a profession
has a long and rich history. But you might also want to know where the profession of social work is going in the future. Where will the jobs be? What will
these jobs pay? What type of preparation will social workers need to be effective
in the coming decades? In this final chapter, we will complete our exploration
of the social work profession by considering the future trends and opportunities for the social work profession, examining the route to becoming a social
worker, and, most importantly, moving toward answering the question Is social
work a career for you?

PROFESSIONAL OUTLOOK FOR SOCIAL WORKERS

*Social work does not exist in a vacuum. As much as any profession, social
work activity is woven into the very fabric of society. Social work
acts and reacts to that which transpires in society.*
—ALLEN-MEARES & DeROOS (1997, P. 384)

As we consider social work practice in the 21st century, the future looks bright for
the profession. Employment opportunities continue to expand, compensation

for social workers is increasing, and society recognizes the valuable contributions that social workers can and do make to the well-being of people they serve.

As the social work profession enters its second century, the profession will continue to be viewed as a major service profession and, as noted in the opening quotation, remain an integral part of society. It will experience growth and expansion in the diversity of the membership and practice settings (Austin, 1997). Projections suggest that the future of social work will have a distinctive focus on the concerns of women, children, and older adults, as these continue to be the persons in our society that are most vulnerable and at risk for negative outcomes. Social work will continue to be somewhat unique among major professions, as its members are predominantly women, and women increasingly hold many of the leadership positions. There continues to be substantial participation by men. Social work will continue to be a profession that emphasizes diversity and will be involved in public controversy, because social workers are often involved in sensitive and highly publicized social issues.

Employment Trends and Opportunities

The future appears extremely promising in terms of increasing employment opportunities for social workers. Increases in diversity of all kinds—ethnic, cultural, age, and family structure—will continue to provide expanded opportunities for social workers. For the first decade of the 21st century, the availability of social work positions is expected to increase at a greater rate than the average rate for all occupations (U.S. Department of Labor Bureau of Labor Statistics, 2002b). Social workers in the United States already number approximately 600,000, and the Bureau of Labor Statistics projects a 30 percent increase for the profession by 2010 (2002b). Employment prospects are expected to be most competitive in urban areas, but social work positions in rural communities will continue to provide significant opportunities for social workers, in general, and BSWs, in particular.

Projections for growth have been consistent in recent years. The popular press has proclaimed social work to be one of the hot careers on the rise. Here is a sampling of these reports:

- One of four hottest fields created by the aging of the baby boomers, with opportunities in patient advocacy and gerontological social work (McCleary, 2002).

- One of "seven hot sectors in these hard times" by *Rolling Stone* (Mulrine, 2002).

- One of the careers with the largest expected growth between 2000 and 2010 (Eisenberg, 2002).

- Number 25 of 50 hottest jobs in *Money* (Marable, 1995).

- One of 20 "hot job tracks" in *U.S. News and World Report* (Beddingfield, Hawkins, Ito, Lenzy, & Loftus, 1996; Brindley, Bennefield, Danyliw, Hetter, & Loftus, 1997).

Increases in the overall U.S. employment market are projected at approximately 15 percent, suggesting that social work and the various related fields will fare well in future years due, in large part, to increasing opportunities to work with older adults and their families (U.S. Department of Labor, 2002a). For the social service delivery system, in general, which includes social work and other related professions, growth is anticipated to range from 36 percent to 74 percent (Begun, 2000; Braddock, 1999). Estimates from the U.S. Labor Department suggest increases from 2000 to 2010 will be 18 percent for counselors, social and religious workers, and up to 54 percent for "social and human service assistants" (2002a, 2002c). For social workers, specifically, growth is anticipated in virtually every field of practice and setting.

For the fast-growing older-adult population, social workers will be needed particularly in the areas of mental and physical health services. In addition to increasing opportunities to work with older adults and their families, other settings expected to experience growth and employ larger numbers of social workers at all levels in the early part of the 21st century include agencies that provide services in child protection, disabilities, HIV/AIDS, and chemical dependency and addictions. Social work employment opportunities in the criminal justice system, particularly with adolescents, will continue to grow, as will social work positions within elementary and secondary school systems. Private practice (in which self-employed clinical social workers provide individual, family, and group treatment) will be another growth area for social workers with MSWs. The focus will be on the provision of intensive, short-term interventions, increased group interventions, and advocacy, particularly at the policy level (Austin, 1997).

The funding crises that have plagued the social work profession for much of its history will continue to dictate the growth that is realized in these settings. The need for social workers will remain constant, however. Our legislators and funding sources will determine whether the resources required to meet the need will be present as well, making advocacy efforts critical as an area of social work focus.

Areas of Practice   The provision of mental health services is expected to remain the primary area of practice for social workers, as evidenced by the fact that students enrolled in social work programs identify mental health as the largest area of concentration (Gibelman & Schervish, 1997). Approximately 40 percent of NASW members report their primary area of practice as mental health (NASW, 2004a).

As noted, a significant area of growth for social workers is in the area of gerontological social work, especially in community-based and hospital-based medical and residential services (Rosen & Zlotnik, 2001). As a result of increasing pressure on physicians to maintain shorter hospitalizations, patients are being returned to their homes with greater needs for in-home health services. Social workers serve as key members of the multidisciplinary team of health professionals that work with older adults and their families to provide adequate home- and community-based care. Funding has been made available to social work educators in recent years to provide students with knowledge, skills, and values so they may work effectively with older adults and their families regardless of the area in which they specialize.

With the privatization of many social service systems, a number of social workers are expected to leave the public and nonprofit sectors to work in for-profit and nonprofit organizations. Privatizing social services shifts administrative responsibility for delivery to a privately owned company that contracts with governmental agencies and private insurance companies. These contract agencies then provide the services at a lower cost, as there are typically fewer bureaucratic requirements. In particular, employment opportunities are expanding in the for-profit sector of mental health, medical facilities, and home-based care for persons with disabilities and older adults (Gibelman & Schervish, 1997).

Salaries   Almost all students want to know the salaries they can expect when they choose social work as a career. Although it is common knowledge that social work salaries, like many other human service–related careers, have historically lagged behind other professions, the salaries for social workers are improving. In recent years, the profession as a whole has united to campaign for higher salaries and compensations and has realized some success in this area. The statistics presented here are broad-based, nationwide salary ranges that differ considerably by region, field of service, educational level, and experience; but they serve as a useful reference point.

The U.S. Department of Labor reports that median annual salaries for all social workers in 2000 ranged from the low $30,000s to mid-$40,000s. Specifically, the median annual salary for social workers employed in child, family, and school settings was $31,470; in medical and public health settings it was $34,790; and in mental health and chemical dependency services, $30,170 (2002b). To give you an idea of the range of salaries for particular fields, Box 12.1 lists salaries for several categories within the main divisions of child, family, and school services; health care services; and mental health and chemical dependency services.

A 2000 NASW survey projects the median annual salary for the profession in coming years at $49,500 with the majority of social workers earning over $40,000 a year (*NASW News,* 2003). Exhibit 12.1 provides a breakdown of projected social work salaries.

BOX 12.1

Social Work Salaries in 2000

Child, Family, and School Services
  $26,780/year (residential care facilities)
  $27,170/year (individual and family services)
  $32,860/year (state government, except education and hospitals)
  $35,780/year (local government, except education and hospitals)
  $41,700/year (elementary and secondary schools)

Medical and Public Health Care Services
  $29,730/year (individual and family services)
  $31,580/year (nursing and personal care facilities)
  $35,300/year (local government, except education and hospitals)
  $36,230/year (health and allied services)
  $40,020/year (hospitals)

Mental Health and Substance Abuse Treatment Services
  $26,620/year (residential programs)
  $28,160/year (individual and family services)
  $28,270/year (health and allied services)
  $33,150/year (hospitals)
  $33,950/year (local government, except education and hospitals)

Source: U.S. Department of Labor, 2002b

In examining the differences between the salaries of social workers with BSWs and MSWs, geographic locale and type of setting influence salaries. However, according to the U.S. census, BSWs typically earn about 18 percent less than those social workers with a graduate degree (Barth, 2001).

Overall, U.S. census data suggests that social work professionals earn approximately 11 percent less when compared with all professions (Barth, 2001). A variety of explanations have been offered for these lower salaries. Professions that are made up largely of women (for example, nursing and education) routinely receive lower levels of compensation. The social work profession is approximately 85 percent female. Secondly, social workers are typically employed in organizations that may struggle for financial stability, thus paying lower salaries. As many social workers feel drawn to the profession out of a commitment to working in services for and with the disenfranchised, social workers are undervalued by dominant society in the area of compensation. Although social work employment opportunities are increasing, there is often an ample pool of persons to fill vacant positions, thus keeping the salaries lower (Barth, 2001). However, those in the pool may not always be degreed social workers.

Although these explanations may be, to varying degrees, a valid commentary on the state of the social work profession's salary status, they can also serve as a call to social workers to engage in more aggressive advocacy for the profession.

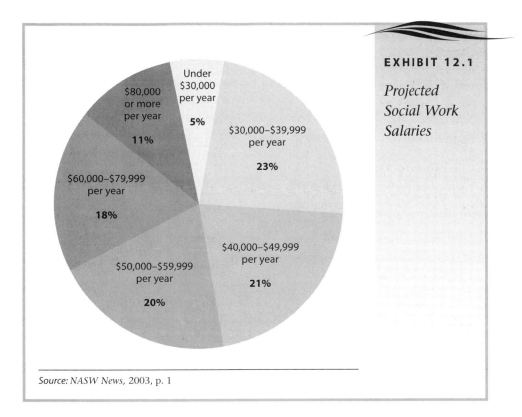

EXHIBIT 12.1

Projected Social Work Salaries

Under $30,000 per year — **5%**

$30,000–$39,999 per year — **23%**

$40,000–$49,999 per year — **21%**

$50,000–$59,999 per year — **20%**

$60,000–$79,999 per year — **18%**

$80,000 or more per year — **11%**

Source: *NASW News,* 2003, p. 1

Social workers provide valuable, much-needed services to a large segment of our population and therefore deserve recognition and compensation for the work they do. Social workers routinely focus professional advocacy efforts on behalf of client systems, but to maintain high-quality education and training opportunities, social workers also need to advocate for salaries that recognize the valuable services provided.

The Social Work Library

For a more in-depth look at the future of the social work profession, read Gibelman and Schervish's "Where Are We Going?"

Societal Perceptions of the Social Work Profession

Social work is a profession that is visible and valued within our society. Validation of that statement comes from the fact that social workers are employed in an increasingly wide-ranging number and type of settings and are being sought to fill needs in the social service delivery system.

In addition to the traditional settings that have been described throughout this book, social workers are entering the political arena. Over 170 social workers have been elected in recent years to political office at the local, state, and national levels. For a listing of social workers in elected office and information on getting involved, visit the NASW-PACE Web site at http://socialworkers.org/pace. Social workers are also being called on to use their knowledge and skills to develop national policy. As an example, a social worker was added to the staff of Senator Hillary Clinton to design policy on older-adult issues.

State government officials also recognize the need to increase the number of social workers. For example, measures are being taken to address the ongoing need to fill over 25,000 social work positions in California. Recommendations have been made to the state legislature that include developing tuition reimbursement and loan forgiveness programs, increasing recruitment efforts and enrollment in social work programs, and expanding reciprocal licensing programs with other states to attract social workers to California (O'Neill, 2003a).

Additional support for the positive perception of the social work profession comes from a recent study conducted by a group of MSW students in a research class at Arizona State University. Using randomly selected telephone numbers, students conducted 386 telephone interviews with local residents in their community and asked questions about the respondents' knowledge and perceptions of the social work profession (LeCroy & Stinson, 2003; O'Neill, 2003b). Viewed as a boon to the profession, here are some of respondents' perceptions:

- 97 percent perceive that social workers are valuable to the community.

- 96 percent see social workers as a source of comfort in times of need.

- 92 percent believe that social workers work with all socioeconomic groups.

- 91 percent perceive social workers as protectors of children.

- 82 percent report they would be generally happy if their children became social workers.

- 80 percent feel social workers are important for society's social problems.

- 79 percent responded that social workers engage in family therapy.

- 67 percent personally know a social worker.

- 59 percent view social workers as agents of social change (for example, have the ability to influence policy).

- 59 percent report that the information they have received about social workers is positive.

- 56 percent have had personal experience with a social worker.

- 53 percent believe that a bachelor's degree is appropriate for the practice of social work.

- 8 percent view the role of social workers being to disburse "welfare payment."

Although this profile of public perceptions of social workers is encouraging, social workers will continue to advocate for the profession by educating the public regarding the role that they play in society. They do this by taking every opportunity to represent the profession favorably in the public eye. For instance, they write letters, make telephone calls, and send e-mail messages when social workers are negatively portrayed in the news, on television, and in the movies. They can ensure that when the media highlight social workers, they are identified as degreed social workers. Conversely, when a person who does not possess a social work degree is identified in the media as a social worker, professional social workers challenge that label and provide clarification that only those persons who have been awarded social work degrees from CSWE-accredited programs are social workers.

PROFESSIONAL SOCIALIZATION

Developing the knowledge, skills, and values needed for social work practice is only one aspect of becoming a social work professional. Along with learning the theories and methods of practice, becoming a social work professional involves being socialized into the profession. Professional socialization involves becoming acquainted with the rules, norms, and culture of the profession, establishing a professional identity, identifying with the social work profession, feeling comfortable with that self-identity, and understanding the role of social work within the community and society. Being a social worker becomes part of who you are.

You have begun your socialization process by gaining an overview of the profession; experiencing social work through class discussions and exercises; possibly volunteering or working in a social service agency; and hopefully, interacting with other social work students and social work practitioners. In the following sections, we explore the next steps in the professional socialization process.

Social Work Education: Pursuing a Degree

Do you see yourself as a social worker? Some students know before they begin their first social work course that they want to be a social worker. For others, the feeling of connection comes later in other courses or their field experience.

Professional identification begins with introspection and soul searching. Essentially, you are asking yourself "is social work the right career for me?" "Do I see myself working in those settings that I have been learning about and doing the work I have been reading about and seeing?" The decision to become a social worker lies solely in your hands, but if you are unsure, a number of activities may help you determine whether you identify with the social work profession.

As you learned in the discussion on the social work degree in the first chapter of this book, to become a social worker requires a bachelor's or master's degree in social work awarded by a college or university accredited by the CSWE. In 2004, there are 642 social work programs accredited by the CSWE—168 MSW and 437 BSW programs, with 19 and 18 programs, respectively, in candidacy (an application for accreditation is in process) (CSWE, 2004). In 2000, over 11,000 persons were awarded BSW, 15,000 received MSW, and over 200 social work doctoral degrees were granted.

Bachelor of Social Work   Social work courses at the BSW level focus on preparing generalist social work practitioners. A brief description of each content area of the social work foundation curriculum follows. The Council on Social Work Education *Educational Policy and Accreditation Standards* (2001a) provides guidelines for social work curricula.

- *Human behavior and the social environment:* Understanding the reciprocal and dynamic relationships between a person's behavior and the social environment in which she or he lives is key to practicing social work. Therefore, this curriculum area emphasizes learning theoretical frameworks for understanding human behavior across the life span of an individual and family and the role of the organization and community in the life of the person or family. The impacts of the biological, sociological, cultural, psychological, and spiritual perspectives on development are interwoven throughout this course.

- *Social welfare policy and services:* Gaining an understanding of the history of social work and the social welfare system is the focus of this curriculum area. Students are exposed to social justice issues and current policies designed to address social injustices. Students learn about the ways in which those policies impact the lives of the individuals, families, groups, organizations, and communities with which they will work and how to analyze those policies.

- *Social work practice:* Learning to practice social work with individuals, families, groups, organizations, and communities is the focus of the practice curriculum area required for all social work students. In one or more practice-oriented courses, students learn about engaging client systems; assessing needs, resources, and strengths; developing with the client system a plan for intervention; and evaluating and terminating the intervention process. The learning of appropriate and culturally competent communication skills is key to these courses.

- *Research:* To engage in effective social work practice, social workers need research skills in the areas of qualitative and quantitative research. Research courses prepare students to understand and interpret research methods as well as to conduct research to better inform their social work practice.

- *Field education:* The integration of theory and practice occurs when the student is able to apply the knowledge and skills learned in the classroom in an agency-based social service setting. Under the supervision of social work practitioners, students gain experience in engaging, assessing, intervening in, and evaluating client systems that include individuals, families, groups, organizations, and communities.

Content for BSW courses builds on the content of the other courses required in a liberal arts curriculum. Although programs vary considerably, courses typically taken by social work majors at the bachelor's level include English, human biology, history, mathematics and/or statistics, political science and/or economics, fine arts, sociology and/or anthropology, foreign language, psychology, and philosophy. Each of these areas of study is key to becoming an articulate, effective social worker who has a broad base of knowledge about people, culture, and society. The competent social worker understands the way in which the human body and mind function, the role of culture in our society, the impact of the economy and the political system on the lives of the people that social workers serve, and the use of statistical analysis for the purposes of funding and evaluation. The arts and humanities courses that social work students take provide an understanding of the motivations of human beings.

In addition to the general liberal arts courses and required social work courses, social work students complete elective coursework in individual areas of interest. Most BSW programs offer electives, but students can also choose to take their elective coursework in other departments to round out their knowledge base. Using our past to look into the future, you can seek out elective coursework, readings, projects, and experiences to enable you to approach your social work career armed with a broad-based repertoire of skills. There are a variety of areas you may want to cultivate during your social work training.

- Critical thinking skills, which are essential for effective social work practice, come from a broad understanding of the liberal arts. They empower the social worker to question, discuss, and test assumptions and knowledge in the quest for social work practice competence (Gambrill, 1997).

- Coursework in economics can strengthen your understanding of the impact of a shifting labor market on psychosocial issues (for example, chemical dependency and addiction, domestic violence, multiculturalism, and physical and mental health problems) (Reisch & Gorin, 2001).

- Having an understanding of the legal system can be invaluable to a practicing social worker. Most fields of social work practice intersect at some point with the legal system. Client systems may encounter the legal system as a victim of crime or the accused, when they need guardianship, have end-of-life decisions that require legal intervention, or need legal help with immigration concerns.

- The integration of policy knowledge and skills into social work practice places individual, family, and group concerns within a larger societal context (Jacobson, 2001).

- Knowledge of aging and effective practice methods for working with older adults and their families will be essential for social work practice in the coming decades as the baby boomers become older adults (CSWE/SAGE-SW, 2001b).

- Knowledge of community practice education is needed, particularly in classrooms that promote multidisciplinary education and communication and in assessment and intervention at the community level.

- Social workers need leadership skills to be on the forefront of policy development instead of reacting to established policies.

- Communications skills, such as public speaking, working with the media, and providing testimony, are essential for being effective advocates for the social worker's constituencies.

- Applied research skills are important for conducting agency or community-based research, including the ability to conduct needs assessments and develop and evaluate programs with measurable outcomes.

- The time has come for social workers to be particularly skilled in the areas of collaboration, coalition building, and service coordination skills to strengthen the voice of those client systems often unheard by policy makers and to serve as a bridge between those in power and those not in power (Reisch, 1997).

In order for social workers to maintain knowledge and skills that are relevant for societal needs of the time, they require regular, ongoing education. Completing a BSW degree involves a comprehensive education based on the foundations of generalist social work knowledge, skills, and values. Areas for intervention and employment opportunities are extremely varied and constantly in a state of change. Social workers require education and training to enable them to be responsive to the changing society.

Master of Social Work   At the graduate level, coursework is delineated into two levels: foundation and concentration. The foundation coursework, comparable to the generalist courses completed as part of the BSW, consists of social work practice with individuals, families, groups, organizations, and communities; human behavior and the social environment; social policy; research methods; and the field experience. Also infused and integrated throughout the foundation coursework are the areas of social work values and ethics, understanding and respect for diversity, populations at risk, and social and economic justice.

At the master's level, following the successful completion of the foundation coursework, students select an area of concentration in which to focus their course of study. Each social work program establishes these areas of specialized study, but the curriculum always includes advanced coursework in the areas introduced at the foundation level: practice, human behavior, policy, research, and field experiences. Although the diversity of concentration areas is wide ranging through MSW programs, typical areas of specialization include children, youth, and family practice; mental and physical health practice; gerontology; administration; community practice; and social and economic development.

Many schools offer **advanced standing** into MSW programs to students who have graduated from a CSWE-accredited BSW program. Their coursework may be applied to part or all of the foundation coursework, thus decreasing the total number of credits required to complete the MSW degree. With advanced standing, students may complete their master's degree in a shorter period of time or take more elective coursework in areas of interest.

Additional options for completing both the BSW and MSW degrees are the five-year and Bridge programs offered at some institutions. The five-year program typically involves the student's completing a joint BSW and MSW degree within a structured five-year plan. The Bridge program typically enables the student to complete three years in another major or institution and begin MSW coursework during the senior year of the undergraduate experience.

Current Issues Influencing Social Work Training for the Future

Because social work is a profession that responds to the personal and societal needs and concerns of the times, social work knowledge and education must also reflect current societal changes and needs. As we progress through the 21st century, some new opportunities are emerging for social workers.

Changes in Health Care   Social work is becoming more integrated within the health care delivery system; therefore, social workers need knowledge, skills, and values to understand the biopsychosocial and spiritual dynamics that impact people's lives. For example:

- As social workers become more involved in end-of-life issues, in prolonging life, in psychopharmacology, and genetic counseling, knowledge of biochemistry, neuroscience, and genetics will be a marketable asset.

- As researchers investigate the biological causes of some mental illnesses, social workers, as primary providers of mental health treatment, need an understanding of the interrelatedness of the biological and psychological aspects of mental illness (Austin, 1997).

- Social workers already play a significant role in the provision of multi-disciplinary health and social services to persons with HIV/AIDS and their families and caregivers; therefore, knowledge of this illness and an understanding of its effects are critical.

Technology   No longer a novelty, but a part of our daily lives, technology is a necessary skill area for social workers. Social workers must have increasing levels of technological sophistication for record keeping, data analysis for funding and program evaluation, communication, and distance education. Computer technology has enabled social workers to conduct online therapy and support groups, facilitate discussion/chat rooms for clients interested in similar issues, provide long-distance social work education and training, maintain up-to-date knowledge of legislation and policies, and reach numerous policy makers in a matter of seconds. In short, technology has enhanced social workers' abilities to reach more people in less time. However, we must use technology in an ethical and responsible manner. Social workers are ethically obligated to ensure integrity at all times when using technology. For example, confidentiality is essential when communicating with or about client systems via a cell phone or e-mail, and Web sites should be checked to ensure they are credible sources of information.

Crisis Intervention   Social workers are increasingly on the scene in times of disaster to provide support and mental health services. For example, over 40 percent of the volunteers trained by the American Red Cross to provide mental health services in emergency and disaster situations are professional social workers (NASW, 2004a). Social workers' knowledge and skills in crisis intervention make them valuable assets for working with persons traumatized by a disaster. In a related area, social workers are needed to work with those members of the military and their families who are involved in military deployments. Social workers have accompanied troops in virtually every deployment in recent times and are working with the families on the home front as well.

Multilingualism   As the U.S. population continues to become increasingly diverse, having proficiency in multiple languages enables a social worker to communicate more effectively with client systems. When we think about being bilingual in the United States today, Spanish is typically the first language that comes to mind. Although Spanish follows English as the second most common language spoken, there is a need for social workers who are fluent in other languages as well, including Russian, Bosnian, and American Sign Language.

Child Welfare Services   The professionalization of child welfare services is at a critical point in the United States. Historically, due to large caseloads and inadequate salaries, child welfare agencies in nearly every state are challenged to have competent and appropriately trained professionals to work in the area of child welfare. Although turnover rates are considerably less for degreed social workers that work in child welfare, many states do not require a social work degree for these positions; thus, the national turnover rate is 30–40 percent annually (U.S. General Accounting Office, 2003). High turnover results in less effective and inconsistent services for children and families.

In response to the need for more degreed social workers to work in child welfare, federal funds are available through Titles IV-B and IV-E of the Social Security Act and have contributed to the development of university-agency partnerships in over 40 states to provide support and training for social work students interested in this area. However, more social workers, at both the BSW and MSW level, are needed to develop knowledge and skills to work in child welfare services.

Making Social Work Your Career

Having gained insight into some of the societal and social work practice challenges and opportunities that are on the horizon for social workers in the future, let us end the journey by turning our attention to your socialization as a social work professional within this context of future needs and issues. Box 12.2 provides an array of possibilities for you to gain more information and experience with the social work profession. Key to your success in determining whether the social work profession is for you is gaining experience. Volunteer and service-related activities are valuable opportunities for developing insights into the world of social work. Working as a volunteer in a social service setting can provide you with access to social workers who can share with you the rewards and realities of being a social worker.

Although formalized education is an essential part of your professional socialization as a social worker, many informal aspects of your educational experience are equally important for your professional development. One group of graduating BSW students share their wisdom for optimizing your social work professionalization experience during your time as a social work student (Clewes, 2001):

- Be prepared to grow and change by being open minded and having your values and beliefs challenged, but do not plan to change anyone but yourself.

- Maximize your learning opportunities by challenging yourself and recognizing that every person that comes into your life can teach you something. Venture into areas of learning that are new for you.

- Ask for help when you need it, and see mistakes as opportunities for learning.

- Be prepared for your social work program to change you and provide you with the tools to go out and continue this change.

- *Network:* Through social work organizations, get acquainted with other social workers who have interests similar to your own. Join a social work listserv or chat room for the opportunity to converse with other social work students and faculty. See if your school has a student social work association or student/faculty special interest groups (for example, social workers interested in working with older adults or a group for students that are gay, lesbian, bisexual, or transgendered). If you join a group, get involved! There is no better way to get connected than to serve in a leadership position.

- *Join NASW:* You can get a discounted student membership rate as well as a transitional rate following graduation. As a member, you receive a monthly newspaper, *NASW News,* the journal, *Social Work,* your local chapter newsletter, and the opportunity to join one of the Specialty Practice Sections, including aging; alcohol, tobacco, and other drugs; child welfare; health; mental health; poverty and social justice; private practice; and school social work. Membership in one of the Specialty Practice Sections provides several benefits: two newsletters per year that include sections on the trends, specific activities, and practice updates of interest to members of that section and online forums for section members to network with one another. In addition, each NASW chapter and the national chapter have student representation—think about running for one of those positions.

- *Get more experience:* You may have been required to complete a community service experience for this introductory course, but consider the value of gaining even more experience in the social service field. You can continue volunteering at the site where you completed your community service, gain a different experience by volunteering at another organization, or even seek paid employment at an agency. Many social service organizations have part- or full-time positions for students seeking to gain social service experience.

Your social work training will be a lifelong process; therefore, the list of educational and professional socialization opportunities provided here is just the beginning. Our society is in a constant state of flux, and the knowledge and skills needed by social workers must be regularly updated and refined over the course of their career. The social worker of the 21st century will need a broad array of knowledge and skills to enable her or him to work with equal effectiveness on private issues (individual, family, and group work) and public issues (organizational and community practice) (Reeser, 1996).

CONCLUSION

Is a career in social work for you? Social work is a unique helping profession that is dually committed to providing social services, such as emergency shelter, while advocating for change to alleviate social problems, such as lobbying for affordable housing policies. Social work is a profession striving to make a difference as its members work for positive social change and serve vulnerable groups within our society. It is a fulfilling profession shaped by the totality of the social worker's life experiences and professional knowledge, skills, and values. You can begin the process of identifying with the social work profession as early as this first social work course and revisit that process many times throughout your career.

You are almost at the end of your first social work course. You have been exposed to a wide range of information about the profession of social work and have, hopefully, gained a sense of what a career in social work would entail. Your task now is to determine how your journey will continue. I would like to end our time together by asking you to consider the inspirational theme for Social Work Month 2004 (NASW, 2004a):

The Social Work Library

Now that you have developed a beginning understanding of contemporary social work, read William Gordon's 1962 "Critique of the Working Definition."

The Power of Social Work: Pass It On:

- We pass the power of our work on to the people whom we help, giving them renewed hope.

- We pass the purpose of social work on to the community to show how our role benefits everyone.

- We pass the passion of social work on from one generation of social workers to the next.

MAIN POINTS

- The outlook for the social work profession is promising. Employment trends suggest that social work jobs will be expanding into new areas, particularly related to aging and racial and ethnic diversity, although provision of mental health services will continue to be the primary area of practice for social work professionals.

- The current median annual salary for social workers is in the low $30,000 to mid-$40,000 range, but it is projected to grow to $49,500 in coming years.

- Societal perceptions of the social work profession are improving, but social workers must stay focused on self-advocacy efforts to ensure that such perceptions continue to improve.

- The BSW prepares social workers to function as generalist practitioners. Both the BSW and MSW foundation curricula encompass a broad spectrum of content that includes human behavior, social policy, research, and social work practice and is integrated through the field experience.

- Socialization as a social work professional encompasses the formal educational process along with the informal strategies for developing a professional identity. Be prepared for a lifelong process of growth and change if you decide to pursue a career in social work.

EXERCISES: PRACTICING SOCIAL WORK

Review

Click on Evaluate. Review the Evaluation Introduction and complete Task #1 for the entire Sanchez family case (notebook review).

Reflection

To conduct an overall review of the Sanchez family case, complete Task #2 which includes intervention evaluation, case closed, and final thoughts. In the final thoughts section, reflect on the work you have done with the Sanchez family throughout this class. How would you know that you were effective in your work? For example, would you ask the family to complete a satisfaction survey? Would you review the goals the family set for themselves and measure progress against those goals? If you failed to reach certain goals, how would you respond?

Case Closed

Complete Task #3 and bid farewell to the Sanchez family and consider all that you have learned from them.

EXERCISES: THE SOCIAL WORK LIBRARY

A Critique of the Working Definition

From the Social Work Library, select the article "A Critique of the Working Definition" (Gordon, 1962). Read the article and answer the following:

1. How does the working definition of the 1950s and 1960s compare with the current definition?

2. Is the definition still relevant? Describe your rationale.

3. Discuss the ways in which your perception of social work has changed (or not changed) as a result of this course.

Where We Are Going

After reading "Where We Are Going: Trends and Issues" (Gibelman & Schervish, 1997), reflect on your perception of the observations and predictions presented by the authors.

OTHER EXERCISES

Connecting with the Field

Along with completing an introductory social work course and learning about the social work profession, talking with practicing social workers is an excellent strategy for determining if social work is the right career for you. With the help of your instructor for this course or other faculty in the social work program, identify a social work practitioner that you can interview in person at her/his agency. Consider an area of social work that is of interest to you and select a practicing social worker that works in that area. Examples might include:

Health/Medical	Child Welfare	Gerontology
Policy	Community Organizing	Administration
Advocacy	Mental Health	School Social Work
Law/Justice System	Children and Families	Adoption
Substance Abuse Treatment	Domestic Violence	Youth

After you have identified a social worker to interview, contact the person by telephone or e-mail to request the interview. Be certain to discuss a convenient time and duration for the interview. Confirm the interview time and location. You may want to e-mail or mail your questions to the interviewee before the interview. Don't forget to send a thank you note after the interview.

Upon completion of the interview, reflect on the information that you learned from the social worker and submit that to your instructor. Summarize the information you gained, but also reflect on your thoughts and reactions to what you learned. Note: You may want to consider audiotaping the interview to help with your reflection paper.

Here are some suggestions to get your started in your interview. Do not feel limited to these suggestions. Be creative and inquisitive!

1. Tell me about your journey into social work. What about social work appealed to you? How did you decide to become a social worker?

2. What is your educational background for being a social worker?

3. What social work experiences have you had, including practical and paid employment?

4. How did you determine the area(s) in which you wanted to work?

5. Tell me about your current social work position. What are your responsibilities? How long have you been employed in this position? What do you like/dislike about your job?

6. What are the positive aspects of being a social worker?

7. What are the negative aspects of being a social worker?

8. What suggestions would you offer to someone who is considering a social work career?

9. Based on what you now know, what suggestions do you have for courses or field experiences that a social work student might seek out during training?

Here are some suggestions for you to consider as you reflect on this experience:

1. Before the interview, how would you describe/define social work?

2. Did the social worker you interviewed confirm or change your perception of the social work profession?

3. What about the social worker's job appealed or did not appeal to you? Can you see yourself working in the area or job of the social worker you interviewed? Why or why not?

4. What new information did you learn about social work that you did not previously know?

5. Did the social worker discuss how she/he applies the values of the social work profession?

6. Did the social worker discuss any ethical conflicts that she/he has encountered? How would you handle similar situations?

Journal Entry #5—Looking Back and Forward

Discuss your current perception of social work. Issues to consider: has your attitude/perception changed since the beginning of the semester; if so, how; what is your perception of the future of social work.

REFERENCES

Abramovitz, M. (1997). Temporary assistance for needy families. In R.L. Edwards, *Encyclopedia of social work* (19th ed., 1997 supplement) (pp. 311–330). Washington, DC: NASW Press.

Akin, J. (1998). *100 skills of the professional social worker.* Tallahassee, FL: NASW Florida chapter.

Albelda, R., Folbre, N., & the Center for Popular Economics. (1996). *The war on the poor. A defense manual.* New York: The New Press.

Allen-Meares, P. (2000). Our professional values and the changing environment. *Journal of Social Work Education, 36*(2), 179–182.

Allen-Meares, P., & DeRoos, Y. (1997). The future of the social work profession. In M. Reisch & E. Gambrill (eds.), *Social work in the 21st century* (pp. 376–386). Thousand Oaks, CA: Pine Forge Press.

Association for the Advancement of Social Work with Groups, Inc. (2004). Standards for social work practice with groups [Online]. Available: http://www.aaswg.org.

Austin, D.M. (1997). The profession of social work in the second century. In M. Reisch & E. Gambrill (eds.), *Social work in the 21st century* (pp. 396–407). Thousand Oaks, CA: Pine Forge Press.

Bakely, D.C. (1976). *If . . . a big word with the poor.* Newton, KS: Faith and Life Press.

Baldino, R.G. (2000). Wearing multiple hats as a social worker. *The New Social Worker, 7*(2), p. 25.

Barker, R.L. (1999). *The social work dictionary* (4th ed.). Washington, DC: NASW Press.

Barker, R.L. (2003). *The social work dictionary* (5th ed.). Washington, DC: NASW Press.

Barth, M.C. (2001). *The labor market for social workers: A first look.* Prepared for the John A. Hartford Foundation, Inc.

Beddingfield, K.T., Hawkins, D., Ito, T.M., Lenzy, T., & Loftus, M. (1996, October 28). 20 hot job tracks. *U.S. News and World Report,* 89.

Begun, B. (2000, January 1). USA: The way we'll live then. *Newsweek,* 34 35.

Berg, I.K. (1994). *Family based services.* New York: W.W. Norton & Company.

Blank, B.T. (1998). Settlement houses: Old idea in new form builds communities. *The New Social Worker, 5*(3), 4–7.

Boyd, K. (1996). There IS a job market for BSW graduates. *The New Social Worker, 3*(2), 18–19.

Braddock, D. (1999). Occupational employment projections to 2008. *Monthly Labor Review, 122,* 51–77.

Brieland, D. (1995). Social work practice: History and evolution. In R.L. Edwards, *Encyclopedia of social work* (19th ed.) (pp. 2247–2257). Washington, DC: NASW Press.

Brindley, D., Bennefield, R.M., Danyliw, N.Q., Hetter, K., & Loftus, M. (1997, October 27). 20 hot job tracks. *U.S. News and World Report,* 96–98, 100, 104–105.

Brown, J. (1933). *The rural community and social casework.* New York: Family Welfare Association of America.

Burkemper, E. (2004). Informed consent in social work ethics education: Guiding student education with an informed consent template. *Journal of Teaching in Social Work, 24*(1/2), 141–160.

Center on Budget and Policy Priorities. (2003a). A hand up. How state earned income tax credits help working families escape poverty in 2003 [Online]. Available: http://www.cbpp.org/3-3-03sfp.htm.

Center on Budget and Policy Priorities. (2003b). An introduction to TANF [Online]. Available: http://www.cbpp.org/1-22-02tanf2.htm.

Center on Budget and Policy Priorities. (2003c). Poverty increases and median income declines for second consecutive year [Online]. Available: http://www.cbpp.org/9-26-03pov.htm.

Chace, W.M. (1989). The language of action. *Wesleyan LXII*(2), 36.

Clark, E.J. (2003). The future of social work. In R.A. English, *Encyclopedia of social work* (19th ed., 2003 supplement) (pp. 61–70). Washington, DC: NASW Press.

Clewes, R. (2001). Experto credite: New social work graduates share their wisdom. *The New Social Worker, 8*(4), 14–16.

Collins, D., & Coleman, H. (2000). Eliminating bad habits in the social work interview. *The New Social Worker, 7*(4), pp. 12–15.

Corey, M.S., & Corey, G. (1998). *Becoming a helper* (3rd ed.). Pacific Grove, CA: Brooks/Cole Thomson Learning.

Council on Social Work Education. (2001a). *Educational policy and accreditation standards.* Washington, DC: Author.

Council on Social Work Education/SAGE-SW. (2001b). *Strengthening the impact of social work to improve the quality of life for older adults and their families: Blueprint for the new millennium.* Washington, DC: Author.

Council on Social Work Education. (2003). Draft of NASW rural policy statement [Online]. Available: http://www.cswe.org.

Council on Social Work Education. (2004) [Online]. Available: http://www.cswe.org.

Dale, M.L. (2001). Your summer vacation—or is it? The value of experiential learning as part of the new social worker's career campaign. *The New Social Worker, 8*(1), 4–6.

Damron-Rodriguez, J., Villa, V., Tseng, H., & Lubben, J. (1997). Demographic and organizational influences on the development of gerontological social work curriculum. *Gerontology and Geriatrics Education, 17*(3), 3–18.

Danziger, S. (2002). Approaching the limit: Early national lessons from welfare reform. In B.A. Weber, G.J. Duncan, & L.A. Whitener (eds.), *Rural dimensions of welfare reform* (pp. 25–49). Kalamazoo, MI: W.E. Upjohn Institute for Employment Research.

D'Aprix, A.S., Boynton, L.A., Carver, B., & Urso, C. (2001). When the ideal meets the real: Resolving ethical dilemmas in the real world. *The New Social Worker, 8*(2), pp. 20–23.

Day, J.C. (1996). *Population projections of the United States by age, sex, race, and Hispanic origin: 1995 to 2050.* U.S. Bureau of the Census, Current Population Reports, P25-1130. Washington, DC: U.S. Government Printing Office.

DeWeaver, J.L., Smith, M.L., & Hosang, M. (1989). Has social work education abandoned preparation for rural practice? *Human Services in the Rural Environment, 11*(4), 28–32.

Dickinson, N.S. (1997). Federal social legislation from 1994 to 1997. In R.L. Edwards, *Encyclopedia of social work* (19th ed., 1997 supplement) (pp. 125–131). Washington, DC: NASW Press.

Doelling, C., Matz, B., & Kuehne, J. (1999). *Job market of 1998 MSW graduates.* Prepared by the Social Work Career Development Group.

Dunlap, K.M., & Strom-Gottfried, K. (1998a). Everyday ethics and values for social workers (Part 1 in a series on ethics). *The New Social Worker, 5*(1), pp. 16–18.

Dunlap, K.M., & Strom-Gottfried, K. (1998b). Maintaining confidence in confidentiality (Part 3 in a series on ethics). *The New Social Worker, 5*(3), pp. 10–12, 19.

Dunn, C. (2002). The importance of cultural competence for social workers. *The New Social Worker, 9*(2), 4–5.

Dunn, J.H., Flory, B.E., Berg-Weger, M., & Milstead, M. (2004). An exploratory study of supervised access and custody exchange services: The children's experience. *Family Court Review. An Interdisciplinary Journal, 42*(1), pp. 60–73.

Eisenberg, D. (2002, May 6). The coming job boom. *Time,* 40–44.

Flexner, A. (1915). Is social work a profession? Proceedings of the National Conference of Charities and Correction (pp. 576–590). Chicago: Hildmann Printing.

Flory, B.E., & Berg-Weger, M. (2003). Children of high-conflict custody disputes: Striving for social justice in adult focused litigation. *Social Thought, 22*(2/3). (Also published in Stretch, J.J., Burkemper, E.M.,

Hutchison, W.J., & Wilson, J. (2003). *Practicing justice* (pp. 205–219). New York: Haworth Press.)

Flory, B.E., Dunn, J., Berg-Weger, M., & Milstead, M. (2001). An exploratory study of supervised access and custody exchange services: The parental experience. *Family and Conciliation Court Review: An Interdisciplinary Journal, 39*(4), 469–482.

Frumkin, M., & Lloyd, G.A. (1995). Social work education. In R.L. Edwards, *Encyclopedia of social work* (19th ed.) (pp. 2238–2246). Washington, DC: NASW Press.

Gambrill, E. (1997). Social work education. Current concerns and possible future. In M. Reisch & E. Gambrill (eds.), *Social work in the 21st century* (pp. 317–327). Thousand Oaks, CA: Pine Forge Press.

Garvin, C.D. (1997). *Contemporary group work.* Boston: Allyn & Bacon.

Germain, C.B., & Gitterman, A. (1980). *The life model of social work practice.* New York: Columbia University Press.

Germain, C.B., & Gitterman, A. (1995). Ecological perspective. In R.L. Edwards, *Encyclopedia of social work* (19th ed.) (pp. 816–824). Washington, DC: NASW Press.

Gibelman, M., & Schervish, P.H. (1997). *Who we are. A second look.* Washington, DC: NASW Press.

Ginsberg, L. (1995). *Social work almanac* (2nd ed.). Washington, DC: NASW Press.

Ginsberg, L. (1998). Introduction: An overview of rural social work. In L. Ginsberg (ed.), *Social work in rural communities* (3rd ed.) (pp. 3–22). Alexandria, VA: Council on Social Work Education.

Ginsberg, L.H. (2001). *Careers in social work* (2nd ed.). Boston: Allyn & Bacon.

Gitterman, A., & Knight, C. (2000). The power of group work. *The New Social Worker, 7*(2), 15–18.

Green, G.P., & Haines, A. (2002). *Asset building in community development.* Thousand Oaks, CA: Sage Publications.

Gummer, B. (1995). Social planning. In R.L. Edwards, *Encyclopedia of social work* (19th ed.) (pp. 2180–2186). Washington, DC: NASW Press.

Gutiérrez, L., & Nagda, B.A. (1996). The multicultural imperative in human services organizations: Issues for the twenty-first century. In P.R. Raffoul & C.A. McNeece (eds.), *Future issues for social work practice* (pp. 203–213). Boston: Allyn & Bacon.

Gutiérrez, L.M. (1994). Beyond coping: An empowerment perspective on stressful life events. *Journal of Sociology and Social Welfare, 21*(3), 201–219.

Hartman, A. (1978). Diagrammatic assessment of family relationships. *Social Casework, 59,* 465–476.

Haynes, K.S. (1996). The future of political social work. In P.R. Raffoul & C.A. McNeece (eds.), *Future issues for social work practice* (pp. 266–276). Boston: Allyn & Bacon.

Hopps, J.G., & Collins, P.M. (1995). Social work profession overview. In R.L. Edwards, *Encyclopedia of social work* (19th ed.) (pp. 2266–2282). Washington, DC: NASW Press.

Horejsi, C.R. (2002). Social and economic justice: The basics. *The New Social Worker, 9*(4), 10–12.

Jacobson, W. (2001). Beyond therapy: Bringing social work back to human services reform. *Social Work, 46*(1), 51–61.

Johnson, N. (2001). A hand up. How state earned income tax credits help working families escape poverty in 2001: Summary [Online]. Center on Budget and Policy Priorities. Available: http://www.cbpp.org/10-18-01sfp.htm.

Kendall, K.A. (2000). *Social work education: Its origins in Europe.* Alexandria, VA: Council on Social Work Education.

King, M.L. Jr. (1963, June 23). Speech at the Great March on Detroit.

Kosberg, J.I., & Kaufman, A.V. (2002). Gerontological social work: Issues and imperatives for education and practice. *Electronic Journal of Social Work, 1*(1), February 15, 2002.

Kosmin, B.A., & Mayer, E. (2001). *American religious identification survey, 2001.* New York: The Graduate Center of the City University of New York.

Landon, P.S. (1995). Generalist and advanced generalist practice. In R.L. Edwards, *Encyclopedia of social work* (19th ed.) (pp. 1101–1107). Washington, DC: NASW Press.

Lazere, E., Frernstad, S., & Goldberg, H. (2002). States and counties are taking steps to help low-income working families make ends meet and move up the economic ladder [Online]. Center for Budget and Policy Priorities. Available: http://www.cbpp.org/5-18-01wel.htm.

LeCroy, C.W., & Stinson, E.L. (2003). Public's perception of social workers. Paper presented at 2003 Society for Social Work and Research, Washington, DC.

Leighninger, L. (2000). *Creating a new profession. The beginnings of social work education in the United States*. Alexandria, VA: Council on Social Work Education.

Living Wage Resource Center [Online]. (2003). Available: http://www.livingwagecampaign.org.

Loewenberg, F.M., Dolgoff, R., & Harrington, D. (2000). *Ethical decisions for social work practices* (6th ed.). Itasca, IL: F.E. Peacock Publishers.

Logan, S.M.L. (2003). Issues of multiculturalism: Multicultural practice, cultural diversity, and competency. In R.A. English, *Encyclopedia of social work* (19th ed., 2003 supplement) (pp. 95–105). Washington, DC: NASW Press.

Longres, J.F. (1995). Richmond, Mary Ellen (1982–1928). In R.L. Edwards, *Encyclopedia of social work* (19th ed.) (p. 2605). Washington, DC: NASW Press.

Mackelprang, R.W., & Salsgiver, R.O. (1999). *Disability: A diversity model approach in human service practice*. Pacific Grove, CA: Brooks/Cole.

Marable, L.M. (1995, March). The 50 hottest jobs in America. *Money,* 118.

Marson, S.M., & MacLeod, E.H. (1996). The first social worker. *The New Social Worker, 3*(2), 11.

Martinez-Brawley, E. (1983). *Seven decades of rural social work*. New York: Praeger.

McCleary, K. (2002, October). Help wanted. *Good Housekeeping, 235*(4), 77–78, 80.

Meyer, C.H. (1995). Assessment. In R.L. Edwards, *Encyclopedia of social work* (19th ed.) (pp. 260–270). Washington, DC: NASW Press.

Minahan, A. (1981). Purpose and objectives of social work revisited. *Social Work, 26*(1), 5–6.

Mindell, C.L. (2001). Religious bigotry and religious minorities. In G.A. Appleby, E. Colon, & J. Hamilton (eds.), *Diversity, oppression, and social functioning. Person-in-environment assessment and intervention* (pp. 195–216). Boston: Allyn & Bacon.

Mizrahi, T., & Baskind, F. (2003). Social work education and the future. In R.A. English, *Encyclopedia of social work* (19th ed., 2003 supplement) (pp. 137–149). Washington, DC: NASW Press.

Mulrine, A. (2002, March 14). Where the jobs are. *Rolling Stone, 891,* 62.

Murdock, S.H., & Michael, M. (1996). Future demographic change. The demand for social welfare services in the twenty-first century. In P.R. Raffoul & C.A. McNeece (eds.), *Future issues for social work practice* (pp. 3–18). Boston: Allyn & Bacon.

Naparstek, A.J., & Dooley, D. (1997). Community building. In R.L. Edwards, *Encyclopedia of social work* (19th ed., 1997 supplement) (pp. 77–89). Washington, DC: NASW Press.

NASW News. (2003, February). Practitioners surveyed; incomes increased. *NASW News, 48*(2), 1, 8.

National Association of Social Workers. (1973). *Standards for social service manpower*. Washington, DC: NASW.

National Association of Social Workers. (1996). *Social work myth busters*. Washington, DC: Author.

National Association of Social Workers. (1998). *Milestones in the development of social work and social welfare*. Washington, DC: Author.

National Association of Social Workers. (1999). *Code of ethics*. Washington, DC: NASW.

National Association of Social Workers. (2000–2003a). Deprofessionalization and reclassification. *Social work speaks: National Association of Social Workers policy statements 2000–2003*. Washington, DC: NASW Press.

National Association of Social Workers. (2000–2003b). Temporary assistance for needy families: Welfare reform. *Social work speaks*. Washington, DC: NASW Press.

National Association of Social Workers National Committee on Racial and Ethnic Diversity. (2001). *NASW standards for cultural competence in social work practice* [Online]. Available: http://www.naswdc.org.

National Association of Social Workers. (2003). Government relations update [Online]. Available: http://www.naswdc.org/advocacy/updates/default.asp.

National Association of Social Workers. (2004a) [Online]. Available: http://www.naswdc.org.

National Association of Social Workers. (2004b). *Issue fact sheets. Diversity & cultural competence* [Online]. Available: http://www.naswdc.org.

National Association of Social Workers. (2004c). *Social work profession* [Online]. Available: http://www.socialworkers.org/profession/overview.asp.

National Association of Social Workers. (2004d). Social work profession and issue fact sheets [Online]. Available: http://www.naswdc.org.

National Center for Health Statistics. (2003) [Online]. Available: http://www.cdc.gov/nchs.

National Public Radio/Henry J. Kaiser Family Foundation/Harvard University Kennedy School of Government. (2001). *Poverty in America* [Online]. Available: http://www.kff.org.

Okun, B.F., Fried, J., & Okun, M.L. (1999). *Understanding diversity: A learning-as-practice primer.* Pacific Grove, CA: Brooks/Cole.

O'Neill, J.V. (2002, May). Better labor data on social work sought. *NASW News,* 1, 8.

O'Neill, J.V. (2003a). California's worker shortage. *NASW News, 48*(10).

O'Neill, J.V. (2003b). Profession perceived favorably by public. *NASW News, 48*(3).

Ozawa, M.N. (1997). Demographic changes and their implications. In M. Reisch & E. Gambrill (eds.), *Social work in the 21st century* (pp. 8–27). Thousand Oaks, CA: Pine Forge Press.

Paraquad. (2002). *Words with dignity* [Online]. Available: http://www.paraquad.org, or 311 N. Lindbergh Blvd., St. Louis, MO 63141.

Peck, S. (1999). Who are we? *The New Social Worker,* 6(1), 4–6.

Peterson, J. (2002). Feminist perspectives on TANF reauthorization: An introduction to key issues for the future of welfare reform [Online]. Institute for Women's Policy Research. Available: http://www.iwpr.org.

Pinderhughes, E. (1995). Direct practice overview. In R.L. Edwards, *Encyclopedia of social work* (19th ed.) (pp. 740–751). Washington, DC: NASW Press.

Quam, L. (1995). Addams, Jane (1860–1935). In R.L. Edwards, *Encyclopedia of social work* (19th ed.) (pp. 2571–2572). Washington, DC: NASW Press.

Raffoul, P.R. (1996). Social work and the future. Some final thoughts. In P.R. Raffoul & C.A. McNeece (eds.), *Future issues for social work practice* (pp. 293–300). Boston: Allyn & Bacon.

Ramanathan, C.S., & Link, R.J. (1999). Future visions for global studies in social work. In C.S. Ramanathan & R.J. Link, *All our futures: Principles and resources for social work practice in a global era* (pp. 219–237). Belmont, CA: Wadsworth.

Rank, M.R. (1994). *Living on the edge: The realities of welfare in America.* New York: Columbia University Press.

Rank, M.R., & Hirschl, T.A. (2001). Rags or riches? Estimating the probabilities of poverty and affluence across the adult American life span. *Social Science Quarterly, 82*(4), pp. 651–669.

Rank, M.R., & Hirschl, T.A. (2002). Welfare use as a life course event: Toward a new understanding of the U.S. safety net. *Social Work, 47*(3), 237–248.

Rauscher, L., & McClintock, M. (1997). Ableism curriculum design. In M. Adams, L.A. Bell, & P. Griffin (eds.), *Teaching for diversity and social justice* (pp. 198–229). New York: Routledge.

Reamer, F.G. (1995). Ethics and values. In R.L. Edwards, *Encyclopedia of social work* (19th ed.) (pp. 893–908). Washington, DC: NASW Press.

Reamer, F.G. (1998). *Ethical standards in social work.* Washington, DC: NASW Press.

Reamer, F.G. (2001). *Ethics education in social work.* Alexandria, VA: Council on Social Work Education.

Reeser, L. (1996). The future of professionalism and activism in social work. In P.R. Raffoul & C.A. McNeece (eds.), *Future issues for social work practice* (pp. 240–253). Boston: Allyn & Bacon.

Reid, P.N. (1995). Social welfare history. In R.L. Edwards, *Encyclopedia of social work* (19th ed.) (pp. 2206–2225). Washington, DC: NASW Press.

Reisch, M. (1997). The political context of social work. In M. Reisch & E. Gambrill (eds.), *Social work in the 21st century* (pp. 80–92). Thousand Oaks, CA: Pine Forge Press.

Reisch, M. (2000). Social work and politics in the new century. *Social Work, 45*(4), 293–297.

Reisch, M., & Gorin, S.H. (2001). Nature of work and future of the social work profession. *Social Work, 46*(1), 9–19.

Reisch, M., & Jarman-Rohde, L. (2000). The future of social work in the United States: Implications for field education. *Journal of Social Work Education, 36*(2), 201–214.

Richmond, M. (1897). The need of a training school in applied philanthropy. In the Proceedings of the (1897) National Conference of Charities and Correction (pp. 181–186). Boston: Geo. H. Ellis.

Richmond, M. (1917). *Social diagnosis.* New York: Russell Sage Foundation.

Richmond, M. (1922). *What Is social casework?* New York: Russell Sage Foundation.

Rose, N. (1997). The future economic landscape: Implications for social work practice and education. In M. Reisch & E. Gambrill (eds.), *Social work in the 21st century* (pp. 28–38). Thousand Oaks, CA: Pine Forge Press.

Rosen, A.L., & Zlotnik, J.L. (2001). Demographics and reality: The "disconnect" in social work education. In E.O. Cox, E. Kelchner, & R. Chapin (eds.), *Gerontological social work practice: Issues, challenges, and potential* (pp. 81–97). New York: Haworth Press.

Rothman, J. (2001). Approaches to community intervention. In J. Rothman, J. Erlich, & J. Tropman, *Strategies of community intervention* (6th ed.) (pp. 27–64). Itasca, IL: F.E. Peacock Publishers.

Saleebey, D. (1992). *The strengths perspective in social work practice.* New York: Longman Publishing.

Saleebey, D. (1996). The strengths perspective in social work practice: Extensions and cautions. *Social Work, 41*(3), 296–305.

Sanfort, J.R. (2000). Developing new skills for community practice in an era of policy devolution. *Journal of Social Work Education, 36*(2), 183–185.

Scharlach, A., Damron-Rodriguez, J.A., Robinson, B., & Feldman, R. (2000). Educating social workers for an aging society: A vision for the 21st century. *Journal of Social Work Education, 36*, 521–537.

Schlesinger, E.G., & Devore, W. (1995). Ethnic-sensitive practice. In R.L. Edwards, *Encyclopedia of social work* (19th ed.) (pp. 902–908). Washington, DC: NASW Press.

Schmidley, A.D., & Robinson, J.G. (2003). Measuring the foreign-born population in the United States with the Current Population Survey: 1994–2002. Population Division Working Paper No. 73 [Online]. Available: http://www.census.gov/population/documentation/twps0073/twps0073.pdf.

Schneider, R. (2002). Influencing "state" policy: Social work arena for the 21st century. *The Social Policy Journal, 1*(1), 113–116.

Schopler, J.H., & Galinsky, M.J. (1995). Group practice overview. In R.L. Edwards, *Encyclopedia of social work* (19th ed.) (pp. 1129–1142). Washington, DC: NASW Press.

Seccombe, K. (1999). *"So you think I drive a Cadillac?" Welfare recipients' perspectives on the system and its reform.* Boston: Allyn & Bacon.

Segal, E.A., & Brzuzy, S. (1998). *Social welfare policy, programs, and practice.* Itasca, IL: F.E. Peacock Publishers.

Segalman, R., & Basu, A. (1981). *Poverty in America: The welfare dilemma.* Westport, CT: Greenwood Press.

Senkowsky, S. (1996a). Religion and social work. *The New Social Worker, 5*(4), pp. 8–9.

Senkowsky, S. (1996b). Social work's religious roots. *The New Social Worker, 3*(2), 10.

Sherraden, M. (1990). *Assets and the poor: A new American welfare policy.* Armonk, NY: M.E. Sharp, Inc.

Shulman, L. (1999). *The skills of helping individuals, families, groups, and communities* (4th ed.). Itasca, IL: F.E. Peacock Publishers.

Siegel, J. (1996). Aging into the 21st century. Washington, DC: Administration on Aging, Dept. of Health & Human Services.

Southern Regional Education Board Manpower Education and Training Project's Rural Task Force. (1998). Educational assumptions for rural social work. In L. Ginsberg (ed.), *Social work in rural communities* (3rd ed.) (pp. 23–26). Alexandria, VA: Council on Social Work Education.

Statistical Abstract of the United States. (2000). [Online]. Available: http://www.census.gov/statab/www.

Strom-Gottfried, K., & Dunlap, K.M. (1998). How to keep boundary issues from compromising your practice (Part 2 in a series on ethics). *The New Social Worker, 5*(2), pp. 10–13.

Strom-Gottfried, K., & Dunlap, K.M. (1999). Unraveling ethical dilemmas. *The New Social Worker, 6*(2), pp. 8–12.

Syers, M. (1995). Flexner, Abraham (1866–1959). In R.L. Edwards, *Encyclopedia of social work* (19th ed.) (pp. 2584–2585). Washington, DC: NASW Press.

Tropman, J., & Erlich, J. (2001). Introduction to Part II. In J. Rothman, J. Erlich, & J. Tropman, *Strategies of community intervention* (6th ed.) (pp. 233–250). Itasca, IL: F.E. Peacock Publishers.

Turner, F.J. (1995). Social work practice: Theoretical base. In R.L. Edwards, *Encyclopedia of social work* (19th ed.) (pp. 2258–2265). Washington, DC: NASW Press.

U.S. Census Bureau. (2001). Households and families: 2000. Census 2000 Brief [Online]. Available: http://www.census.gov.

U.S. Census Bureau. (2003). *Poverty in the United States: 2002.* Current Population Reports, Series P60-222. Washington, DC: Government Printing Office.

U.S. Census Bureau. (2004). United States Census 2000 [Online]. Available: http://www.census.gov.

U.S. Department of Health and Human Services. (2002). *Women's health USA 2002.* Washington, DC: U.S. Department of Health and Human Services, Health Resources and Services Administration, Maternal and Child Health Bureau.

U.S. Department of Health and Human Services. (2003). The 2003 HHS poverty guidelines [Online]. Available: http://www.aspe.hhs.gov/poverty/03poverty.htm.

U.S. Department of Health and Human Services. (2004). Protecting the privacy of patients' health information [Online]. Available: http://www.hhs.gov/news/facts/privacy.html.

U.S. Department of Labor. (2003). Minimum wage laws in the states [Online]. Employment Standards Administration Wage and Hour Division. Available: http://www.dol.gov/esa/minwage/america.htm.

U.S. Department of Labor Bureau of Labor Statistics. (2002a). *Career guide to industries 2002–2003 edition* [Online]. Available: http://stats./bls.gov/oco/cg/cg1006.htm.

U.S. Department of Labor Bureau of Labor Statistics. (2002b). *Occupational outlook handbook* [Online]. Available: http://stats.bls.gov/oco/ocos060.htm.

U.S. Department of Labor Bureau of Labor Statistics. (2002c). *Occupation report* [Online]. Available: http://stats.bls.gov.

U.S. General Accounting Office. (2003). *HHS could play a greater role in helping child welfare agencies recruit and retain staff (GAO-03-357)* [Online]. Available: www.gao.gov.

Urban experience in Chicago: Hull House and its neighborhoods, 1889–1963 [Online]. Available: http://uic.edu/Jaddams/hull/urbanexp/contents.htm.

Walton, S. (1996). Getting real: Mastering the art of helping others. In *America's best graduate schools* (p. 63). Washington, DC: *U.S. News and World Report.*

Wambach, K.G., & Van Soest, D. (1997). Oppression. In R.L. Edwards, *Encyclopedia of social work* (19th ed., 1997 supplement) (pp. 243–252). Washington, DC: NASW Press.

Wilshere, P.J. (1997). Personal values: Professional questions. *The New Social Worker, 4*(1), p. 13.

Worldbank Group. (2003). Understanding poverty [Online]. Available: http://www.worldbank.org/poverty/mission/up1.htm.

Yeskel, F., & Leondar-Wright, B. (1997). Classism curriculum design. In M. Adams, L.A. Bell, & P. Griffin (eds.), *Teaching for diversity and social justice* (pp. 231–260). New York: Routledge.

York, R.O., Denton, R.T., & Moran, J.R. (1989). Rural and urban social work practice: Is there a difference? *Social Casework: The Journal of Contemporary Social Work, 70*(4), 201–209.

CREDITS

Akin, Jim, "100 Skills for Social Workers." (1995) NASW-Florida Chapter. Reprinted by permission of the National Association of Social Workers, Inc.

Bakely, Donald C. (1976). "If . . . A Big Word with the Poor." Faith and Life Press. Reprinted with permission.

Barker, R.I. (2003). "Twelve Skills for Social Work Practice," *The Social Work Dictionary*, 5th Edition. Washington, DC: NASW Press. 409–410. Reprinted by permission of the National Association of Social Workers, Inc.

Branding, Ronice E. "Action Continuum." Adapted from the National Conference for Community and Justice—St. Louis Region. Reprinted with permission.

Collins, D. & H. Coleman. (2000). "Eliminating Bad Habits in the Social Work Interview," *The New Social Worker*, 7(4).12–15. Reprinted with permission.

D'Aprix, A.S., L.A. Boynton, B. Carver & C. Urso. (2001). "When the Ideal Meets the Real: Resolving Ethical Dilemmas in the Real World," *The New Social Worker*, 8(2). 20–23.

Germain, C.B. & A. Gitterman. (1995). "Ecological perspective." In R.L. Edwards, *Encyclopedia of Social Work*, 19th Edition. Washington, DC: NASW Press. 816–824. Reprinted by permission of the National Association of Social Workers, Inc.

Hartman, A. (1978). "Diagrammatic Assessment of Family Relationships." *Social Casework*, 59(8). 470. Reprinted with permission from *Families in Society* (www.familiesinsociety.org), published by the Alliance for Children and Families.

Lynch, Darlene and Robert Vernon, "You'll Need a Social Worker." © 2001. Reprinted with permission. For free distribution information visit http://hsmedia.biz.

Saint Louis University, Department of Marketing and Communications.

Saleebey, Dennis. (1996). "The Strengths Perspective in Social Work Practice: Extensions and Cautions." *Social Work*, 41(3). 296–305.

Schneider, Robert, "Influencing State Policy." Reprinted by permission. For more information visit http://www.statepolicy.org.

Wesleyan University Library, Special Collections & Archives.

Photo Credits Chapter 3, p. 28. Jane Addams © Bettman/Corbis; p. 37: Octavia Hill: The Granger Collection, New York; p. 38: Mary Richmond: Courtesy of Columbia University School of Social Work.

GLOSSARY/INDEX

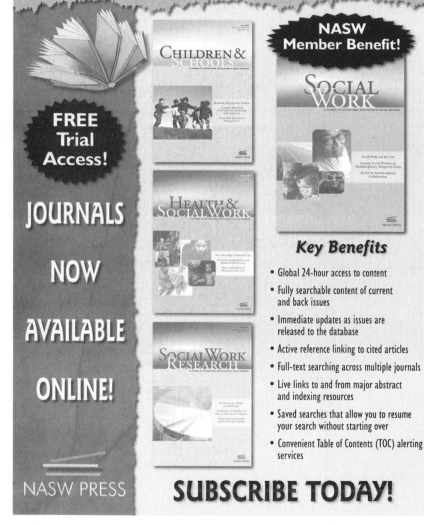